A MAN CALLED MIKE

A MAN CALLED MIKE

the inspiring story
of a shy superstar

CHRISTOPHER HILTON

MRP

MOTOR RACING PUBLICATIONS LTD
Unit 6, The Pilton Estate, 46 Pitlake, Croydon CR0 3RY, England

First Published 1992

British Library Cataloguing in Publication Data

Hilton, Christopher
    Man Called Mike: Inspiring Story of a Shy
    Superstar
    I. Title
    796.7092

    ISBN 0-947981-65-9

Typeset in Great Britain by
Ryburn Publishing Services, Halifax, West Yorkshire

Printed in Great Britain by
Hartnolls Limited, Bodmin, Cornwall

CONTENTS

To Les Nick. I didn't even know you were ill, never mind that you'd crossed the finishing line; I didn't even know until long after it was far too late. Not that it matters now, but sorry.

A MOMENT IN TIME

"Nooooo. You're joking."
"No", Nichol said, "you did it."
"Bloody hell, I wasn't even trying very hard." – Dialogue, the Isle of Man

Coming fast towards the right-hand corner at Ramsey, a stone-clad outpost of a town butting onto the Irish Sea, the crowd behind the simple wooden barrier craned, and leant, and began to wave in a short, intuitive ripple. They'd already heard the sound of the Suzuki 500 being pressed down through the gears – rasping, rasping, rasping – they'd already seen the man on it in his blood-red leathers holding himself in the classical tuck position as he approached them, reaching for the apex of the corner at the entry to Ramsey; and now, hands and programmes and hats and scarves fluttered as he cranked the Suzuki over, dipped down another gear so that for an instant the engine shrieked in pain, held the bike vertical, cranked it over the other way to curve round the left-hand corner just across the little town square. The road whipped in front of a white-painted house there. The house front, sheer as a cliff wall, was the corner.

And he was gone, gone so suddenly that he might have kicked the bike through the right, upright, left; was gone in a fluid, raucous cascade of sound and tight movement which bore within it a certain majesty, a certain grace; was gone, with the cheers from the barrier already melting into the echo of the engine, gone to where he had been so many times before in another life: to face The Mountain.

The man who turned the bike through the hairpin at Elfin Glen, fled round Waterworks Corner and began the climb to the Goose Neck was no longer young. The face beneath the helmet remained broad and open; it was tanned, but worn now. The hair nestling under the helmet had receded over the crown of the head, and to compensate he'd grown it so long it hung in thickets over the ears, but that didn't unbalance his appearance, only accentuated it. He had a moustache which drooped; it was whitening at the edges, and any self-respecting Mexican adventurer would have been proud of it. Somehow it suited him perfectly. But the smile was the same as it had always been, impish, boyish, easy, natural, charismatic in a way nobody could define and never had been able to define.

Mist hung like a shroud out on The Mountain beyond the Goose Neck. The road was cut into a ledge, and a hillside covered in coarse grass climbed to one side, the drop ran away to the other. There was no barrier, no protection from this drop, and he was a thousand feet above sea-level. The Suzuki wailed long and low and, as it travelled so fast, fast, fast down this ordinary road, the pitch was moving up and up a scale until it became sharp as a yearn. The crowd waited here, too, some strung out just beyond the rim of the road in the coarse grass, others gathered in vast groups at the bends. As the Suzuki passed, the same ripple followed it: a people communicating directly with one man through gesture and distant, unheard cheering alone. It was a deep subterranean current surfacing, born of their memories, but existing now, spontaneous and helpless and profound.

And he was gone, gone towards the Guthrie Memorial.

Did he see it then? Did he glance back just this once and see not a ribbon of road unfolding behind him as it had always done but the whole of a life? Twenty-one years before he'd been precisely here, so young and being pushed so hard by his father that people worried he'd kill himself; and then there had been the wins and the world titles, a whole clutch of them, and genuinely epic races, too, here and at plenty of other places on four continents of the earth. Did he remember any of those, even as glimpses which fled from him? And then there had been the cars. Did he remember Monza, when he'd led the Italian Grand Prix? Did he remember the great ones he'd raced – Surtees and Brabham and Graham Hill and Clark in one era, Stewart and Hunt and Lauda in another? Did he remember the forays into the Le Mans 24-hour sportscar race? Did he hear the echoes of a life, the girls, and the riotous good times and the outrageous pranks and tricks? Did he remember the fist-fights as well as the crashes, the lonely times playing the clarinet in his childhood, when the only audience had been butlers and maids hearing it echoing down oak-panelled corridors? Did he remember the games of patience in anonymous hotel rooms, just chugging his way towards tomorrow, just waiting for tomorrow?

Maybe, maybe not.

As with Stan Hailwood, his father, nostalgia held little interest until later in his life.

And he descended The Mountain, the altitude tumbling away from him, and skimmed through the right curve at Hillberry. He forced the bike way over to the grassy verge on the inside and held it there, only moving out when he needed to position it for the left curve flowing so fast at him beyond the tall trees whose branches stooped across the road, fashioning a high triumphal arch.

He was almost home now. He had covered 224 miles at an average speed of over 110mph. Two miles remained, the sharp right at Signpost Corner, the sharp right at Governor's Bridge, then the big hammer, hammer, hammer to the line, where an official held the chequered flag and described great, final circles in the air with it. As the man in the blood-red leathers reached the line he raised his left hand to acknowledge the crowd in the grandstand, every one of them on their feet. It was a small, polite, modest movement he made, nothing more. He was like that.

Mike Hailwood had just won the Senior TT at the Isle of Man, the most frightening course in the world. He was 39. It was the last win of his life, and in its context very probably the best. Essentially he'd stopped racing bikes in 1967, then moved to cars, but that had ended in 1974 when he crashed in the German Grand Prix at the Nurburgring, the most frightening car circuit in the world. He damaged his leg so badly (the foot fused into a sort of lump) that afterwards he had to be coaxed to get onto friends' ordinary, innocent road bikes. He was concerned that he simply wouldn't be able to ride them any more at all.

Now this.

When it was over he stood hemmed-in by journalists and well-wishers, a garland round his neck, a green Castrol cap at a jaunty angle, and someone said "You know you've done the lap record?".

"Really?" He was genuinely astonished.

Somebody else (the late, lamented Leslie Nichol of the *Daily Express*) told him the speed, sharp and hard. "114 miles an hour."

"Nooooo. You're joking."

"No", said Nichol, "you did it."

"Bloody hell, I wasn't even trying very hard." He almost dropped the 'h' of hard; he was speaking plain-man speak, he could speak no other way. Mike had always been dismissive of his achievements, and maybe those words should stand as his epitaph, although he always tried very hard. Always.

No man had ever taken a 500cc bike round the Isle of Man course faster than he had just done, lap three of the six-lap race, and that, too, could stand as his epitaph.

114.02mph.

There would be a further race on The Island later this same week – the Classic – and then absolute, final retirement beckoned, safe after it all, a thousand races, two thousand races, who truly knows how many. He'd be tempted to race just one more time after The Island, but would break his collar bone practising for it and would have to go to Derby Infirmary instead. And that was it.

He'd work at his bike dealership in Birmingham and face the problems of middle-age, the problems of the daily grind which to such a man would inevitably be more difficult in the sustaining than for other people. He wouldn't have seen it like that. It was life in another chapter, whatever that chapter would be.

His fame was secure forever, and would increase in the telling, not diminish. Not that he would do the telling. He had a deep horror of discussing himself, even to his sister. He genuinely thought he was uninteresting. Others would do the telling, generation after generation carefully passing down the legend. They wouldn't have to amplify a thing. The legend was too big to need that.

As he left The Island at the end of the week after the Classic – he lost that final victory by an absurd three seconds over the 226 miles – he had just 20 months to live. It was June 1979.

■ ■ ■

Mike's life is revealed by what he did and by how he touched the lives of so many different people. Without exception they hold to his memory with an affection and loyalty which can only be described as fierce. When I was making a 'cold' call to try to arrange an interview with one of these people he burst into tears at the mention of Mike's name and needed several minutes to compose himself. This is not, I hope, an ordinary book because it is not about an ordinary man.

It is, I hope, an honest portrait, an attempt to capture all of a life – although this by definition is impossible – and you will have to judge for yourself how close I have come. Some aspects of any human being are secret unto themselves and will always remain so.

I have been astonished by a groundswell of good wishes and active co-operation, often extremely touching. Chris Buckler, Mike's sister, insisted that I cut a colour picture of their father out of a precious personal photograph album with scissors. I protested at this potential piece of vandalism, but no, she wanted me to have the picture, and it is here in this book. She lent many more, and the book would have been infinitely poorer without them. She also spoke candidly of their childhood, of the sadnesses as well as the joys of that. At moments it was an uncomfortable experience for her, but she did it, and I am deeply grateful. The interview ended as it should have ended, happily.

Pauline, Mike's widow, also faced what must have been an uncomfortable interview. If it was, she didn't betray that. You could see why she and Mike married. She has stature of her own as well as genuine elegance. I thank her publicly for making the book more complete than it could conceivably have been without her and, just as nice, for selecting her own favourite photographs.

Pam Lawton, one of Mike's first girlfriends, squarely faced the fact (to herself) that this was an interview she ought to give, and again the book would have been seriously diminished without her. Her overriding concern was for Mike's memory and, yes, there were tears, too, but also lovely laughter and great sensitivity.

A simple list of the names of others who helped or broached their memories will suffice here because in most cases you will see the depth of their contributions in the text. That is the measure of the groundswell. Some also provided precious memorabilia as well as talking at great length, and often enough interviews disintegrated into riotous laughter as some wild and wonderful tale was recounted. There are many things in this book, but a lot of laughter.

Those people (some of whom were conduits to other people) are listed in no particular order: Chris Barber, Nobby Clark, John Dee, Eoin Young, David Fern, Charlie Rous, Brian Hart, Linda Patterson, Guy Edwards, David Mills, Iain Mackay, Jerry Wood, Richard Attwood, Valerie Singleton and Pat Thornton of the BBC, Ken Sprayson, Stuart Graham, Tommy Robb, Ralph Bryans, Carol and Lewis Young, Rob Walker, Percy Tait, Shirley Robinson of Rothmans, John Cooper, Peter Stayner of Marlboro McLaren International, Ken Lawrence, Rod Sawyer, Derek Bell, Leo Wybrott, Dave Clark, Sonia Ball (who did invaluable and voluntary research), Phil Read, Nigel Roebuck, Jim Redman, Michael Knox of Oxford and County Newspapers, Doug Hailwood, John Surtees, Kiyoshi Kawashima (Supreme Advisor to Honda Motor Co), Shoichiro Irimajiri (Executive Vice-President of Honda and President of Honda R and D), Derick Allsop, Mick Grant, Ted Macauley, Martyn Pass, Innes Ireland, Alan Trim, Maurice Hamilton, Andrew Marriott, Nick Harris, Gary Taylor, Martin Ogborne, John Watson, Jody Scheckter, John Bromley, David Hobbs, Greg Hobbs, Simon and Douglas Plummer, Giacomo Agostini, Alex George, Paddy Driver, Mikihiko Aika, Mamoru Haji, Ikuo Nagashima, Katsumasa Suzuki, Katsutoshi Oshiro, Jacky Ickx.

Murray Walker gave a candid interview and read the manuscript, pointing out inaccuracies. For his care and concern, sincere thanks. That said, any mistakes in the book are mine, not his.

Honda, via Yoichi Harada of their Public Relations Division in Tokyo and Iain Mackay, helped above and beyond the call of duty in securing interviews and photographs; and on the subject of photographs I've credited each with the lender's name. Many have not been published before.

Peter Bolt, editor of *Motor Cycle News*, very kindly gave permission to quote from a supplement they produced in the Sixties entitled *The Hailwood Story* in which Stan recounted how it all began. It is a fascinating document and I have used it extensively because as far as I'm aware it is the only one of its kind and thus of genuine historical importance.

Ted Macauley, of the *Daily Mirror*, has already written three personal accounts of Mike's life (*Hailwood*, and *Mike The Bike Again*, by Cassell, and *Mike*, by Buchan and Enright). I have consulted these for background and poached a phrase here and there. To Ted, a friend, my thanks for his time and his candour.

I've quoted from *No Time to Lose*, the story of Bill Ivy, by Alan Peck (MRP) and leant heavily for basic information on the *Marlboro Grand Prix Guide*, *Rothmans' Grand Prix Motorcycle Yearbook*, *Great Motor-cycle Riders*, by Peter Carrick (Hale), *Directory of Classic Racing Motorcycles*, by Brian Woolley, and *Manx Norton*, by Mick Walker (both Aston), *The Story of Honda*, by Carrick (PSL), *From TT to Tokyo*, by Tommy Robb and Jimmy Walker (Courier-Herald Printers), *Wheels of Fortune*, by Jim Redman (Century Hutchinson), *Suzuki*, by Jeff Clew (Haynes), *The McIntyre Story*, by Bob McIntyre (Arthur Barker), *Racing and All That*, by John Thompson (Pelham), *Barry Sheene: A Will to Win*, by Michael Scott (Star), the *Marlboro (car) Grand Prix Guide*, *Grand Prix!*, by Mike Lang (Haynes), *History of the Grand Prix Car*, by Doug Nye (Hazleton), *Great Motor Races*, by Bruce Carter (Weidenfeld and Nicholson), *Flying on the Ground*, by Emerson Fittipaldi (William Kimber), *Grand Prix British Winners*, by Maurice Hamilton (Guinness), and *The Day I Died*, by Mark Kahn (Gentry). *Motor Sport*, *Autocar* and, particularly, *Autosport* gave the nuts and bolts of Mike's career in cars.

The BBC have allowed me to use two extensive interviews by Brian Johnston and Valerie Singleton and, equally kindly, the Managing Director of Manx Radio, Stewart Watterson, gave permission to reproduce one of their transmissions.

Duke Marketing have produced an invaluable cassette, *Tribute to Hailwood*, and two videos, *One Day in June*, and *Champions*, while *TT Tribute* (Castrol) was closely scrutinized, too. These videos bring it all alive, and that's a good word to use. Virtually every minute of his 39 years Mike was that.

Once upon a time and long ago, another great Englishman, Samuel Pepys, wrote a diary, and in the introduction to the definitive published version (by Bell and Hyman) – paradoxically the edition I bought came out in 1979, the year of Mike's final TT victory – a gentleman called Robert Latham wrote that "in the end the historian's debt to the diary will not be calculated by simply adding up the subjects on which it can yield significant information. Its total value is something greater than the sum of the value of its parts. This is not only one man's history of a decade – this is what it felt like to be alive."

Yes.

The total value of Mike Hailwood's life is also greater than the sum of the value of the parts, and yes, this is what it felt like to be alive. Mind you, if he'd ever read such mellifluous words about himself he'd have smiled that broad open smile and shaken his head and said how alarmingly serious it sounded, then shifted the conversation quickly away. You can almost hear him saying it in that soft London-influenced voice which was almost a verbal caress: "Come on then, you bastards, who's for a drink?".

STAN

"If young Stan is to die I'd sooner he died with his leg on." – George Arthur Hailwood

"I'll tell you this, my lad. If somebody offers me a cigarette I never refuse it. That's why I'm a millionaire." – Stan Hailwood

"Mike never ever mentioned his mother." – Charlie Rous

"At 16 Mike said he'd never live to 30. That used to worry us, my stepmother and I. I think it probable that he saw he was going to do things which could kill him. So this explains everything: he crammed everything into his life." – Chris Buckler

1

That forgotten day in 1924, a strong, handsome man moved away from Oxford Station down New Road. He limped, but he had a dogged gait. With each step he was leaving his past behind except the single part of it he bore with him: himself. Stanley William Bailey Hailwood didn't look back because he wasn't the kind. He was 21.

He kept on all the way to the end of New Road and turned into a coalyard which bordered the wharf of a canal. A small garage stood in a corner. He opened the door and went in.

He'd come from Manchester and he came from solid stock. His father, George Arthur, had worked in the mines as a kid and would subsequently be a warehouseman. George was a gymnast who gave of his time freely – and for free – teaching the poor of Salford how to become gymnasts, and naturally enough George Arthur's sons – the first named George after him, the second Stan – were good at it. There was also a sister, Maude, and 15 years later a third son, Doug. They lived in Leigh, itself a solid place. George Arthur was known as "honest, sober and trustworthy"; he was a bell-ringer at the local church and his 5,000-change bell-ringing was something to hear. His wife Elisabeth did the catering at the church hall.

"We were a very close family", Doug will say, "not so much religious as bound together by the hardships of the era. Stan wasn't born with the leg. He and my other brother were playing about at Guy Fawkes' time and it was a simple domestic accident. He fell on a needle my sister was knitting with and it broke in his knee. We didn't have any money for X-rays or anything, and in those days accidents like that could be dangerous. In hospital they broke and set and rebroke his leg several times; there was a risk of gangrene and a surgeon said he wanted to amputate. My father said 'if young Stan is to die I'd sooner he died with his leg on'. I do know Stan lay on his back for two years and so he had very little schooling. He educated himself." The leg would never be allowed to interfere with whatever Stan wanted to do. He wasn't that kind, either. Did it stop his gymnastics? "Oh no, you should have seen him go up a rope."

He'd left school at 13 to join the Foden wagon-works – "we called them the steam wagon-works. I don't know how he managed to get a job with Foden; nobody wanted to employ a cripple." Stan left at 16 to join a motorcycle firm where he repaired the bikes of the day, mainly Zeniths, Rudge Multis and Triumphs. As a hobby he used to buy bikes – there were a lot around after the First World War – and take them to bits and put them back together in the kitchen. He'd strip them, get them going again and sell them, although he wouldn't have made much. When Stan was 17 he raced for the first time, riding a single-speed Norton at a meeting at Axe Edge, Buxton. Later, perhaps, he'd somehow milked a living by selling ties and quite possibly brushes direct from a suitcase to tailor's shops.

One other forgotten day he saw an advertisement in a motorcycling magazine. It announced that a Mr King of Egrove Farm, Kennington, Oxford, wanted a mechanic. The mid-Twenties were a time of depression, and the connotation of the word was not then as it is now. The Welfare State was still fully two decades away, and a depth of poverty unrecognizable today stood on every northern street corner. Sometimes there would be children in bare feet or hand-me down clothing which had been handed down a long way; bitter, distant memories of it live on.

Stan wrote in answer to the advertisement and received an invitation to come down. He would say that he walked and hitch-hiked from Manchester and, if it is true, you have a measure of the man already. More properly he limped from Manchester. In his pocket he had a few shillings George Arthur had managed to save to help him on his way.

Motor dealers, selling both cars and bikes, inhabited New Road. The arrangement was common enough and sometimes still is, on one street a grouping of jewellers, another of tailors, another of antique shops. Perhaps the concentration helped trade, perhaps they all felt more comfortable together. Safety in numbers.

Howard King, who placed the advertisement, had founded the business in 1918 with family money. His father had given him enough to do it when Howard returned from the War. Howard seems to have been a cautious man who knew little about how motorbikes actually worked. He didn't need to. He didn't manufacture them, he sold them, and in an unusual way. He established a very early mail order and credit system so people could buy the bikes "through the post". Stan faced him and said, in an echo of the times: "You need me and I need work. I don't want a wage. I'll do up old bikes and you pay me a percentage of what you sell them for."

But Howard was looking at the leg. "There in the coalyard", Doug says, "they saw he was a cripple and said they couldn't take him on. Stan said 'you see those blokes over there loading bikes onto a wagon? I can do anything they can do' – and he started hoisting the bikes on to it. They said 'Alright, we'll give you a month's trial'." He stayed 38 years.

Stan's daughter Chris distils memory into a single sentence capturing everything. "Howard had the money and didn't have the brains, my father had the brains and no money."

Stan bought in bikes for a few pounds, renovated them and sold them. Stan received only a fraction, but that was money, real money, and it increased proportionately as Stan got his hands on more expensive bikes and sold them for more. He also sold new bikes on commission, and in time King's of Oxford would grow and need to do direct selling, would move into number 34 New Road, where small outlines of bikes were set into frosted glass above the showroom window. In retrospect, as with so many stories of success, it all seems easy, inevitable. Stan's position within the company strengthened, and soon enough he was moving towards a dominant position. He became sales manager, then Managing Director. He had restless energy until the day of his retirement, and he only retired at all because doctors advised him that he should. They must have been very insistent.

Where Howard remained cautious, Stan took chances. In lean times he'd buy enough bikes to fill the whole of the top floor, getting them at knock-down prices, and when the good times came back there they were, dozens of them available and ready to go. If you have enough capital to buy when others can't, ride out a long wait and then sell for more than you paid, you are going to make money and keep on making money; and the more you make the more you make. King's grew again and expanded, opening branches as far afield as Glasgow and Manchester and Yarmouth and Hastings. The ultimate figure was 50 in 21 towns and monthly sales of 1,000 bikes. King's began to buy up other dealers until they were the biggest in the land, and that 1,000 a month may have been the largest in the world by any single dealer. They grew into selling cars. Stan became authentically rich in a way which is difficult to imagine now when financial and other statistics mean so little.

To confront this, here are two examples: Inflation did not exist and a bottle of Scotch cost 12s 6d (62½p) in 1919 and all the way to 1939; for well over a decade you paid 2½d (1p) per mile on the railways wherever you went. Stan made a million, a gigantic sum which allowed every conceivable luxury and indulgence. The million also allowed him to do what he wanted, when he wanted, how he wanted, and to a man with the character of Stan it meant he ran his world as an emperor would have run his. Former employees of King's are agreed that if Stan said jump you jumped, or as Dave Clark, one of those former employees, puts it more graphically: "If Stan said the blue car over there was pink, it was *pink*".

Here in essence is a Victorian concept, the commercial baron wielding power, but do not judge Stan by that alone. He inspired affection, loyalty and respect in equal measure. "We worked hard for him because we liked him so much", his former secretary, Sonia Ball, says. "On a Sunday morning I might be up a ladder decorating and the phone would ring. He'd need something doing and I'd be in the office in 20 minutes. I didn't think anything of that. I remember when Peter Thorneycroft was Chancellor of the Exchequer (1957–58), and in his Budget he was going to shorten the period for which you could have hire purchase agreements, from I think three years to 18 months, and it would obviously have a profound effect on selling bikes (by heightening the repayments beyond what many ordinary folk could afford). The Sunday morning after the Budget we were all in the office and we sent letters to every motorcycle dealer in the country saying: *Fire off a telegram to Thorneycroft telling him what will happen.* In the end the Budget was changed, and that never happens, does it?

"In some ways Stan was a modest man. He didn't like driving his Rolls down to Cannes for the summer holidays (registration SWB5 because even he couldn't get SWBH 1), so my husband and I used to do it, spending a couple of days on the way down. If you went into a restaurant with him in Cannes he wouldn't snap his fingers and say 'waiter this and waiter that'." At the office he was always known as SW, simply that, and the use of the initials implies unmistakable presence. In the early Thirties he found George Arthur, Elisabeth and Doug a rented house in Oxfordshire and looked after them. Doug went away to the Second World War, George Arthur died during it, and when Doug returned (he was a mechanic) Stan took him on at King's and he rose to become manager of the Bristol branch before he retired.

What Stan had he had hewn with his bare hands. Until he was 60 he worked 12 hours a day six and a half days a week and regularly covered 1,000 miles during those weeks. Before motorways, this could be a slow and agonizing distance; to average 30mph over a journey was a desirable norm, but not always attainable. On the single-carriageway roads which passed through all the towns traffic moved as a naval convoy moves – at the speed of the slowest. Once, when Stan crossed double white lines to overtake three vehicles, he told Banbury magistrates "I always try to drive so carefully". They fined him £10. He could afford to pay, let us say. We cannot know now what he thought during those lonely hours out there in the Rolls or the Bentley Continental (he had both), building, building the business. We do know that he demanded of others what he demanded of himself. Everything.

Inevitably he was drawn into racing bikes when he had settled in Oxford. Up to 1927 he took part in road races, but meetings on grass were becoming popular, so he'd have a go at that. He had a special metal rest built for his leg and ran 500cc sidecars. He is still remembered for his pristine appearance. Years later he would say: "When I was riding I always wore white overalls, as did my sidecar passenger. Leathers were not necessary in those days. We had to put up with a few sarcastic remarks, but this, plus immaculate machines, paid off in goodwill and reputation." Stan's style on a bike has been described as "spectacular and forceful", and surely it was. *The Oxford Mail* reported wistfully: "Many of the meetings were held at Marston in a field now covered with houses. Mr Hailwood would corner so fast round the short, bumpy track that he often had the crowds gasping." Stan also said "In three years we were hardly ever beaten, except by that marvellous sidecar racer Jack Surtees, father of the one and only John Surtees". (The folklore, as John Surtees says, is that Stan raced only around the Oxford area, whereas Jack, who travelled further afield, went up there and put Stan's nose out of joint by going faster! I believe this.) Four decades hence John Surtees would prepare a Formula One car and Michael Hailwood would ease himself into it...

Stan was "no star on a bike by himself", Doug says, "but at sidecars he was virtually unbeatable. They called him Hoppy Hailwood because of his leg – because he used to hop."

In 1930 Stan moved to car racing, buying an MG and having it properly prepared by a team of enthusiasts at the MG factory in Abingdon. Three times he competed in 500-mile races at Brooklands[1] and at a time when 100mph was still a bit like going through The Sound Barrier he lapped that circuit at 114mph during an attempt on the world one-hour record. He had to abort it when the weather turned nasty. Many years later he recounted this revealing story to *Motor Cycle News* after (evidently) he had broken the lap record while practising for the 1931 Ulster TT for cars at Ards: "A pretty Irish nurse was standing beside an ambulance on the approach to the sharp right-hander into Comber Village. Every lap she waved as I passed and I had visions of dating her. I was using her ambulance as a braking and changing-down point. A couple of laps later – by then I was concentrating more on her than the driving – to my horror I realized that the ambulance had moved nearer the corner. It was too late to do anything. The MG crashed into a butcher's shop and sausages, kidneys and shoulders of beef landed on my mechanic (who of course was also in the car)." With the mechanic injured, Stan embarked on and completed a 1,000-mile race alone.

In 1932 he took part in the Brooklands 500, of which Barre Lyndon wrote in *Great Motor Races*: "When the official announcements were made for the last really big race of the season it was discovered that all handicaps had been increased with the exception of that for 'unblown' 750cc cars. This suggested that such machines had a real chance for victory since they had to do only the same speed as a year before while everyone else had to travel faster. Norman Black and Hailwood promptly removed their blowers and announced that they would run unsupercharged, and their lead was followed by three other MG entrants. The rest decided to tune their machines to the limit. No other race has quite the same atmosphere as the Five Hundred. Every really enthusiastic driver tries to get the wheel of the fastest machine in sight. Hailwood again had his machine prepared by Lacey." Note the name, please: Lacey, Bill Lacey.

Such races attracted an amazing variety of cars. Earl Howe entered a straight-eight Bugatti, Count Stanislaus Czaykowski another. R.T. Horton had had his MG streamlined in the style of Sir Malcolm Campbell's Bluebird which had broken the World Land Speed Record in 1931. There were Austins and Rileys and Talbots and a couple of Maseratis and an 8-litre Bentley. It was a handicap race.

"On the chill, hazy Saturday morning of September 24, 1932 the flag fell at 11 o'clock and released one 'unblown' Austin and five MGs. The Austin took the lead in the rush and the bunched MGs behind included Lieutenant Low's TT machine, Norman Black's car and Hailwood's entry. For half an hour they had the track to themselves, then the flag fell again and released the single-seaters. They went away as if strained leashes had suddenly been slipped and the merged blare of their exhausts was like the yelling of metallic voices as cars surged momentarily into leadership, fell back and were replaced by others on the rush to the banking."

There is rare archive film of this race and when the Bentley was unleashed it dwarfed the others, particularly the MGs, as a whale would dwarf a swordfish. The Bentley pitted for fuel – you can glimpse the ordinary pits housed under a

1. A 3.25-mile circuit near Weybridge, Surrey, and the centre of British motor racing between 1907 and 1939. It was patronized by the upper classes in much the same way as Ascot and Henley. Murray Walker puts it thus: "The right crowd with no crowding". The circuit itself has been described as "a sort of concrete saucer" (Bruce Carter, *Great Motor Races*, Weidenfeld and Nicholson), with high, intimidating banking.

corrugated iron roof, people in raincoats and plus-fours wandering about – and Jack Dunfee handed over to his brother Clive. The sun had come out, glinting. Clive set off and lost control on the rim of the banking, the Bentley plunged over into trees, shearing through them before it fell onto the road below. He was killed. They did not stop the race, which Horton won at an average speed of 96.29mph. After that rush at the start Stan wasn't mentioned again.

Stan did trials and hillclimbs, too, but retired from combat in 1933 because the business was taking up too much time, although he would say: "Racing is a disease. Once it is in your blood you can never get rid of it." Interesting words, very interesting words...

Clearly the leg had not inhibited Stan during this hectic career. Later he would have it straightened in a hospital at Oxford, but it remained stiff; he had a shoe with a thickened sole for balance, and whenever he sat he positioned it straight ahead. In an armchair he rested it along the arm. Sonia Ball says that the leg didn't prevent Stan doing whatever he wanted. Nothing did that.

Stan was authentically dynamic as well as rich. They speak in hushed tones of a day after the War when money was tight everywhere and Stan bought *6,000* Enfield bikes from the War Department, who understandably would not allow him to sell them in their khaki colours. No problem. The spraying of them red began immediately.

In time there would be marriage and a family. The first born, a son, died soon after birth, the second was Christine – we'll hear how and why she shortened it to Chris in a moment – and on April 2, 1940 a son again. He was christened Stanley Michael Bailey, and from his first moments he was photogenic. He would remain so all his days.

2

Stan made money, but used it as it was intended to be used. He spent it. He lived in impressive houses, one called Langsmead, one at Goring on the Thames, then Highmore Hall, set in 52 acres at Nettlebed, not far from Henley. Highmore Hall was a proper country mansion built in the reign of Charles II. It had 10 bedrooms, it had the dignified atmosphere of oak-panelling, and Stan became what he was always going to become, Lord of the Manor. "There were servants", Chris says. "We had a butler and a housekeeper and a cook and maids and three gardeners. We had a beautiful dining room and we did eat there at times, Sunday lunch and so on. I certainly didn't find having a butler intimidating to family life. They were reasonably friendly butlers. We had a little room called The Study, and familywise everything happened there."

The woman Stan married, who bore Chris and Michael, exists in the shadows. She must have been a striking woman because both her children were, one genuinely beautiful with a figure to turn heads at Cannes, the other genuinely handsome with a physique to make hearts flutter. "I remember her", Chris will say carefully, "but I don't talk about her very much." The woman Stan married left and returned several times, and one day did not return. The children were very young. Evidently she doted on Michael. Others would all his days, too.

Whether Michael cultivated a degree of secrecy about his family or prefered simply not to discuss it, is something lost forever. Charlie Rous was a journalist who saw one of Michael's first races, became close, and once at Daytona would be pressed into active service when Michael was going for a world record. "I did not know anything about his family, except Stan. Mike never ever mentioned his mother and I still don't really know what happened. I think they were divorced because Stan was remarried to a woman called Pat. Some years after Stan died I did in fact meet Mike's sister. I didn't even know he had a sister."

"My first memory of Mike", Chris says, "is him bawling in the pram. I remember vividly one particular day. I thought 'Poor chap, he's obviously hungry' and I picked a gooseberry and popped it in his mouth, and of course he nearly died. I was not very popular among the household." Forgive her and her good intentions. She was only three.

"I think it must have affected Mike to a certain extent when my mother left, although I'll tell you what, my father was a most wonderful father and mother. He did replace her with his love and he was everything towards us, and it must have been a very difficult time for him. My mother must have missed Mike in the early days and he must have missed her. She started to go away when he was still a baby. We did have wonderful nannies and housekeepers along the way who really loved and looked after Mike, so at the end he must have had the love, but I'm quite sure it can take into adulthood to get over the sense of insecurity, which is probably why Mike did a lot of solitary trumpet playing in his bedroom. Lonely? Yes. Even years later, if you went to a race meeting he was often shut away in his caravan with perhaps only one other person. Nobody else was allowed near him. He just needed to be alone." There may well have been other reasons for that. Fame crowded him and fame brought endless, endless people to do the crowding, and the torment to someone shy scarcely needs underscoring.

Living in a mansion must lead to a certain isolation. Most kids of that age aren't even sure what a butler does, never mind have one. But however lonely he remained into maturity he rarely betrayed it except to those very near to him, but the isolation increased as the fame mounted. At the time when that handsome face had become instantly recognizable anywhere on the Continent he spent many hours playing cards in hotel rooms, sometimes pressing himself into the ultimate refuge with games of patience. He would be happy in company who did not know who he was, but as the years flowed by such company was harder and harder to find. Everybody knew who he was, and in deep, personal moments he would wonder who his true friends really were. All else aside you could make money out of him, you see.

He *was* shy, sometimes painfully so, and this too would remain with him all his days. When his very name had become synonymous with bravery – authentic bravery, the real thing, and the George Medal to prove it after, himself on fire, he hauled a driver from a racing car – he found extreme difficulty travelling across a room to meet strangers. How much of this was fashioned in those formative years is anyone's guess. Perhaps he was simply born with it and it had lingered, but it existed and most people found it as charming as it was inexplicable.

Nor is boarding school necessarily an answer to this, and in some cases it can militate against it; and Mike went to boarding school when he was six. "He was shipped off at that age", Chris says, "because my father had to go to The States on business and he didn't want the housekeepers to have the responsibility. I was at boarding school at Ipswich and he joined me. I don't know why Ipswich: maybe there wasn't a school nearer at hand which took anybody that young. He stayed at boarding school from then till he went to Pangbourne." [2]

This was no orphanage of an upbringing, however. "In fact I think we had a happy childhood, actually. We had a marvellous stream which ran through this garden of ours and a big tree trunk had fallen over it onto a small island, so we could use that to get across. We had a tree-house there and everything else. He was just a normal lad. My father was slightly larger than life. He was a wonderful father, but a very hard taskmaster and he demanded an awful lot of those around him. He required you to be good at everything. If you showed the least ability – even at, say, ice skating – you didn't just do it, you had to do it better than anybody else. We grew up under that fairly stern sort of countenance. He was equally hard with me. One might have thought he might have been softer. But he was very fair, and he wouldn't treat me any differently to Mike because he felt we both had to have the same treatment all the way through. I suppose we behaved quite well because dad was such a stern taskmaster.

"We didn't actually do anything too terribly wrong apart from write off the odd car. Well, I did, and I hid in my room for a day and a bit. I'd been away and I sneaked inside the house – you could do this in our house, it was big enough – and I daren't come down the stairs because of the reaction I was going to get. Dad had bought it for me, a beautiful Sunbeam Alpine, and although I hadn't actually written if off myself – somebody else had done that for me – I didn't have the courage to tell my father. When I did tell him he went mad, of course. *Chrrristine* (mimicking a low, rising bellow of anger). That's why I hate the name Christine. *Chrrristine.* I prefer Chris."

Stan had done Brooklands, had done motorbikes, and it remained in the blood, just as he said it did. "I suppose dad was able to get little bikes for us. They were more than toys, but they were the size of toys. They were proper bikes. He had them properly made, and we were just sort of put on them and told to get round the lawn. We had a little car which was the same." The bikes had 12-inch wheels, three speeds and Michael wore leathers, goggles and a crash helmet. The gardeners were less than enthusiastic about what he did to the lawn.

Christine Hailwood was nine, Michael was just seven.

Stan had the kickstart removed because "I believed he should learn to push-start; he became an expert at it". Mike would always remember this very first bike, would remember riding it round the lawn, but "I didn't know how to stop the thing, I just used to go round and round until it ran out of petrol".

3

In time Stan would remarry. "We had a wonderful stepmother who joined us in the early Fifties", Chris recalls. "She was marvellous and we loved her dearly. She was beautiful and a lovely lady; she loved us both so we only really missed out on the early formative years." By then Michael was at Pangbourne and disliking it. His reports were daunting documents, the only favourable comments being, as Stan would recall, "about cricket and football and particularly boxing". This was something else he carried with him into adulthood: a non-violent man by nature who habitually avoided arguments

---

2. Pangbourne Nautical College, set in over 200 acres near Reading, Berkshire; it prepared boys for the Royal and Merchant Navies.

which could lead to more, but if they did lead to more, anyone laid a hand on him at their peril. Near Rimini one time, he would hit an Italian 'hood' so hard that he broke a finger (and missed a race the following weekend because of it) and he established his own philosophy: "If you have to hit them, hit them as hard as you can. If they get up, run like hell!" He always smiled when he said that. Generally they didn't get up.

On Sundays, after Church Parade, Stan used to drive to Pangbourne, collect Michael and take him home, where an old James trials bike[3] awaited him. He had outgrown the lawn. For four hours at a time Michael would circle an eight-acre field within the grounds; he did it so repetitively that he wore an oval track.

There is a great and natural temptation to read too much into this, to say that he saw his future and went for it as hard as he could. Almost certainly that is false. Virtually all kids played then, in however simple a way, and the streets were full of them, not traffic: cricket in summer, football in winter, and everywhere you'd see a lad held by some lonely compulsion kicking a tennis ball against a wall, trapping it at whatever angle it came back to him, volleying it again, hour after hour, hypnotized by movement and the control of movement; see a lad cast a ball against a wall and hit it with a home-hewn bat when it came back time after time, fascinated by co-ordination and the strange primitive fulfilling power of striking something which is moving fast. It was what kids did, it came with the summers and the winters, goals and wickets crudely chalked on walls, and they needed little more. Imagination and the ritual of the thing itself were enough. Television, for those who had it at all, was a big cabinet in the corner of the room with a small screen which carried amateurish black-and-white pictures as if taken from afar, and these were only transmitted a few hours a day. The rest of the time the screen was blank, and there was only one channel. The clever bric-a-brac of today, the video games and computer games and ghetto blasters and Walkmans, were completely unknown, remote as man landing on the moon. So you kicked a ball against a wall, or if dad was rich you enacted the same ritual but on a bike, round and round and round until you'd cut the oval groove. It was a different context, but the same thing.

There was a subconscious gain. If you begin something early enough and do it often enough you store up an immense and profound experience of the basics. In another time altogether, Ayrton Senna, who bestrode Formula One, would quietly confess that he had an advantage over all the others. He'd been given – by a rich dad – a kart when he was four, so the feel of movement, the currents of movement, were all within him. Michael had first known them slightly later, when he was six.

Michael brought friends home from Pangbourne and they rode the bike, too, and Stan worried in case they injured themselves. Stan also said he was worried about the neighbours' reaction to a bike minus silencer doing interesting things to the sacred slumber of English Sunday afternoons, although it is extremely hard to imagine anyone getting satisfaction if they journeyed up the drive to complain.

Michael was now 14.

One forgotten afternoon around 1955, Stan secretly timed him out of curiosity, and then "one of the boys who used to work for me and who was a very

---

3. Trials is a form of cross-country with observed sections tackled with great deliberation.

good grass track rider, came out to my home. I asked him to ride the James round the same track and I was flabbergasted at his time. It was much slower. When the boy found out what I was doing he had a really good go and was rather crestfallen and amazed when I told him what time Mike was going round in.

"Some time later I heard the bike revving away in an old quarry we had, and I walked across with the idea of telling him to pack it up so the neighbours could have a Sunday afternoon nap. He had marked out a course with stakes and string and was riding those rocks like an expert. I hid behind a tree and then quietly disappeared."

At 16 Michael asked if he could leave the College and Stan agreed. Michael went to his room, packed and simply got in the car. He didn't look back. The future, whatever it was, would not be cold showers, iron discipline and at least one beating he would remember all his days. It is so with many who become great sportspeople. They rarely accept discipline imposed because they impose their own, and it is much more rigid, more all-embracing. This has a meaning to them that square bashing can never have. It is taking them to where they want to go, not to where somebody else wants them to go, and in absolutely their own way. It may be that Stanley Michael Bailey Hailwood inherited more from Stanley William Bailey Hailwood than even he appreciated.

In time, few human beings would live life as fully as Michael, succumb so effortlessly and willingly to so many temptations in so many places, and yet discipline themselves so completely when it was important. Sometimes he would arrive with a hangover, unkempt and unshaven, but he'd always do the business and do it well. Most times he just arrived and did the business. He would break his body mightily in accidents, but was never once heard to mention pain, and if he was caught taking aspirin for a hangover he would say sheepishly that it was only for a headache; and even aspirins he took only rarely. Some mistook him for being casual because he gave that appearance, laid-back about it all, easy about it, yes, even dismissive. But it was totally different the instant an engine fired up, and what he did then was his own discipline, nobody else's.

Perhaps he foresaw this and the consequences of it. "Yes, at 16 Mike said he'd never live to 30", Chris recalls. "That used to worry us, my stepmother and I. We used to think 'Poor little lad, he's only 16 and he's saying this'. Whatever he did, if it was wrong he'd say 'I have to do it to get it all in because I'm not going to live longer than 30'. It's a very peculiar thing for a 16-year-old to say, isn't it? It wasn't a tease or anything, he was serious. I think it was probable that he saw he was going to do things which could kill him. He knew he wouldn't have a long life. So this explains everything: he crammed everything into his life, he lived to the hilt."

Stan took Michael into King's, but soon suspected him of malingering, of being too keen to just run errands, offering to fetch the lads cigarettes or whatever so he could escape on his bike to do the fetching. Dave Clark remembers that. "Go and get yourself a job, you lazy so and so", Stan would say to him, and occasionally there would be a clip round the ear to accompany it. Others had already formed a true impression about how shy he was, how normal he was. They knew only this most superficial part, the part you couldn't mistake. His inner fibre Michael revealed only to himself, if that. Perhaps he just lived intuitively, with no pretentions to a future at all and would accept it whatever it would be.

He was moving towards physical maturity, but true adulthood in the sense that he would become his own man would have to await Stan's departure to retirement in Nassau several years hence. "My father and Michael were both strong-willed, but there was only one winner and that was my father. So Mike's will had to bend to his, as did all of ours in a way. When my father lived abroad Mike started to develop his own strengths in his own way because he didn't have the overriding factor of my father always being there."

One final glance at childhood. "We both went to school, we saw each other in the holidays and it was good to see each other", Chris says. "I don't really remember that Mike and I scrapped, ever. Our relationship was close, it was solid when we saw each other. There was a sort of understanding because of what we'd been through together, I suppose, a sharing of experiences from an early age."

Stan decided to get Michael a job at Triumph, who made motorcycles at Meriden, near Birmingham. "I suppose he thought he was going to be a tester, but I made sure he was given the dirtiest job in the factory", Stan would say typically and inevitably. You may think you've got kid gloves, but if you have they'll be dirty kid gloves.

Percy Tait was a test developer, and soon enough he would come across "this lad with a wonderful personality who just wanted to race motorbikes. That was all he wanted to do, although he was very talented musically. He went through the whole factory, on the track[4] and then in the repair shop. He was only earning peanuts, but I don't think that was the point of it." It wasn't.

Twenty-four years later Percy Tait's telephone rang and Mike Hailwood invited him out for a meal. It was Saturday, March 23, 1981. Tait said he couldn't make it, but would be delighted to on the Monday, after he and Mike had finished the road safety lecture they were due to give at Stratford on Avon...

4

At first there was an hotel, then digs in Meriden, and at the weekends there were bikes and trials and scrambles to leaven the daily grind, which he didn't like (factory discipline this time). Somehow he got a Triumph. After all he did work there. At 17 he competed in the Scottish Six Days Trial in the Triumph team, his first event. Stan had been 17 when he'd first done it, at Axe Edge, Buxton. Stan would remember these Scottish trials. "Mike retired with ignition trouble. He had been doing very well considering he was the youngest rider there and it was his first effort, and I do not think he was too unhappy. The sight of those massive rocks and boulders frightened even me, but Mike, with his phlegmatic outlook on life, just shrugged them and his retirement off." It was a gesture which would become as famous as the man, and again people mistook it for what it was not. He bore disappointment privately, and many years later, when he was under merciless pressure, just once he revealed it to another human being. This witness to it, a hardened Ulsterman and a hardened rider, was shocked. "He had been pestering me", Stan would say, "to let him have a go at racing, but I thought he was too young, and finding a small machine was most difficult. However, my good friend the late Bill Webster of Crewe had two 125cc MVs.

4. Not of course a racing or testing track, but the area of the factory where the assembly of bikes and cars took place, vehicles moving along to have parts fitted.

I asked if he would sell me one, but Bill explained that Count Agusta[5] let him have them on condition that top riders only were allowed to buy them. But he offered to lend Mike a single-overhead-camshaft model and he was entered for Oulton Park on the Sunday following the Scottish". The date was April 22, 1957.

He blew it at the flag, was left on the line, and Stan, who'd had the kick-start removed from that very first bike so Michael would become expert at push-starts, thought: "Oh well, that's that". But Stan watched as the MV spluttered and coughed and gurgled and began to roar, and soon SMB Hailwood was moving up the field, although "Bill and I agreed to overgear and overjet the machine[6] to save the motor and slow Mike up a bit. It was also decided that Mike should try and follow Bill around. Stan was in a 'sweat', convinced that Michael would fall off, and if he had "believe me it would have been the end of his racing. Bill was glancing over his shoulder, and although in sixth or seventh position was obviously waiting for Mike. After four laps he caught up and went ahead of Bill, who followed behind to see how he was shaping." Michael finished 11th. Laconically, Michael would say years later that "I enjoyed it so much I decided to carry on". Perhaps it was all as simple as that.

Murray Walker, now a famous BBC commentator, was there with his father Graham, who preceded him in commentary and was a journalist, too. "I remember it well", Walker says. "We went to do a broadcast. I didn't know Stan Hailwood, but obviously my father did. Dad was editor of *Motor Cycling*, and King's of Oxford used to take a double-page advert in every issue, 52 issues a year. To tell you the truth I cannot remember if I was aware of Mike before the meeting. Bill Webster was a pugilistic-looking chap with a broken nose, a flattened face, but he was the MV importer for the UK and provided the bike. Mike got on it and everyone was flabbergasted. Nobody had heard of him except through Stan and they hadn't seen him in action. It was clear then that Mike was a natural.

"Stan realized on that day the property he had on his hands. I have always had the private theory that Stan, who had been a reasonable competitor, but no superstar, tried to live through Mike what he had wanted to be himself. So Stan would proceed meticulously and ruthlessly and enormously to develop what Mike had. That, incidentally, was not only going to satisfy Stan's ego, but would do King's of Oxford no harm whatsoever."

Webster judged Michael already good enough to have a bike of his own, and if Stan couldn't get bikes who could? Stan got the 125 MV, a 196 MV which he bored out to 240cc, and a 50cc Itom, which was made by a Milanese company and would prove so successful as a marque that 50cc class racing was internationally recognized in 1962. Stan and Michael roamed the land, racing wherever they could get entries. Michael might be enjoying himself in an innocent way, enacting the impulses of his late teens, but Stan wasn't doing that, Stan was taking it so seriously that the whole world would know of Michael. He would tell them.

---

5. Count Dominico Agusta founded Meccanica Vergera in Italy in 1945. It became known universally as MV. Between 1952 and 1977, when production ceased altogether, MV won 37 world titles and it remains as a thunderous name. Of the Count and the thunder, much, much more later. The company's main occupation was (and still is) making helicopters.
6. Altering the jets in the carburettor to make it run richer, cooler and not so quickly.

"When Michael started riding his father used to come and pick me up in his Rolls-Royce at the small farm where I lived to get me to test the bikes, sort out the sprockets and so on", Percy Tait says. "The funny thing was, after the first time we went down to Silverstone to do some testing and fix some gearing problems, Stan said 'How much do I owe you?', and I said 'Nothing'. It was a pleasure to do it, I didn't want anything. He said: 'I'll tell you this, my lad, if someone offers me a cigarette I never refuse it. That's why I'm a millionaire. Look, I'm going to give you some money', and I think he paid me £10 or £20, which was a lot then; and that's how it went on.

"We'd go to, say, Castle Combe. He always picked me up and took me there while Mike went in the van from King's of Oxford. I'd go off on a 250 and show him the different lines on corners, show him the way round. He was easy-going, down-to-earth, never big-headed. I think it was his calmness, really, he wasn't erratic. If you are an erratic kind of person you can't control the thinking, control the thought-processes.

"In the early days he would change into his leathers in the back of the van or outside. We had no facilities. Many a time we've changed on one side of the van. There was always a bit of a snack bar, but after a meeting we stopped at an hotel or somewhere to have a meal.

"Mike always thought I taught him a lot. I suppose *I* was quite calm, *I* wasn't erratic. I used to say to him 'I'll do a couple or three laps, follow me and then you take over. I'll follow you and see where you're making the mistakes.' We did that and we had a lot of fun. Obviously, when he first started he wasn't getting the lines right, but he was one of those people who could learn a course very, very quickly. He didn't have to go round lap after lap, he'd got it, you know. Could he make the bikes go fast in those days? Oh crickey, yes! And there was a lot of joking. He'd speak broken Italian to Bill Webster, who'd speak it back – no, they couldn't speak Italian, and it was very, very funny ..."

One of the meetings in 1957 was at Crystal Palace, "a lovely circuit which circled the present athletics track. The Press Box was in fact a caravan, one of those things they take round for workmen when they repair the roads, little wooden steps up to it, nothing lavish about it." The words are those of Rous, who found himself sitting in the caravan to cover the meeting. He had never heard of Hailwood. "A colleague got fed up with this old boy with a club foot coming up the steps into the Press Room and telling us how good his son, in the last race, was. In fact we got very fed up. This was the start of the big sell. Hailwood pushed his son right from the start, and it was unheard-of how he did it.

"Stan had three or four mechanics handling this and that, and he did the PR in the hope that it would make news, and it worked. Gradually I noticed that items which weren't usually printed – bike racing was the poor man's sport, there was no money in it and the only national coverage was the Isle of Man TT – were being printed about him. This was a young lad who nobody knew at all, but who very quickly started winning races" – and Stan made sure everyone knew, everyone.

Jerry Wood became a friend. "I was working in a factory making diesels. I was living in north London and doing the night shift and I hated it. One night Mike had driven down from Oxford for a jazz concert and he called in. 'Come with me', he said. I said 'You know I can't, I've got to go to work'. He said 'I'll make the money up to you'. So I did..."

Iain Mackay became a friend. "He lived in Boars Hill, I lived in Aylesbury, and he used to come over to a jazz club around 1957, 1958. He had a very wry sense of humour, but he was shy, desperately shy. He had a 'Milliganesque' sense of humour, for want of a better term, based very much on the Goon Shows. He listened to the Goon Shows, oh yes."

This was cult territory on BBC radio. Starting as Crazy People in 1951 and largely written by Spike Milligan, an original comic genius, the programme evolved into The Goon Show and by 1957–58 was at its height. It was quintessentially British and comprised a sequence of bizarre characters fumbling, stumbling and scheming a path through a wildly improbable storyline, like climbing Mount Everest from the *inside*. The dialogue was based around the characters taking a logical series of steps to reach an illogical conclusion, or taking an illogical series of steps to reach a logical conclusion, and all of it heavily loaded with puns and innuendo, some extremely *risqué*. It was so far-out that even many British people couldn't comprehend it, or gave up trying for fear of their sanity. It was also excruciatingly funny if you happened to have a certain sense of humour, and to define that sense of humour I'd say it would actively enjoy making fun of itself, never take life too seriously and be exceedingly irreverent.

By contrast, "Mike got a lot of criticism in the Press because of his father, who on the one hand was a great asset, and on the other a great liability. Mike had the best equipment, although Mike got nothing, nothing, for free, but people didn't know that. I met Stan on a couple of occasions and he was a tough guy, brash and hard." The speaker is Phil Read, who had already begun a riding career. Asked whether Mike had a philosophy about life, Read responded "Oh, he just lived, and that's the truth, but I never knew him do anything if he didn't do it properly. He was a very competitive person. As a rider he worked very hard."

Quite how much Michael did get for free is unprovable now. Stan himself, writing in *Motor Cycle News*, said "I should like to finally kill the myth that it was money and backing that made Mike. I am opposed to parents who spoil their children by giving them everything they want. In business, and this applies to Mike, I believe in the theory that if anybody wants anything badly enough they must earn it. Whatever Mike has got he has earned by his own natural ability as a rider. The only thing I gave him was my enthusiasm, encouragement, advice, and a temporary loan towards that first 125cc MV.

"He had saved some money from working at King's and at Triumph and this went towards the purchase. Then he won sufficient to buy the Itom for £90. From the two he again earned enough to buy on hire purchase the 196 MV, and so it grew and grew. The idea was prevalent that I was spending money like water on Mike and his machines – a ridiculous notion. All I did was try and run the racing like a business. It was also a great pleasure, because I believe it should be done properly or left alone. The fact that the backing was there if required was obviously a great comfort, but apart from Mike being in the red to me for the first 18 months there was only my guidance and management during that newcomer period. I think the fallacy was fostered by two things: A slight feeling of envy and jealousy on the part of a few people who hated to think that a kid of 17 or 18 could come along and win, and my belief that showmanship goes a long way towards success." (The truth of what Mike did and did not get probably rests where the truth generally is to be found, somewhere between the two positions.) "When Mike first began there was no start money and everything had to be saved from winnings. The first machines we looked after ourselves. When we had two or three machines earning money we engaged a mechanic ..."

Stan would judge the moment, the real moment when it began, as a 250cc race at Cookstown, Northern Ireland, where Michael won and broke the lap record. Stan decided that a winter racing in South Africa was just what Michael needed, and what Michael needed Michael got. (If Michael was doing it out of winnings, did they pay for the trip? Hmmm.) Stan rang John Surtees and inquired if Surtees would lend Michael his NSU to take with him. "I'd used it in 1955 and then kept it and run it in a number of races, which I'd won", Surtees says. "Stan came on and said 'Can I borrow it for the South African season?'." Surtees said "Yes".

"He was riding an NSU and he had a 350 Norton with him", Jim Redman recalls. Redman, who was born in Britain but had left for Southern Africa on the grounds that if he did National Service the pay wasn't good enough, had designs of his own on conquering the world and would do so. "Mike was very young, you know, but a mature guy for his age because he'd lived in an environment with the Old Man pushing him. He was quiet and modest. We got him drunk for the first time in his life in Durban. You saw the overall result ..." (Of this, more, much more, later.)

"He came out with the late Dave Chadwick"[7], Nobby Clark says. He also came with his own mechanic. Clark himself was to become a superb mechanic, and he'd be there on The Island 20 years later. Clark was a Rhodesian (now Zimbabwe) and "Rhodesians used to dominate the racing scene out here. Mike and Dave had come out to do the local season, which was off-season in Europe. The circuit where I met them was called Grand Central and was near Johannesburg. After the meeting we all went to the local hotel and had a few drinks before all the Rhodesians headed north – we had a 300-mile trip to get back home and be at work the next morning. The beer was flowing pretty well and Mike put a spoonful of sugar in my beer, then a spoonful into someone else's and so on. This resulted in the beer frothing, the froth went in all directions and the place looked like a snowstorm had hit it." This lovely little tale is instructive and blends perfectly with Webster and the mock-Italian. Michael was full of fun and would remain so all his days.

"He didn't ride the 350 Norton until right towards the end of the season", Redman says. "There was a race called the Port Elizabeth 200 where they closed the roads. I lived halfway between the town and the circuit, and to save putting the bikes on the trailer I used to ride across. This day I pitched up with me riding a 350 and my wife Marlene riding a 500 Norton. Michael couldn't believe his eyes and started riding his 350. He thought: If a woman can ride a 500 I can ride a 350!

"He had all the potential in the world, and of course the backing. Mike was the poor little rich boy, but it just so happened that contrary to what usually happens – the poor little rich boy is bloody useless and wastes a lot of dad's money – this poor little rich boy turned out to be the best rider in the world."

There's a postscript to this trip which tells us a little more about Stan and may give you a smile. "Stan wouldn't give the NSU back because Mike had won races in South Africa on it", Surtees says. "The argument went on and on, and in the end he paid out for it, but I never did get the bike back."

---

7. An experienced rider from Manchester.

5

Unheard of. That completely covers the assault Stan was poised to unleash, and unleash is not a word I've chosen carelessly. Mike, you see, had returned from South Africa with a lot of trophies. Stan hired Bill Lacey, the tuner, or more properly brought him out of retirement, the same Lacey who had tuned the MG of Brooklands days. Lacey worked full-time preparing Michael's bikes and was given a workshop at Tymore Hall with everything in it he might need. Stan bought a "large old van" for £200 and it became a mobile workshop. He had *Ecurie Equipe, For the Love of The Sport* emblazoned across its flank in bold lettering, and nobody had seen such a thing before. They imagined the van must have cost a fortune.

"Stan was the first to have a transporter", Walker says. "It was gigantic, and on the back doors in gold-edged red lettering he had *Here come Mike's bikes*, and in my pedantic way I thought it should have read *There go Mike's bikes*. The van and the facilities were absolutely unheard of then, and it was very much resented among a lot of the motorcycle fraternity because they used to turn up in the equivalent of a Transit van with a bike stuck in the back or on a trailer. There was nothing lush and luxurious like that transporter."

Stan described it thus: "Whereas others were buying new light vans at £500 I went the other way. We had the large van painted cream with red lettering and it was big enough to carry welding equipment, bench and vice, a wash basin and beds for the mechanic and Mike. In fact, a mobile workshop. I know this colourful innovation really shook everyone, but I was always a believer in good showmanship. It heightened the tone of motorcycling, which for years had been regarded as synonymous with dirt and grease. In this respect Mike failed me. I got so tired and angry at his worn-out boots, tatty leathers and odd gloves, but anything I did or said made no difference so I stopped trying." (This is difficult to believe; not that Michael was indifferent to what he wore – that rings very true – but that Stan was forced to accept it. If *that* is true, it is the only recorded instance of Stan not getting his own way.)

Of this transporter Surtees says "When it came in painted with *For the Love of the Sport* people used to wince and say 'Oh, well, that's Stan', but so what? Stan had decided that this was going to be the chosen path. Stan went to meetings and took times, and if three or four machines were faster he'd go along the line of the grid before the race and try to buy them. He ended up with an enormous group of bikes. Stan went to Ducati and commissioned a total design and build of bikes and did a commercial deal so that King's of Oxford would buy X number of Ducati (road) bikes in return. This is how the 250 and 350 Ducati twins were made. I raced against Mike in those early years at places like Scarborough, Silverstone and Crystal Palace on my own bikes, which to a large degree ended up with Mike. I sold them to Stan, who wanted them for Mike.

"Stan was an extreme man, he was on a massive family thing with Mike, and from his own point of view an ego trip, too, but again so what? Was he living it through Mike? Don't a lot of people? Isn't that a question of dreams, of achieving things? You can't be critical of him that way. OK, there is a certain degree of hypocrisy about the whole thing, but dear me, that's life. I don't doubt that if my father had had the same purchasing power as Stan he would have used it to try and further my career, although he wouldn't have got up to the same sort of things because he was a different sort of man."

Read had started his career on May 13, 1956 (riders remember dates like that). "We thought, there's a rich boy being brought by his dad in a Continental Bentley. This big transporter arrived, this artic, with the writing on it. I suppose Mike was rather resented in a way. Here was this young lad and he had two mechanics to every bike, and he'd crash it, and they'd wheel another one out, and he'd jump on that. It was an extraordinary thing. We were a bit gobsmacked. Stan was – what shall we say? – aggressive and forceful in looking after Mike's interests. He was also helpful to the people who would help Mike, but aggressive to the people who were threatening Mike's publicity."

Rous amplifies this sense of amazement. "People like Stan set a ball rolling which led to the modern coverage of the sport. He was the one who let the world know that motorbike racing was something. At the time it was big business for the motorcycle dealers, but otherwise the business aspect was totally different. There was no sponsorship in the sense we know it now. What you had was support from the oil companies and tyre companies and that was all. You got peanuts and you had to earn them as well. Gradually the oil companies withdrew their support and moved into the background while at the same time the sponsors – principally, I suppose, Marlboro – began to put millions into it."

Ah, yes, but this is still 1958, when motorbike racing was surrounded by the rudimentary, where many tracks were even more basic than they are now, and the Bentley or Rolls and the transporter, and the mechanics and the array of perfect bikes provoked such strong reactions. This is a direct comparison, vintage 1958, drawn from the memory of Tommy Robb, a warm, perceptive and delightful Ulsterman who was so representative of the era:

"I put my NSU on the boat at Belfast lugging it up the gangplank. The crew then lashed the bike down with ropes – it was exposed to the elements – for the crossing to Liverpool. I could not afford a berth. I had got to know all the crew, and when the Captain was on the bridge the crew used to smuggle me forward and I slept where they did. The tide was in at Liverpool, so I had to lift the bike step by step up the gangplank." Robb had guts, ambition, skill. What he didn't have was money. This day in 1958 he had crossed the Irish Sea to race at Aintree.[8] "I was not a professional then, and I didn't turn professional for another couple of years. I was just starting to come to England to race amongst the fast men. I had been reading in the Press that this teenager from Oxford had been to South Africa, and how well he had been doing there, and it was the son of millionaire Stan Hailwood of King's of Oxford. I thought: this is some lad, this is – I was older, you see.

"In those days I was met by Ralph Rensen, a Norton rider who was later killed at the Isle of Man. He'd take me to Oulton, or Aintree, or wherever and bring me back to the boat, and I'd sleep on the way back, and I'd do the same for him when

---

8. Site of the Grand National at Liverpool where there was also a motor racing circuit, which ran in the opposite direction to the steeplechase course. Aintree hosted the Formula One British Grand Prix between 1955 and 1962 and it was here that a certain Nigel Mansell saw his first F1 race. Here, too, Stirling Moss won the 1955 British Grand Prix in a Mercedes-Benz, narrowly beating Juan-Manuel Fangio, and the question remains: did Fangio, a most gracious man, allow Moss, a Briton driving in Britain, to win? Nobody knows except Fangio and he isn't saying – or rather, he says, in much the same way as Michael would later in other contexts, that the best man won on the day.

he came to Belfast. At Aintree I was walking up the pits in my leathers and I saw this young fellow walking towards me. I had seen photographs of him in *Motor Cycle News* and he must have seen photographs of me. We sort of looked at each other and just as I was about to say 'Mike Hailwood' he said 'Tommy Robb'. From that day a friendship began which became bonded throughout my racing career. The only difference was that I was doing it on my one old NSU whereas Mike started with a 350 or 500 Norton, a 125 Ducati, a 250 NSU and I thought: My God how can I compete with that?"

"Paddy Driver and I came over in March 1958", Redman says, "and my first race meeting was at Brands Hatch. I had a tremendous day and the Old Man was one of the first to come over and say you did really well. I'd saved up the glorious sum of £1,500 to conquer the world, and at that stage, by the time I'd paid my fare, bought a van, bought some bikes and some spares I had 50 quid left in the world.

"I won £75 that day. I had a fourth, a third and a second – the second was behind Derek Minter, known as The King of Brands. Stan said 'Come up and stay at our place on the way to Silverstone', and Stan also said 'You've had such a wonderful day, don't take the money, get them to give you a big silver tray engraved with your first-ever meeting in Europe.' My answer was: 'Stan, I can't eat a silver tray, I've just got a 150% increase in my bank account!'

"Paddy and I did go and stay for a couple of weeks. It was a magnificent place in its own grounds, and all that. I remember it: the curved drive, the crunchy gravel, the garages which were old stables, the butlers and maids. Lounging back in there we thought we were the king of the kids. In later years the Old Man told me what he paid for it when he'd bought it in, I think, 1954 – £40,000 for this estate. It was a fortune, it was like someone telling you today they've paid £10 million for somewhere.

"I always got on very well with Mike. We were friendly because we had come from South Africa and we'd look after him down there. He'd stayed with Paddy in Johannesburg. We became even more friendly when we had gone through the mill together."

In time Graham and Murray Walker were also guests, and although I've recounted this in another book (*Honda: Conquerors of the Track*, Patrick Stephens) it will bear repeating verbatim. "Stan had been known to turn Mike out of the house", Murray Walker says. "Sometimes he threw him out in the middle of the night if they'd had a row, and Mike would go to Bill Lacey's home until it was sorted out" – and in time Lacey himself would storm out, and only return because racing was really all about Mike, not Stan. "Stan's house was fairly close to Silverstone, and it was a tradition that when there was a big meeting there, if my father and I were doing the commentary Stan would invite us to stay. The cynic in me suggests that Stan was asking us not only because my father was editor of *Motor Cycling* and therefore not at all a bad bloke to be on the right side of, but because Graham and Murray Walker could give an extra amount of publicity to his gifted son. It worked, because I'm damn sure we did without realizing it!

"I arrived one evening and Stan had a vast armchair, and he sat there with one leg up along the arm of it. I asked how everything was. 'Not too good, Murray. We had a bit of a problem today. We were testing the Norton at Silverstone and Mike came off and he's hurt his leg quite badly, but he's insisting on riding tomorrow. You know Mike likes you, go up and have a word with him.'

"Mike was also a gifted musician, and I went upstairs and he was sitting half-on half-off the bed with the leg all bandaged up playing the clarinet. I said 'How's the leg?'. 'Not too good.' 'What's all this about riding tomorrow?' 'Well, the Old Man says I've got to, so I suppose I have.' I knew who was telling the truth. Mike started from the back, he had a pusher to get the bike moving, and he won..."

Walker assesses Stan as "a most peculiar mixture. I found out he could be – and very often was – hard as the proverbial nails and utterly ruthless, a brilliant businessman, but he could also charm the proverbial birds out of the trees, and he'd got this putty-like human being in his hands. I don't mean Mike was submissive or hadn't got any character of his own – God knows, we all know he had – but Stan had a very, very forceful personality, and at that age Mike took the line of least resistance. Mike was friendly and cheerful, but peculiarly withdrawn.

"My father used to run meetings at Donington; they were called Donington Days and were a publicity thing for *Motor Cycling*. They had a big string of races and I think everybody got in for free. One day my father went up to Stan and actually put his arm round Stan's shoulder and said jokingly – because my father was a bit blunt – 'I like you, you know, Stan, but I don't like the way you run your business', and the next day the magazine's advertising director got a cancellation for all of King's advertising. My father was called in by this manager and told he had to apologize to Stan, which my father was not at all anxious to do.

"Apart from being a businessman Stan was a public relations man and an advertising man, and he saw the opportunity to develop King's through all sorts of ways. I think it was Stan who made them the biggest in the country."

Rous first spoke to Michael at Silverstone on what he thinks was a test day. "I was working for the *News Chronicle* (a British national newspaper that folded in 1960) and doing bits and pieces of freelancing. He struck me then as a very keen young boy, by no means macho. It was almost as if he'd be more interested in books than bikes, although no way was he actually academic. My feeling was that he was dominated by Stan, and I don't think he realized how much. It then became apparent to him that this was a very easy thing to do. He suddenly found motorbike racing very, very easy and didn't put any great store by being able to do it. I think this was a surprise to him. He seemed to come to the front so easily; within a very few months he came from nowhere on the 125 his father plonked him on, but you have to bear in mind that he never rode rubbish machines. That is a most important thing. Yet he progressed from 125 to 350 and 500 Nortons, where instantly he was quick. Bill Lacey was brought in, so Mike always rode machines which were capable of winning, but equally you had to know how to use them in order to win."

This, as we have seen, was the Lacey who "in the early Thirties had tuned my Cotton bike which had a dirt track JAP engine", Stan would say. "Bill was my ideal of a tuner, and I had so much faith in him that I asked him if he would tune Mike's bikes. He replied 'I've lost touch, Stan. The last motorcycle I tuned was yours 25 years ago.' But I knew that if I could only get the whiff of racing oil into his nostrils again I could persuade him. He agreed to come to Silverstone where we were testing machines. After seeing Mike ride he simply said: 'OK, I'll have a go at them'. People imagine that it was backing which brought Bill in, but there again it was only the winnings which paid the bills, plus Bill's enormous enthusiasm and craftsmanship. Agreed I spent a lot of money experimenting with various things, but this was purely for my own amusement. If the experiments were successful I passed them on to Mike." As I say, the truth rests somewhere between the two.

Minter noticed the full force of the assault, although it was difficult to miss, and now we'll have to live with a word, a single word, because it will come back again and again as stabbing as a pneumatic drill. I shan't tell you what it is, but you can't miss it. "Stan was exactly the same as John Surtees' father," Minter says. "His Old Man was always pushing John and Stan was doing it to Mike, pushing him all the time. Stan was push, push, push all the time, almost literally. He told the boy he had got to go out and win. How you can detail somebody to do that I don't really know. It was so obvious what was happening because Stan just turned round and said: Money's no object, anything you want we'll buy, you've got to have the best of everything. But as a person there couldn't have been anyone better than Mike. He was ideal. He was on a Mondial the first time I saw him, it was at Castle Combe or somewhere like that. He was alright, but just a youngster, just a novice, and you didn't see the potential in the first few meetings. That would come later."

Many, many years further on, Michael confided to a friend, Rod Sawyer, about how Stan hardened him. "When he was down in the South of France with his father", Sawyer says, "and he was six years old he was made to compete in swimming matches. His father entered him at distances he'd never even swum. His father made him do the most extraordinary things which largely he didn't want to do. Mike got into boxing, he learnt how to look after himself at a very early age so he had no fear that way. He did a number of hard things in his schooling, like going to the naval college. We talked about it loosely and he said 'Yes, they did prepare me for a lot of things'. If someone was being antagonistic Mike was not the first person to pick a fight, but he was certainly the first person to stop it, leaping in there and smacking the guy so hard he wouldn't get up. Quite a few times we were involved in a little fracas and it was always Mike getting in there first but he never went looking for it. Far from it."

"I wasn't surprised that he took up bikes", Chris Buckler says. "My father was determined that that was the way it was going to go, and whatever he was determined about happened. I did feel my father was living it through Mike. Mike was the success my father wasn't. My father had broken the odd lap record, but he was never at the top. It always worried Mike that everybody would think it was because he had the best bikes that he was good, and because my father was who he was and what he was. In the early days Mike was worried he would never come up to scratch, never be successful enough. Geoff Duke[9] was worried about Mike being pushed too hard because he thought with Mike's inexperience and the way he was being pushed something really serious could happen, that Mike could kill himself. Duke felt sorry for this little lad and took him under his wing a bit. Mike used to talk to him occasionally because Duke had been through it, and he gave time to Mike.

---

9. A famed and fabled figure in motorbike racing history. Between 1951 and 1955 he won six World Championships on 350s and 500s. He was perhaps the first 'modern', appearing in one-piece leathers and employing a deliberate style on a bike. Before Michael, his name was synonymous with motorbike racing, and if you're of the era it still evokes speed. He won a total of 33 Grand Prix races and in the early Fifties dominated the Isle of Man. He was a notable ambassador for the sport and, in Murray Walker's words, "one of the greatest riders of all time".

"As he got older he became more confident and relaxed and a happier person. I don't think those early days were terribly happy because he had so much to do, so much to prove, so much to achieve. It wasn't good enough to go in and win the odd race, he had to be World Champion, no question of it. Mike knew that, and it's difficult for a young man to cope with, so there must have been awful feelings inside him. Maybe they came out in the racing, maybe he got it out of his system just by getting on the track.

"He found it extremely difficult to talk about himself, even to me. It was always embarrassing for him; he'd rather talk about somebody else. He never talked about himself really; you had to ask him point blank and then perhaps he would, although with difficulty. It was not an easy subject for him. He'd talk about the family, but I don't think he thought himself as being interesting enough to talk about. *What's all the fuss about*, you know? *It's just me doing my job*. That's basically how he saw it. Mike didn't see himself as others saw him, I suppose. He saw himself as doing the job, and he was pleased if he did it well because that would have the Old Man's approval. He was pleased at the end of the day that he had done what the Old Man expected of him."

"Mike was relatively timid", Surtees says, "and his public appearances were dominated by Stan. Quite possibly the push which Stan gave was not at times that welcome because it was an enormous pressure being exerted."

Of course, you can argue this another way. Stan knew Michael, Stan knew Michael was a Hailwood, and Stan knew Hailwoods – starting with his own father George Arthur – and Stan knew that what they could all take was enormous pressure. Many who did not know Michael well when he was still a teenager misjudged him because they could not see behind his facade of diffidence. Stan did not misjudge him. Perhaps (and it happens with parents) when Michael was 17 Stan understood him better than he understood himself. It's only a thought, no more, and anyway we'll never know now.

6

Michael went to the Isle of Man for the first time in 1958 and The Island was as it remains: a deeply alarming place which can be deadly. The Island was all roads and telegraph poles and stone walls and kerbs and houses and, rising through its 37.75 miles, The Mountain you had to go up and down. At its highest point it stood 1,384 feet above sea-level. The best protection you could hope for anywhere round the course was bales of straw here and there placed in little screens.

"I had an hotel called The Arragon out at a place called Santon", Duke says. "Stan, Mike and the mechanics stayed with us the first time they came to The Island. Stan struck me as driving his son too hard. I think Mike felt he was being driven too hard, and he most certainly was. Stan realized that Mike had a lot of potential, but that's always a problem between father and son: the father is living through the son. I was fortunate that my father was the complete opposite and if anything tried to discourage rather than encourage me. When Mike was young he was a very nice lad, but quite shy. That first year we sat in the bar of the hotel one afternoon – we weren't drinking, of course – and Mike was worried about his riding. Whether it was because he was being pushed so hard or not I don't know. Fortunately he survived those pressures – and he was no slouch on a bike in those days, either."

Robb gives a variation of this. "Stan pushed him to the hilt." Mind you, Stan had other interests, too. As Robb says, "Stan used to be at circuits with girls, and I'd say to Mike: 'That's a nice girl your father has there', and Mike would say 'Yeah, I've already got my eye on her!'. Typical Mike. I think the relationship was one of devotion both ways, but different in both ways. Stan could buy anything he wanted in any aspect of life to achieve what he wanted, but I don't think Mike wanted him to. Mike wanted to show the world that he could achieve what he was achieving by being Mike Hailwood, rider, not Mike Hailwood, Stan Hailwood's son. There were times, maybe, when he resented everything Stan was doing for him."

On The Island that year Michael was third, seventh, 12th and 13th.

Duke did, perhaps, race against him once, which would be a nice historical conjunction, one whole era overlapping another. Memory is vague, the records too, but they suggest that it was a 250 at Hedemora, about 100 miles north of Stockholm, this same year of 1958, and "it was raining. I overtook him on a right-hand bend, and as a matter of fact I think I went round the outside. Whether he'd been to the circuit or not before I don't know, but I had, and that made a difference." Race reports make no mention of Duke in the 250 so it may have happened in practice. Certainly Duke won the 500, and brilliantly, but Michael wasn't riding 500s yet. He finished second in the 250 to Horst Fugner, who was on an East German MZ two-stroke; Michael would finish fourth in the Championship table.

In 1958, too, an ebullient person called John Cooper had just emerged from his National Service and would have a riding career himself. "The first time I saw him was at Mallory Park when he was more or less learning to ride. I think he had a Mondial. Dave Chadwick was there, whom Stan had employed to go with Mike to South Africa to learn the trade. Dave Chadwick was a bloody good 125 rider. My first impression? It was obvious Mike could ride. When did I first get close to him? In the bar at Mallory! He liked to go in and have a bit of fun afterwards, that was one of the nice things about him."

There were a lot of nice things about him.

"The first time I spoke to Mike was at Snetterton in 1959. I'd gone with friends who were running a Norton and it was oiling up the plugs. They dared me to go and ask 'ol' Hailwood' if he had any plugs, so I did. He was only an up-and-coming rider then. I went over to this big van and he was in the back and there were pin-up pictures all the way round the inside. I thought *whoops*. I asked if he had any spare plugs, and he looked at me as if to say *you cheeky monkey*. Anyway, he gave me some and I said 'Thank you very much'. After the race I took them back and he said 'Don't worry, forget about it'." She was called Pauline and she was strikingly beautiful. Years hence they'd raise a family.

What initial impression did Michael make on her because, after all, he was so handsome? "Ah, that's difficult for me, that's difficult for me. He wasn't good-looking to me so much as having animal magnetism, lots of that. Of course, after that, whenever I saw him at a race meeting he always nodded and said 'Hello'."

In time she would come to know Stan, too, and "I liked him very much. Yes, he must have been very hard to live with, but he cared a great deal about Mike and Chris. He was a determined sort of person. If he set his mind on achieving something he would. I think that's where Mike got it, or got a lot of it. Stan was a total charmer. He could play people very much to his tune. You could see that happening. Everywhere he went he would charm people, and very successfully.

"I saw something of Stan in Mike, oh very much. Mike did have a lot of respect for his father; he thought he was a bit of a tyrant, but he still had a lot of respect for him. Was it mutual respect and affection? I think that's pretty accurate.

"Mike did refer to him as Stan, he usually called him Stan or The Old Man. Stan was Stan and Pat was Pat. She was lovely, such a lovely personality. She must have done very well to (pause, chuckle) cope with Stan. She told me a few stories. Apparently Stan had a stack of photographs of other women in a bottom drawer of his office. Every time she went in there she took one off the bottom, but the pile never went down." (Laughter.)

In 1959 Michael won his first Grand Prix, a 125 at Dundrod, Northern Ireland, on a Ducati. Incidentally, he'd won the 125, 250 and 350 classes at the British Championships in 1958 and now added the 500 in the 1959 Championships. You can pass this off in a paragraph and miss the point. To get the point the paragraph demands to be expanded. In 1958 he won the 125 on a Paton, the 250 on an NSU, the 350 on a Norton; in 1959 he won the 125 on the Ducati, the 250 on a Mondial, the 350 and 500 on Nortons.[10] A great truth was being revealed and within it lay his true greatness; he could ride anything and make them all win.

Stan saw a glimpse of this greatness on the Island in the 250cc race, which was run over the Clypse Course, a much shorter version of The Mountain, but daunting enough and no mistake. Michael had what Stan would describe as an eight-year-old privately-entered Mondial,[11] and he faced two Italians, Carlo Ubbiali and Tarquinio Provini, both on factory MVs. Ubbiali had been World 250 Champion in 1956, Provini in 1958. They had five 125cc World Championships between them. They were famous riders of the day and knew the Clypse intimately. One or other had won the 125cc race over it for the past four years, Ubbiali had won the 250 over it in 1956, Provini in 1958. Michael was 19 and in only his second full season of racing.

Stan professed himself "amazed" to see that as the riders completed the first lap Michael was "right behind them", and he stayed there for the next three laps. The spectators round the course were "on their toes" with excitement, and a photograph of it has survived: a tight right-hander, the crowd on a grassy knoll on the other side, every eye locked into the duel. Ubbiali is coming through the corner, his crash helmet tall as a dome, his mouth protected by what seems to be a white woollen scarf tight across it. Just behind him the Mondial is turning into the corner, and there beneath the goggles is the broad, open face of Michael.

The positioning of the two bikes would become symbolic of so many positionings in the years to come: Hailwood the predator poised to strike, although mostly he didn't have to. He was already in front.

---

10. Of this variety of makes, three stand as particularly notable. NSU was a German company which raced before the Second World War and between 1951 and 1954; their engines were renowned for their power. Norton was a legendary British company dating back to before the turn of the century and had won almost everything. Their Manx Norton became a classic. Ducati was an Italian company which contested World Championship events in 1958 and 1959. Brian Woolley judges that the 125cc machines were "astonishingly fast and reliable" (*Directory of Classic Racing Motorcycles*, Aston).

11. An Italian company which had begun in 1948 and officially withdrew from Grand Prix racing in 1958. Their most noted rider was Provini.

The commentary echoed, the voice rising and rising, that out on the Clypse Michael had overtaken them both on the *outside*. There was tumult in the grandstand when they came past, the old Mondial 50 yards ahead. Then... Michael's ignition failed. Stan, as worldly-wise as any, wandered across to Provini when the race was over (Provini had won) and wondered aloud if these wily Italians had been playing games with Michael. Provini took a deep breath and said: "God, no ..."

The 125cc race, also on the Clypse, was a race of another sort. Michael was third behind Provini and a small, neat Swiss called Luigi Taveri. They would become such firm friends that to this day Taveri speaks of Michael only in the present tense. Taveri's wife Tilde would become almost a mother-confessor, and whenever Michael happened to be passing their neat little house near Zurich he'd stay the night, play badminton on the lawn. There are many photographs of him there. In each of them he is smiling.

Robb was in that race, and when the telephone rang at his home near Warrington on March 23, 1981 he momentarily lost control of himself and cried and cried and cried.

7

The 125 was not just another race, another entry into the list of TT races which in one form or another had been running since 1907. The Island had been fascinated and amused by the arrival of a totally unfamiliar group of mechanics and riders based in the Nursery Hotel which fronted on to the Clypse Course, and who each day, on frail-looking bikes, did dozens of miles led by their team leader, an American called Bill Hunt. He wore a most bizarre-looking 'space age' helmet. Because he was team leader the riders behind him did not overtake on a point of honour until, in exasperation, he *ordered* them to. Hunt himself seems to have fallen off a good deal and he duly fell in the race itself. The others, each bearing a totally unfamiliar name, pressed doggedly on and finished sixth, seventh, eighth and 11th to take the team prize. They were delighted, and rightly so. This was the first time they had ventured anywhere near Europe.

The name of the bikes they rode: Honda.

British Petroleum produced a booklet covering the TT meeting that year, and in it they said that "Hailwood was trying hard to pass Ernst Degner (an East German who subsequently defected) and succeeded on the fifth lap. Degner was losing speed and Hailwood drew away, but could not get to grips with the leaders. So hot was the pace that Hailwood finished over two minutes behind Taveri."

As Hailwood got himself off his Ducati when it was over he had unknowingly seen his own future. Who now remembers those riders with the unfamiliar names, Taniguchi, Tanaka, Suzuki? Everybody remembers Hailwood and Honda.

Before we leave the Island, Stan in action. Reynolds were a company in the Midlands making tubes, and amongst their uses were frames for bikes. Each year Reynolds dispatched an employee to work in a garage during the TT, welding any bits of frame which required it, and did this simply as a service. Ken Sprayson was the welder, a spade-is-a-spade Brummie who understood frames intimately and profoundly enough to make them as well as weld them together.

"I had a garage behind the Falcon Cliff Hotel. In those days the service was used very, very extensively, it was almost a day-and-night job, and whenever I went to the garage there was always a queue of people waiting for work to be done. Stan came in and came to the front of the queue, his hand full of £5 notes. 'Can you do this for my lad?' I said 'Get to the back of the bloody queue, and if you don't put that money away you'll get nothing.' I didn't look up further, I don't know whether Mike was outside. That was the only dealing I had with Stan."

Nine years later Michael would ask Ken Sprayson to put all his experience, energies and talent into making a very special frame to take a very special engine, the fearsome Honda 500. This engine, circa 1967, had already been in a Honda frame and the result was so frightening that – as all are agreed, particularly Taveri and Cooper, the two other people who got on it – only one man on earth could actually ride the thing, Stanley Michael Bailey Hailwood. And that was the future he didn't know.

MICHAEL

"Stan said: 'You could earn a quick few pounds here', so I said 'Why, what's happened, Stan?'. He said: 'I'll give you £50 if you keep your bicycles in the van'." – Derek Minter

"I took my driving test three times. I just think I was going too fast most of the time. Terrified the examiner? Yes." – Mike Hailwood

"I felt he never feared dying. Yes, I feared dying, or getting hurt, or becoming a paraplegic." – Phil Read

1

The crowd which drank and danced and sang *Auld Lang Syne* in Trafalgar Square as *Big Ben* chimed midnight and its hands moved gently forward into the first moment of January 1960 cannot have known that the new decade would be spiced by youth, power-driven by youth and would surrender to youth. London would swing and the world would watch London swinging, then mimic it themselves.

A complete new way of living came together all at once; music, clothing, life-style, morality, and all of it strewn with the fragile blossoming of Flower Power. The Fifties had been drawn over by the aftermath of the war. Confectionery and coal were still rationed into that decade, and Britain's cities still bore the craters of the bombing, still bore buildings like broken teeth the way the Luftwaffe had left them. The priority had been reconstruction until, under the Tory government of Harold Macmillan, the blossoming had finally begun. A slogan of the time caught this: *You've never had it so good*. That was late in the Fifties, but it set the tone and the expectations for the Sixties. A generation which barely remembered the war and had not been exhausted either by it or by the reconstruction were here, uninterested in engaging in a long struggle to buy a washing machine, unaware that their parents had suffered years of genuine privation, these same parents who dressed soberly as befits a sombre decade. The very notion of coloured shirts (all men wore white ones) was unthinkable. Rock 'n Roll had been imported from the 'States midway through the decade, but no responsible person took such jungle music and such gyrations seriously. It was harmless stuff for the kids.

Within a handful of years Joan Baez would be singing haunting melodies with messages which struck deep chords across the world, the Fab Four would be revving-up the pace, stirring hysteria and mob adulation never seen before, *yeah, yeah, yeah*. The Rolling Stones dealt in raw unconcealed sexuality, and nobody had seen that before, either.

Harold Wilson, by background an ordinary fellow from Huddersfield, would become Prime Minister and bring to the job none of the inhibitions any of his predecessors had had. The American public would seriously question and demonstrate against a war, Vietnam, and that had never happened before, either.

Fashion followed fashion, skirts rose from the mini to the micro, limbs seemed to be everywhere, to sleep with your boyfriend was what girls did and said so; some smoked their pot and saw psychedelic visions of peace and love and beauty; some jangled their love-beads and gave flowers to soldiers, and for the first time to be young was to be genuinely important. If you were single, rich, handsome and becoming famous you'd have done well in any decade, but the Sixties were made for you.

That early January morning, when the chimes died into the revelry Michael was four months short of his 20th birthday. All of the Sixties would belong to him – all their delights, all the freedom they bestowed – and of course when these same chimes rang out the decade at midnight on the last day of 1969 he would not yet be 30. It was a delicious prospect and there were times when he seemed afraid of losing a minute, seemed somehow to be overloading every minute; but he did not emerge as himself until Stan retired and began to live abroad in 1962.

Michael might well have made history in 1960, the kind no-one can take away. Instead, Minter did it – just. There had been an advertisement in a magazine saying that £100 awaited the first man to lap The Mountain course at the Isle of Man at 100mph on a single-cylinder 500cc bike. The symmetry of the offer was obvious, £1 for each mph, but the potential donor was unknown. Minter was not a man to ignore such an opportunity or subsequently forget that the offer had been made. I hesitate to suggest that Minter was mercenary – he would prove otherwise by refusing a bribe from Stan (see quotation!) – but in fair combat he knew his worth and translated that easily into coin of the realm. It was his work, and he wanted paying for it.

The 500cc race was the second World Championship round of the season. The first, at Clermont-Ferrand, had been won by Surtees on an MV, Surtees, who was arguably as famous as Duke, and in a precise, poignant, historical sense the bearer of even more talents. Formula One cars would fall prey to him, too, giving him a unique position which only one other man since has had a genuine chance of equalling.

Stanley Michael Bailey Hailwood.

"Mike started off in front of me. I caught him and passed him on the Mountain Mile", Minter recalls, "and then he tucked in behind me so he was the second rider to do it. It was only that I encouraged him to go quicker because I passed him that made him do it." You must understand the pride of a man and balance it against the man's own memories. Derek Minter has pride and memories and does not necessarily, I sense, allow that Michael was better than he was, certainly in some circumstances.

In fact the first 100mph single-cylinder lap was nothing like so simple. Michael had started before Minter because traditionally riders went in pairs at

10-second intervals. Minter was paired with Bob McIntyre, a Scot, and within the confines of motorbike racing as much of a legend as Duke and Surtees.[1] "I could have done the 100mph lap before but for McIntyre", Minter says in his very own trenchant way. "He and I started off together. I had a better start and led him all the way into Ramsey and he passed me there. I thought 'This is good because I can learn from him going up The Mountain'."

McIntyre was the old hand, and gifted with it, whereas Minter was famed for short circuits like Brands Hatch; and the Island stretched long, the longest circuit in the world, the full 37.75 miles.

"McIntyre was so slow going across The Mountain that I actually rode round the outside of him at the 33rd,[2] which is the long way round. I beat him back to the start-finish line to complete the first lap and I'd done 99mph. It would have been 100mph if I'd passed him up The Mountain, which I could have done. I did 101mph on my second lap." Moments later Michael did it, too, and faster – but later. "My third lap would have been faster still, but unfortunately the oil tank split just before Kirkmichael. I went round the right-angle corner there like a speedway bike. I had a full left lock on doing, I suppose, 70 or 80mph; I looked down and saw the rear tyre was all shiny, so that was it. (The spilling oil made it shiny, and however laconic and phlegmatic Minter may be this was an alarming moment.) I poodled round to finish the lap." Minter is sure he *would* have gone faster still because "the first lap I went down with McIntyre through Greeba[3] and I was convinced in my own mind I could get through there in third gear instead of second; the next lap I did get through in third and I knew then that because I'd already done it I could do it again. So I went a lot quicker through Greeba. That third lap would have been 102mph, I think.

"I didn't go up to Stan afterwards for the £100 because nobody knew who was giving it. I wrote to the Auto-Cycle Union, the governing body, and asked *who's going to cough up?* They told me it was Stan Hailwood. It took me about nine months to get the money, it was paid just before or after Christmas (the race had been in June). He was reluctant to part with it because as far as he was concerned Mike was going to be the one to do the 100mph lap. Daddy was going to give that because he thought Mike was going to do it."

This does not prevent Derek Minter from paying a most sincere tribute and I suspect tributes about other riders do not come easily from him. "To ride against Mike, well, he was one of those people you could trust. You could sit behind him and he'd be on the same line all the time. You got behind Phil Read and it was a different kettle of fish, you know what I mean? He's not on the same line every time. And as you know, there is only one way round a corner and that is a straight line, isn't it? You are holding the bike straight and the corner is unfolding, not the bike, so you are actually going in a straight line. Mike was a difficult man to overtake, but when I was determined I was going by, that was it, and if he was overtaking me I'd do the same thing." In other words, not move over.

---

1. Born in Scotstoun, a suburb of Glasgow, he learnt to ride in 1928 when he bought a bike for £12 to get to and from his job in a garage. He was killed in 1962.
2. A left-right curve on the descent from The Mountain, naturally enough it was 33 miles from the start.
3. Greeba Bridge, a twisting left-hander, about six miles from the start.

This is a very simple, but potent matter. You defend the corner as well as you can, but when you know you've lost it you cede it and you do not endanger yourself or the man overtaking. It is the most curious of things and it spans all motorsport. Once upon a time, which for our purposes we can conveniently fix at 1960 although many another year would do, this was governed by sporting ethics and a sense of self-preservation. To defend then cede a corner was a natural conjunction between the two; racing existed as sport, but the general safety standards were so stark that if you crashed there was a very real chance you'd kill yourself. Plenty did, and soon enough we shall have Redman explaining this in chilling statistics: a simple sum which could have been written on the back of an envelope and which troubled him enough to tempt him to pack the thing in before he did kill himself.

The principle then in a car or on a bike was that if a man with superior machinery or skill, or both, placed himself in a position to overtake you and you could not honourably resist, you chose not to resist. Many were the men who overtook Michael here and there, many, many more whom he overtook, and only once did he betray the ethic. It was at Brands; he was wheeling and dealing all around the dips and rises of that circuit with Minter and couldn't find enough power to legitimately overtake, so he conjured a ploy, drew alongside, glanced down to suggest that Minter had oil on his tyre and Minter naturally slowed. (Once as a speedway rider is enough with full lock on.) Michael won that race, tried to laugh the ploy off to himself but failed, and never did anything like it again all his days. Before a race he would employ gamesmanship,[4] which is perhaps legitimate psychology (psyching in the modern parlance), but when a race began it was straight and fair and to the best man the victory. There were variations on the theme, arrangements between riders about putting on a show for a defined number of laps, but after them it was every man for himself and – to the best the victory. Michael was scrupulous about that and never betrayed the ethic of it.

Oddly, Minter doesn't remember that race at Brands at all, although he does concede it might have happened. I take that as absolute proof that it only happened once because if it had been more Minter would have remembered and other people would have noticed, too.

"After a race he'd come up and have a little chat. 'That was a dirty thing to do', he'd say, but it was all done in good spirit. The sport was as it should be, a sport. If you wanted a bit for your bike you'd go and see Stan or Mike or whoever and they'd lend it to you and you'd give it back to them after the meeting and say 'Thank you very much', and they were glad if it had done you some good.

"Mike was shy speaking to the public, but if he knew you and got on with you he was just like anybody else, just like Tom, Dick and Harry. He liked flirting and so forth. He was always trying to pull a joke on you. We were both staying in the Douglas Hotel in the Isle of Man. His favourite joke was to put in an early morning call for you so that a waiter would arrive at four in the morning with your breakfast on a tray. That happened a couple of times.

"On one or two occasions Stan brought some women with him to a meeting, but you weren't sure if they were his or Mike's because Mike didn't always have girls of his own age. He'd have older girls. All the women were always after Mike

---

4. A term invented in the Thirties by an English author, Stephen Potter, who defined it as "the art of winning without actually cheating".

Hailwood, his name literally attracted them. They were like bees to honey. He was good looking, and I used to feel envy of him with the women who were hanging around him. The only trouble was, he caught a dose two or three times, didn't he? He used to have to go to hospital to have it cleared up. It didn't worry him at all, he was quite happy about it, he was quite open about it. He used to say 'I've caught a dose! That's no problem' and three weeks later he'd be back and say 'I'm on the job again now'. He liked to go to bed with a woman the night before a race because it gave him something extra. It left most people knackered, but with him it was the other way round. I felt exhausted, but with him it just brought a new lease of life. It could have been nervous energy which needed calming down, it could have been. You can never say, that's the thing."

We have come upon it, as we were always going to come upon it; the overt sexuality of Stan and Michael. There is far too much evidence to ignore it, they did a lot of it, and it remains a legitimate topic of conversation for several reasons, not least the fact that they chose not to hide it themselves. They didn't glory in conquest, didn't flaunt it, never boasted about it. They liked it, circumstances allowed them to do it, and they did it. This did not prevent Michael finding a special girl who became a proper girlfriend, but in 1960 she'd just left boarding school where the nearest she'd got to the male of the species was a French pen pal. She was much shyer than Michael and frankly had never heard of him.

2

That summer of 1960 Nobby Clark reached Europe and went to Assen for the Dutch TT. "Mike recognized me but he'd forgotten my name, though he did remember where he had met me! Later I stayed at Mike's flat in Heston for two years and we really had some good laughs. He enjoyed himself if no-one knew who he was, be it at a party, a pub or a restaurant. The one thing that really got at him was when someone pushed a pen or pencil under his nose and asked for his autograph. Most times he would sign, but he always thought that it was intruding into his private life ..."

Stan's determination that Michael won sometimes went too far. "It was at Castle Combe, although I forget the exact year", Minter says. "It must have been around 1959 or 1960. We were going to scrutineering in the morning. Stan came up to me and patted me on the shoulder the way he did, being nice. He said 'I'll tell you what, Derek, you could earn a quick few pounds here', so I said 'Why, what's happened, Stan?' He said 'I'll give you £50 if you keep your bicycles in the van.' It was a lot of money, but I said there was no chance of me doing that. In fact it geed me up, especially on the 500. I went out and broke the lap and race records on it. No, I didn't speak to Stan afterwards and he wouldn't speak to me. He hadn't had his enjoyment."

Minter's relationship with Michael was quite different. "The pair of us never really had what you'd call up-and-downers because we really raced against each other, and if either one of us won it was just good sport. You didn't go round complaining that this and that was wrong, make a bloody protest, anything like that. We got on with it. If I lost it was just one of those things, but it wasn't very often that I lost against him. (There, you see, the pride.)

"A typical example. This was at Brands Hatch some Easter, he was on an AJS[5] and I was on the Norton, he was leading the race and I kept pushing him round Clearways[6] and I found I could get to the line near enough in front of him. I thought: that's alright. I wasn't going into Clearways as quickly as I normally did because I wasn't going to show him I could go quicker. I was waiting until the last lap and then I'd whistle round the outside of him. So on the last lap I pushed him into Clearways and all of a sudden everything was grinding on the AJS and of course he fell off. His head came sailing across and hit the exhaust pipe of my bike. I thought to myself *Christ that was a bit close, wasn't it?* It made my bike shudder a bit. I thought I'd hurt him because I could see his head hitting. When I finished the race I asked him how he was and *he* said 'that was a bit close, wasn't it?' I said it was a bit too close for comfort ...

"Mike was one of those people who just had it gifted to him. I wouldn't discuss anything with him. At Brands testing and practising he used to try and follow me to learn things and I never took the same line. I always had myself timed from Clearways back to Clearways because when you come past Paddock, just after the start-finish line, you're on full noise and everybody's stopwatch is going. I'd go flat-out until I came to the start-finish line, then I'd sit bolt upright and by the time I got to Paddock everybody was thinking *what's happened here? Minter's slow today.* Nobody knew we were doing it, including Hailwood." Michael himself made two estimations of Minter. The first was that of all the riders he ever rode against Minter was the hardest to beat, and the second was that Minter beat him more times than he beat Minter.

Rous watched all this with careful, knowing eyes. "Mike was rapidly up with people like Minter and Read, people who had established themselves. I have a lot of time for Minter, and in the period around 1960 he was considered the best at Brands Hatch and most of the British circuits. At Brands he was virtually unbeatable, at Oulton Park he was nearly unbeatable. Hailwood came on in leaps and bounds when you consider that he hadn't raced anything until 1957. There were Auto-Cycle Union stars, which were really the National Championships, and for two or three seasons he won every class, even competing with people like Minter, because he was good everywhere. He only failed once, in a 500.

"The first TT I ever covered was 1960. Mike had changed a great deal from being not much more than a schoolboy – well, a naval cadet – and he was growing up in a way his father accepted. During 1959 Mike realized that he was the one doing it, not his father. He was becoming very much an adult. He had a few crashes, though not a really bad one. He was stretchered off a few times, but he didn't break any bones. By the time he got to The Island in 1960 he had matured very rapidly and sensed the sort of performances he was returning were big stuff. Other people considered him too young, perhaps that's the best way to put it."

Across 1960 Michael didn't win a Grand Prix. Across 1961 he convulsed The Island and startled the world. The truly great in all sports often do this. They announce themselves early, suddenly and completely. They may or may not be sure why, but they do.

---

5. AJS, a British company which stopped making racing bikes in 1962.
6. Clearways, later renamed Clark Curve, is a long, statuesque, right-handed sweep leading towards the start-finish line.

3

"I just felt that he never feared dying, that he raced to the limit and finished races. Yes, I feared dying or getting seriously hurt, or becoming a paraplegic", Phil Read says. "I think Mike's attitude is best summarized by his statement when we used to leave on the ferry from The Island. As we stood on the rear deck watching The Island disappear he'd say 'Christ, we've made it again. They should pull the plug out of that and sink it'.

"The Island was something you had to do. You built yourself up because you were a works rider and people expected you to win. You had to put your life on the line a bit. Mike had a respectful fear of The Island, but he didn't show it except at times like that. He was basically on his own and lacked the paternal-maternal closeness. I think he felt – how can I express it? – I think he felt it was down to him to survive. What did he have on The Island? He had a feeling for The Island and a feeling to race to the limit and without fear while he was doing it." Read was a very fast rider, and on The Island in 1961 he won the 350cc race. Nothing remarkable about that, however meritorious – any win on The Island was a good win – but this one was remarkable and takes its place in the tableau of winners for a special reason, as we shall see.

Long before that, Michael competed in the Easter meeting at Brands Hatch. "I remember it very well", Pam Lawton says. "I was wearing a Black Watch pleated skirt with knee-length socks which had buttons down the side. It was the fashion then. I used to have long hair and I'd just had my hair cut. I was standing next to the transporter with my father" – Syd Lawton, a well-known figure in the sport and a former Norton works rider. "I didn't know anything about bike racing, I didn't know who Mike Hailwood was, I'd never heard of any of these people. Stan and my father were talking, I was standing there and Mike came up. Stan introduced me to Mike, I shook hands with him and he gave me a great big grin. Then my father said 'What do you think of Pamela's new hairstyle?' I was so embarrassed because I was very shy. The transporter door was open and I hid behind it – they were all looking at me. Later I was walking along the paddock and this person whistled at me – a wolf whistle – and it was Mike, and he came over to talk to me and he kept coming over to talk.

"He got my telephone number – I don't know how – and then he phoned me and asked me out. I remember our first date. My parents lived in Southampton, and we went to a pub for a drink. Mike was my first boyfriend. In those days courting couples would have a kiss and a cuddle in the car. Well, the car was parked outside the Gents' loo, so there were Mike and I sitting in the car, me having my first kiss, and men going in and out of the loo! We then drove down to the water at Southampton and sat there, which we did on several occasions. I bought him a 21st birthday card which I still have because I was too shy to give it to him, which sounds a bit crazy, doesn't it?" Not if you're that shy, it doesn't. (The inscription she'd written inside the card was almost formal: *With very best wishes, Pam.*) He invited her to the Isle of Man, but this was 1961 and the Sixties weren't quite swinging yet. Pam's visit would be one of propriety.

4

In April 1961 Michael celebrated his 21st birthday at a meeting at Snetterton. The champagne flowed between practice and the race and he would remember going to the line feeling "merry". He didn't fall off or anything, but would approach only one other race in his career in a state of inebriation, in a sportscar 13 years hence.

In May the BBC dispatched Brian Johnston, subsequently famous for his cricket commentaries, but actually trained as an all-rounder broadcaster, to interview Mike. Because it offers so many insights I quote it verbatim.

Johnston: "Well, Mike, where do you live now?"

Mike: "I now live just outside Oxford, Boars Hill – strong in the arm, weak in the head (chuckle). I used to live at Nettlebed, near Henley-on-Thames, but it was a bit out of the way so we moved to Oxford."

Johnston: "Your father has got a big motor firm."

Mike: "A big motorcycle firm, actually."

Johnston: "He's got a reputation for being a bit of a big 'bug' in it, hasn't he?"

Mike: "... well-known around the paddock as Stan the Wallet."

Johnston: "Now do you work in that firm?"

Mike: "Yes I do, actually."

Johnston: "When did you start riding a motor bicycle?"

Mike: "When I was seven I used to ride a little ..."

Johnston: "When you were seven! As young as that?"

Mike: "Yes."

Johnston: "Well, how did you do that?"

Mike: "My father built a little motorbike for me and I used to ride it round the lawn."

Johnston: "Was that pretty dangerous?"

Mike: "Not really. I didn't know how to stop the thing, I just used to go round and round until it ran out of petrol."

Johnston: "Sounds a good way of stopping. And how did you get into racing?"

Mike: "About five years ago I thought I should like to have a go, so my father borrowed a 125 machine from a friend of ours and I had my first race at Oulton Park. I enjoyed it so much I decided to carry on."

Johnston: "Now in the 500cc you ride a Norton. Are you always going to ride British machines?"

Mike: "Well, it looks as if I'll have to in the 500 class because there is nothing better."

Johnston: "But if there was something better and it wasn't British you might ride it?"

Mike: "Yes. Well, you've got to take the fastest you can get."

Johnston: "Do you ride motorbikes on the road?"

Mike: "No. I used to ride up until about two years ago, I used to ride a Triumph on the road, but since then I think cars are safer."

Johnston: "Did you have any difficulty getting on the road?"

Mike: "Well, I took my test three times."

Johnston: "Three times?"

Mike: "Yes."

Johnston: "Well that's an encouragement to some people. Why was that?

What did you do wrong?"

Mike: "I don't really know. I just think I was going too fast most of the time."

Johnston: "Terrified the examiner?"

Mike: "Yes."

Johnston: "Before a race are you nervous?"

Mike: "When it's a race I know I stand a good chance of winning I get terrible butterflies, but when it's a race when I don't stand a chance I don't worry so much."

Johnston: "Have you got any particular thrilling moment that you can remember?"

Mike: "Well, my greatest thrill was when I finished third in last year's TT at the Isle of Man (the 500 behind Surtees and Hartle)."

Johnston: "Your big ambition being of course ..."

Mike: "...to win the TT" (self-deprecating chuckle).

Johnston: "When do you think you will give up motorcycle racing?"

Mike: "I suppose I'll give up when I get tired of it or too old or something. I don't know."

Johnston: "Are you going to take up motor racing?"

Mike: "Yes, I might do a bit of motor racing this winter. I've had an offer from a car racing team and it looks as if I might be going over to America to do a bit of racing there."

Johnston: "How do you think the thrill of that compares with the two wheels?"

Mike: "Well, I haven't tried it, but I don't think it's as thrilling as riding a motorbike."

Johnston: "When you're not racing, Mike, what do you do with yourself?"

Mike: "I listen to records, I've got a lot of records at home."

Johnston: "Any particular type of record?"

Mike: "Traditional jazz I love. My favourite clarinetist is a fellow called Ian Wheeler. He plays with Chris Barber. I think my favourite record is *Elisabeth* by Acker Bilk."[7]

Johnston: "Well Mike, after talking to you like this it's obvious you're a very modest sort of chap. Are all your other friends in the motorcycling world – I mean you're dicing with death the whole time – quiet like yourself?"

Mike: "I don't like the dicing with death bit, but on the whole they are very quiet, most of them, yes!" (Author's exclamation mark.)

Johnston: "Because in the motor racing world, you know, they're a bit more exuberant. Is there any reason for this do you think?"

Mike: "I don't think motorcyclists can afford to be otherwise than quiet!" (Author's exclamation mark again.)

Johnston: "Point taken."

---

7. Barber and Bilk were noted exponents of Trad Jazz in the early Sixties; not quite pop stars of their time, but something much more refined. No doubt it is a complete coincidence that Mike's grandmother was called Elisabeth.

5

On The Island Stan decided that what Michael needed was a 125 Honda and betook himself to the Nursery Hotel to get one. Honda were not impressed. They had their own works riders (Redman, Taveri and Tom Phillis) and what would they suddenly be doing lending a bike to him? They were lending 250s to others, including Michael, but that had all been agreed beforehand. Stan launched an assault on them, pestered, nagged, blustered "to the point where they were glad to see the back of me", and finally he played the last piece on the board. If Honda lent Michael a 125, King's of Oxford – the largest dealership in the country, don't forget – would sell Hondas. Checkmate. The bike which Stan hoisted physically into a van to take away from the Nursery Hotel, just the way he'd hoisted bikes in that coalyard to get the job at King's in 1924, was Taveri's spare and was in Michael's words "clapped out" after he'd tried it up and down the road. The mechanics did their best, he did a practice lap round The Mountain and he was staggered by how much sheer power the bike had.

This was a fundamental in Honda's thinking. It was also simplicity itself: more power = more speed = victory. In the years to come he blessed and cursed this equation in equal measure because if you concentrate on power you risk sacrificing handling, and somebody had to *ride* the bikes; and this would lead all the way to Ken Sprayson – who no doubt was welding away in his garage this June day, the queue getting ever longer – and the big Honda 500 and The Bike Which Almost Never Was.

Kiyoshi Kawashima managed Honda's racing team. He'd first met Stan "in 1959 or 1960 and he emphasized aggressively what a good rider his son was and said 'Why doesn't Honda let him ride?'." Kawashima found himself "excited" by Stan's blunt approach, but he also weighed up "Honda's need for a long-term business relationship with this man who had a big motorcycle dealership". Yes, checkmate.

As Michael ran beside the bike at the start you could see his strength, see his stride lengthening, becoming more urgent, the power coming from the thighs; and he was gone. Redman had started earlier and so by 10 seconds had Taveri. At Sulby, Taveri and Michael had caught Redman, at the Guthrie Memorial Taveri was pressing his Honda hard – this neat man who was so small he almost disappeared behind the fairing. At Signpost Corner, a sharp right which was a tarmacadam furrow between two high grassy banks, Michael had tugged this back to perhaps a couple of hundred yards. As Taveri flowed away from the corner Michael was already in it, the bike cranked hard over, and somewhere up the road there it would be: the predator and the prey. At Governor's Bridge they were closer, closer, closer and Michael of course led the race on 'corrected' time. As he crossed the line he had broken the lap record by two miles an hour. He broke it again on the second lap, but Taveri was a canny old campaigner, a merry elf of a man off a bike but mighty on one, and he resisted, squeezed, forced and held Michael just behind, just behind. There was a beauty in this, two bikes within touching distance, twisting and turning, dipping and rising. Michael didn't overtake until lap three and Taveri tracked him and retook him going up to The Mountain.

Michael did not get past again, but he won by seven seconds at an average speed of 86.23mph despite a magnificent, continuing sweep of a challenge from

Taveri, who set a new record (88.45mph) on his last lap. Stan himself, smoking a cigarette and wearing a suit and a bow tie, wheeled the bike away (to return it?). As he moved, there it was in such direct contrast to Michael, the left leg so stiff and awkward.

This was Honda's first victory on The Island and the first of 16 while the TT held its status as a World Championship event. "During his first ride he was OK", Kawashima says. "My initial impression was that his riding was a bit rough. He was just a boy, but when he got onto a bike he was aggressive."

Honda didn't have to wait long for the second of the 16; the 125 had been in the morning, the 250 was in the afternoon.

Bob McIntyre was one of the other riders who had acquired a 250 Honda, via a concessionaire in Dublin. McIntyre was heavy for a 250, 11½ stone, and had not ridden in a 250 World Championship race before. From a standing start he shattered the lap record and on his second lap he forced the speed to 99.58mph. This was a genuine sensation, and as McIntyre pointed out, it was a mere four years since that first 100mph lap of any kind had been set on The Island, by himself on a Gilera 500.

McIntyre wrote in his life story that "on the second lap the 99.58mph smashed the 350 class record held by John Surtees on an MV. People were speculating, I heard later, on whether I would be the first to break the 'ton' barrier on a 250cc model. I could in fact have gone faster, but my bike had given a warning slide on a left-hand bend and when I glanced down I saw oil on the tyre. My machine had suffered a mysterious oil leak from the engine throughout practice and we had been unable to cure it. With oil on the tyre I had to be careful. I slowed to 99.23mph.

"The engine was still running well as I came to the last lap. Spectators were waving me on. Mike Hailwood, lying second to me, was half a minute behind. Then at Quarry Bends[8] my engine seized due to the loss of oil. I was prepared for this and was able to whip in the clutch immediately, but I was out of the race. Hailwood went by to complete the quickest 'double' in TT history, two wins within five and a half hours."

M. Hailwood	Honda	1h 55m 3.6s (98.38mph)
T. Phillis	Honda	1h 57m 14.2s
J. Redman	Honda	2h 1m 36.2s

Of course, Michael *and* Honda had done this, and since Honda have now grown into a racing dynasty rather than being just a multinational company – their engines dominating Grand Prix car racing to a staggering extent, nine wins in 1986, 11 in 1987, 15 in 1988, 10 in 1989, six in 1990, eight in 1991 – there's a fascinating little glimpse of how it all began. Shoichiro Irimajiri explains it, and to readers who are terrified of the technical (as Michael himself was), please relax because I am, too. Irimajiri worked in development, knows about such matters because he contributed to both bike and car engines, and he has the gift of explaining simply. "How could Honda get such high performance? We bought a Mondial to get to know why such power was coming out. We studied the theory of intake and exhaust, and the efficiency of combustion. That was the starting point from which our engine power increased significantly. This resulted in winning at the Isle of Man. The intake and exhaust became a theory in itself (in

---

8. A left-right kink on the run to Ramsey at the 'top' of the course.

layman's terms almost like being able to breathe faster) and Honda used a computer in Research and Development – it was probably Honda who introduced computers into general use in development. We kept increasing engine power *knowing* we could get more rpm. Our competitors used the conventional approach..."

The 350 race was on the Wednesday and every boat brought more and more people to watch Michael, this time on an AJS, go for the hat-trick, something no man had done before. Arguably Gary Hocking[9] on an MV was favourite, although Read and his Norton represented a very real danger, too. These were hard racing men in hard races.

The day began "unluckily" – Michael's own word – when his van, complete with spares, ran out of petrol on the way to the circuit, but with the minutes ticking away someone going by on his motorbike stopped, siphoned off fuel into the van and wouldn't accept a penny for it. In the race Hocking took the lead, but broke down, and Michael found a clear run home spread in front of him. On the final lap his lead was more than two minutes over Read, but at Milntown Cottage, on the approach to Ramsey and some 13 miles from the finish, the gudgeon pin[10] broke and he stood at the roadside and watched Read go by, then Hocking, who was mounting a furious recovery. "I could have wept", Michael confided to Ted Macauley.

The 500 remained, and he was on a Norton which Lacey had cobbled together with some parts as old as 1958. Lacey, who had the thin face of an ascetic, could achieve that kind of thing. Hocking (on an MV, of course) had a much faster bike. Michael estimated the top-speed difference at 10mph which magnifies itself enormously over the 226 miles of a race. Graham Walker, Murray's father, made the astonishing observation (viewed today) that of the 74 starters only Hocking was on a non-British bike.

McIntyre went from the front row, Michael the second, Hocking the third. They caught and pressured McIntyre and by Ramsey Hocking led on the road – the physical order which also happened to be the order on corrected time – from McIntyre, with Michael third. McIntyre was shed and then there were two. Michael caught and clung to Hocking and every time he tried to go by Hocking fought him off; but Michael's pressure forced Hocking into a genuine mistake, he took a corner too fast and vanished up an escape road. Michael was in the lead. Hocking didn't like that, came back at him and retook the lead, Michael clinging on again, and now the misfortune which had struck at him in the 350 claimed Hocking. The plugs let him down, he lost a minute in the pits. Michael had another clear run home and this time he made it. It wasn't the hat-trick because the purists' definition of that is three-in-a-row, but it was three TT wins, and no man had done that before. He was genuinely astonished when he was told that he'd averaged 100.60mph, and no man had done that on a British bike before, either.

"He'd invited me over", Pam says, "but I didn't want to go on my own because in those days you didn't go and stay with a boyfriend, so I went over for race week with a girlfriend, Diane. It was my first visit to The Island and Mike had told me that he would be practising when I arrived and that I should get a cab up to the

---

9. A Rhodesian who over a couple of seasons was as fast as Mike. He died in a car racing crash in South Africa in 1962.
10. A part of the piston.

paddock. The taxi must have dropped Diane and I off at the wrong place because we had to walk across a big field to get to where the cars were parked and from there into the paddock. It must have taken 10 minutes and when we approached the car park I heard a voice shout 'smile for the camera'. It was Mike. He'd been waiting for me leaning against the roof of a car and he'd been videoing me all the time I was walking. I responded – as *he* would have done – by saying I was surprised the camera hadn't broken!

"Of course it was a very successful TT for Mike and he enjoyed every minute of it except the early morning practice sessions. I was very new to motorcycle racing, and whilst I was really pleased for him each time he won I didn't understand the significance of his 'hat-trick' and the media attention it attracted. Mike was obviously delighted himself after the wins, but he'd arrive at the paddock each day and mess around the way he did, joking with everyone. Looking back I realize that he was almost always surrounded by the media during that time. I was unaware of it, but obviously he was because he knew who the Pressmen were. He didn't change, he was totally unaffected by their presence and constant attention. He had many aspects to his character, but his modesty was a very visible and endearing trait.

"I didn't stay in the same hotel as Mike, that wasn't allowed. Mike accepted that because he respected women. He respected all women regardless of who they were and what they were, and I am aware of that because of his respect for me when I was young and unworldly. It's a very important point about Mike that, unlike superstars who have women throwing themselves at their feet, Mike always respected every woman he went out with as a woman, as a person. He never ever to my knowledge took advantage of a woman.

"There was an instance when he took a woman he'd just met to dinner, a load of other people were there and the wife of one of them said something unpleasant – very unpleasant – about the woman, and Mike was so hurt for the woman's sake that he stood up to leave the table. He wasn't making a fuss, wasn't leaving in any nasty way because he wasn't a man like that. The wife's husband said 'No Mike, don't go, she leaves', and pointed to his wife. I think that shows something about Mike the man, I think it shows he was a real, real man – a man who did not treat a woman he'd just picked up, if you like, as a piece of dirt, who did not say: look what I can do with these women.

"Mike was to me and many, many, many women extremely attractive. He had an enormous amount of sex appeal and a very laid-back attitude with women, nicely laid back. He genuinely did not know or understand why women were attracted to him. He'd say 'surely you're not interested in a receding, well-worn, ugly mash of a man!' A woman dislikes a man who falls all over her because it means she can walk all over him. If a man says 'I love you' every five minutes it comes to mean nothing, it's just words. On occasions Mike said things which were as good as saying that, but he'd say 'I love you' very, very rarely and I actually liked that. It meant something when he did. He didn't strike me as shy, not at all; to me he was a worldly man, but remember I was young and naive."

From this moment on we can begin to call Michael Mike. I've very deliberately called him Michael thus far because somehow it suggests youth. The transition to Mike is intended to demonstrate a transition to the man: Mike is shorter, sharper, harder and also, a nice contradiction, more matey.

After June 1961 he became genuinely famous and it happened very quickly: in the brief space of time between the 125 and 500 races. Mike would always be Mike, but the perception of him wouldn't be the same. The pens and pencils would start to be thrust, and he never really accepted them, never mind welcomed them.

"Post 1961, there were times when he would question the validity of the people around him", Pam says. "It wasn't apparent unless you knew him well, he was still the same outgoing Mike, talking and chatting to everyone and anyone, but by the same token he was far from being a stupid man and he was aware that there would be hangers-on who wanted to know him for who rather than what he was. I'm not sure if that in itself bothered him so much. Rather I think it made him toughen-up a little so that he wouldn't be disappointed by people feigning affection – which was totally foreign to him.

"He had a childlike innocence and a childlike faith in people. Children have an innocence and a faith in what you're telling them, and Mike was like that. I suspect he was frequently disappointed because he treated people by his own standards; those standards were high and he expected the same of others. If he didn't get those standards he'd be very disappointed for a time, but he'd carry on and trust the next person. He never dwelt on it or harboured feelings of revenge. He continued as before, albeit with a little more caution. He did have an innocence. These stories you hear about the fun he had, I suspect they are almost childlike. Well, right, that's what he was like. He was innocent, he was childlike." In business he would lose by this time and again. In life itself he would gain so much by it that you have to travel longer and further than I have to find anyone who will say so much as a bad word about him. I haven't found them.

"Stan to me was a lovely man. He was gregarious, and you always knew when he was around – you could hear him! He had a very distinctive voice. Mike didn't always see eye-to-eye with him, mostly on matters concerning Stan's appetite for publicity and exhibitionism; and when this caused some shortsighted and, dare I say, envious people to call Mike the 'little rich boy' it hurt him a lot. But Mike loved his father, and despite these strong differences in their characters he was tolerant of him. Whatever people say, Stan's heart was in the right place, and he was incredibly proud of Mike."

As a matter of record, Pam adds that "Mike didn't like the fact Stan spoke to the Press about this, that and the other. There were wild stories going around, and most of them could be traced back to Stan." (Example: that girls were queuing for locks of Mike's hair.)

The Hailwoods could be chivalrous. One morning at her hotel Pam came down to breakfast and found a huge bouquet of flowers. The card with them read *To Pam. She must be the sweetest, kindest girl in the Isle of Man. (Signed) Mike and Stan Hailwood.*

The fun was quite something, also. There was a mechanic who was terrified of women, but M. Hailwood and Co lured him out of his bedroom and put some strong drink into him while others, who had obtained a plaster model of a female from a fashion shop, put it in his bed complete with nightie. When the mechanic returned and switched the light on he whinnied in anguish and spent the night in the corridor outside. (I'm grateful to Pam for lending the incriminating photograph of the 'model', which appears on page 73).

Stan could be hard, too. "In 1961", Read says, "I won my first TT, although I crashed in the 500 when I was lying third. During the TT I couldn't get Bill Lacey to come and look at my bike because he was contracted to Mike. OK, my performance was, I think, fantastic for a privateer taking my bike there in a van with one mechanic. I rode very well, although Hocking had trouble on the MV (as of course did Mike with the AJS) and on the last lap I caught him up – just. His bike broke and I came up winning. Because I didn't make a point of thanking Bill Lacey, Stan made a point of telling people what an ungrateful bastard I was.

"Mike was brilliant. To survive and win on that course in three different classes is quite unbelievable. Then we went to the Dutch TT, my first ever Grand Prix, with my van and two bikes, myself and my fiance. The Avon tyre technicians were round my bike and we were talking. Stan came up and said 'Thank you very much, lads, for your help in the Island', and he gave them each a £10 note, and in 1961 that was money. It made me feel a bit small. The thing was, when Stan was around he was buying Mike's success. Mike was a terrific bloke, but we didn't really get to know him until the Old Man retired. When Stan departed the scene Mike found his own strengths, he got to drive a road car then, drive himself around and he was a great lad, the life and soul of the party, although he was a bit self-conscious. He had talents, he could speak French and Italian, he could play musical instruments..."

In 1961, Mike won the 250cc World Championship from Phillis [11] by 54 points to 45, but with only the six best results counting the score became 44–38. This was the first of nine World Championships, and to this day only two men have more. One of them had as much charisma as Mike and would bestride the whole world on MVs, but that was much later. He was called Giacomo Agostini.

This summer, Mike raced many times domestically, including at Scarborough. "The commentator", Mick Grant recalls, "was a chap called Eddie Fitch, who was wonderful. He had reams and reams of information on everyone, and any gap in the programme he'd reel it off. He'd talk for ever and ever and it was interesting stuff. I was only in the crowd watching. Mike had a white line on his helmet and I remember Fitch saying 'here comes young Mike Hailwood on a Mondial'. I'm pretty sure Mike won that day. It was the first time I'd ever seen him. I had an affinity with Scarborough, I was 17 and it was watching people like Hailwood that got me going." Grant would find himself on The Island nearly two decades hence, and Mike would pay him the ultimate compliment. Oh, and beat him, too.

During the summer Mike had asked Pam to travel with him to the races abroad. "I said 'Oh God, no, I couldn't possibly, my father wouldn't let me'. Mike said 'I'm going to cast a spell on you and make you into a midget so small that I can put you in my pocket and take you everywhere.' It was a very sweet thing to say and the more I knew him the more I realized how sweet. He didn't say things like that very often. I think he was shy about saying nice things to girls."

5

Faces in the mirror, faces in the mirror, 1961.

"John Hartle [12] and Mike had equally fast 250 Hondas for the Championship meeting at Oulton Park. They stuck together like glue until the last two laps

---

11. Tom Phillis, an Australian, was Honda's first team captain in 1960. He became 125cc World Champion in 1961.
12. John Hartle, from Chapel-en-le-Frith, was a particularly brave rider who'd raced on The Island as long ago as 1955. He won his first World Championship race in 1957. He was killed in a race at Scarborough.

when Mike just got the verdict by a wheel", Stan would remember. "I always signalled Mike how many laps were left with *Go* or *Tea Up* on the board until Derek Minter said one day 'thanks for telling me when to get cracking'. After that we always used secret signs. I often wondered what Bob McIntyre's sign was until I discovered that Jock, his mechanic, would hang out a Castrol R tin for three or perhaps one lap to go, as they had decided beforehand. Personally I think the majority of riders are given too many signals – one can see their mechanics popping out every lap. This is totally unnecessary and merely serves to divert the rider's attention from the job in hand. I signalled Mike every five laps, and at Mallory Park in the £1,000 race, for instance, the sign might be a big *20* and underneath an *x20* so that he knew he had 20 laps to go with 20 seconds in hand. It is a very strange fact, as I discovered myself, that after a rider had done two laps anywhere, even the Isle of Man, he has not the faintest idea how many laps he has done. That is why we always hang a *Petrol* signal out on the third lap at Sulby." [13]

Stan also said that "Mike is very strong, and this is well illustrated in a picture taken at the 1961 TT prizegiving where he is shown holding two of those heavy trophies aloft – one in each hand. Let someone try doing this, especially after a hard day's riding."

By then, Pam says, "Mike used to phone me virtually every day from wherever he was in the world and send me these really crazy postcards – which I've kept. He'd be on the phone for half an hour, and looking back that's an indication that by nature Mike was a home-maker. For example, he adored children and was fantastic with them. You'll hear from all the men about the frivolity which went on, and that was definitely a part of Mike, but beneath all that was a man who liked security. The phone calls were contact with home, with someone who was his girlfriend. He always said to me: 'The thing I like about you most is that you never change'. I knew him when he was young, he became a superstar, but there were people from his past who never changed, who were always there. He trusted them.

"Mike didn't talk about his mother or his stepmother to me. Though he may not have had security and stability, I'm not sure that that necessarily affected his later life. He was a confident person, very, very confident in his own ability. I don't think he could have done what he did without it. If he was kicked down he'd bounce back..."

The third last 500cc race of the 1961 Championship was at Monza. Thus far there had been seven and Hocking had won six. Only the problem with the plugs on The Island had prevented complete domination. At this moment Count Agusta – an imperious aristocrat and lord of his manor – decided to offer Mike 350 and 500 MVs. The offer came "out of the blue", as Stan said, "and Mike grabbed it with both hands. The pundits said it was impossible to come straight off a single and ride a four satisfactorily." [14]

Hmmm.

Guess who won the 500 and was second to Hocking in the 350?

Count Agusta did not, of course, invite Mike to join the MV team for 1962. That would have been entirely untypical of the Count and the way he worked.

---

13. The third lap was mid-distance in the race.
14. The Norton was single-cylinder, the MV had four.

No, Count Agusta *ordered* him to join, and he did, although not as a full-blown works rider. Stan had a hand in it, which will scarcely stretch your credulity.

Hocking had in a sense been nurtured at MV by Surtees. "He'd played around with some small machines, and they'd increased in size to big twins and so on", Surtees says. "I suggested why not bring him in on the fours and in fact they did that, although I had a year of my contract to go. I had already got involved in car racing, I was racing cars one weekend and bikes the next. Gary Hocking was a very good rider." In 1960 Surtees did four car Grands Prix and left MV at the end of it. In 1961 Hocking won the 500cc Championship from Mike by 56 points to 55, although only a rider's six best results counted so the final scores were 48–40. Whatever, Gary Hocking was rather less than delighted at the new arrival.

Always in motorsport there are interconnecting threads to a career because the bike and car communities are small places. It's the same with any sport except perhaps football, which in a global sense is so colossal that you might play a World Cup match against, say, Uruguay and never see any of those players again, or remember most of their names. Even in motorsport, the two branches, four wheels and two, are distinct, complete and self-sufficient unto themselves; they rarely overlap, they exist concurrently but in separate spheres. One example will suffice. In 1991 there were 16 rounds of the Formula One World Championship for cars and 15 rounds of the 500cc World Championship for bikes, but only five circuits were used by both.

Many of the bike people Mike knew did not frequent car races at all, and vice versa, but Surtees himself would become a bridge between the two. In 1962 he drove a Lola-Climax and finished fourth in the World Championship. He had an offer from Ferrari. There was only one answer and that was "Yes". "I decided I'd close down my motorcycle shop, and in fact I sold or swopped all my stock to King's of Oxford. Before that I'd sold Stan one or two of my racing bikes, which he wanted for Mike. In turn, when I sold my stock I took some racing Ducatis which Stan had had commissioned in Italy because Stan got up to many things to promote Mike."

So there it was for 1963, another bridge. The honour of Italy was to be defended in cars by a man from Surrey and in bikes by a man from Oxfordshire, Norman John Surtees and Stanley Michael Bailey Hailwood. That, of course, is another glimpse into the future, but before that we must face 1962, the Sad Season.

6

"In those days there were probably about 200 riders competing on the Continental circus and one rider was sitting on a cross-Channel ferry on the way to a race and he was doing a few little sums. This is what he worked out: on average, a rider crashes three times a year. When he said this I looked back at my career and I'd crashed three times a year for the last fives years. I thought I must be about average. Then he said: six blokes get killed every year.

"When you take it that every year a few guys would retire and a few new ones would be coming along, and of the rest six would get knocked off – well, after our years of that, Mike and I and a few old stagers would look at each other and think: we're on the short list. In fact I came home thinking I'd better give this up before it gets me, but when I did get home I thought *bugger it, I'd rather be dead than doing what some people are doing for a living, I'll go back, but I'll be more careful.*" The speaker is Jim Redman, working his way through memory.

"It was physically more demanding to ride bikes then because of the narrow tyres and the suspensions we had. Today's riders wouldn't get away with the tricks they do. We didn't get away with it. We had the calculation in our minds: three crashes a year, six are going to get killed. You tick off your crashes and you tick off the ones being killed, and once it gets to three and six you start to go a bit harder because the statistics say you should be alright.

"One year I went to Argentina and I needed a first or second to get the title from Provini, and I'd had my three crashes. I thought *I won't fall off because I've already filled my quota!* I was outriding him, I had a lot of trouble with the bike, I was going round him and I flung it up the road. I thought *hey, what the hell am I doing on the floor, that's four*. I got back on and came second. It's funny because the following year I had an accident testing at Suzuka. A 'six' seized on me and I didn't realize it had seized because it doesn't happen. I thought I'd stood on the brake too hard. I shut off and it locked up and I slid to the right and then it flicked back to the left. I skidded to a halt. I didn't actually lie down, I put my foot down, I stopped with the bike on the deck and me sort of straddling it. But that still made five crashes in two seasons so the average was still there, I was virtually back on average.

"Mike used to play the cavalier, happy-go-lucky guy, but he still wet the bed the night before the race. Sometimes he'd get much more wound up than me; I used to be much more relaxed about it. The laid-back thing was his cover-up. You think about this for a moment: Mike and I separately won more Grands Prix than the likes of Wayne Rainey, Kevin Schwantz, Mick Doohan and Wayne Gardner added together. If you look at the 500 class today you've got Gardner and Doohan, Schwantz and Rainey, Lawson, John Kocinski, six guys. The one particular year for the 350 title, 1962, you had five guys who could win it much the same as those six.

"The five guys were Gary Hocking and Mike on MVs, Bob McIntyre, myself and Tom Phillis on the Hondas. In June, Tom killed himself in the Isle of Man, Gary packed up because of it and went back to Africa and crashed in a Formula One car, killing himself in December, and Bob Mac killed himself in August. So out of the five who were contesting the Championship there were two left. I won it with Mike second.

"Six deaths a year? I put it down to the suspensions and tyres plus we raced a lot on road circuits, and today they don't do it. Those big shots won't go to the Isle of Man and places like that. They want run-off areas and ploughed fields and all that before they hit anything and it's right they should, but in our day it went like this: *here's the track, take it or leave it, you ride or you push off*. The Island was a World Championship race, we had to go. I didn't like the place ever. Mike was at ease, he liked it better than I did. Even when I got my first double there they said 'We suppose you like the track better now'. I said 'No, I don't'. I've never in all of my career crashed in the Isle of Man. Never once. I've crashed on all the rest but, The Island I treated with such respect that I never crashed there."

Thus, the background to the Sad Season.

Stan, meanwhile, was actively planning his retirement, and Mike took the major and decisive step towards manhood. He moved out into a flat and he found freedom intoxicating. There were, he would say, too many women, too much drinking, too many all-night parties, and he approached the season "tired". Pam had a job, Mike's racing took him away more and more frequently, and their relationship evolved quite naturally into the friendship of a lifetime (Pauline's first date with Mike was in the Isle of Man in June 1962). "When I'd see him in the pits he'd be surrounded by people and I was still so shy there was no way I'd ever go up to him if there were a lot of people around. I'd think to myself: He doesn't want that. He always spotted me. He would break away from the crowd, and although we weren't going out any more he'd stand with his arms fully stretched out and then he'd pick me up and spin me round exactly as you do with a child. He always laughed when he saw me, and I'd say 'Why are you laughing?' and he'd just say 'Because you're sweet!'. Mike was a very natural person."

Before Pam melts from the story – she will return as a friend later – this is how Mike had regarded her. "Once at Mallory Park a bloke was talking to me, he wasn't chatting me up and I didn't even know who he was. Mike came over and said 'she's with me, leave her alone'. This is the kind of thing Mike didn't do very often, it was the kind of thing that told you that you were special. The man said 'I'm only talking to her'. Mike said 'I've told you she's with me, keep your hands off, she's worth fighting for', and he pushed this man out of the way."

Stan did retire in March and the board of King's decided that the job of Managing Director was too much for one man and promptly appointed two. Stan had already bought property in Nassau and the South of France and would divide his time between them, although often enough he'd still come to the races with Mike.

"Mike obviously got closer to a lot of other people than his family", Read says. "His father went to Nassau and we never really saw much of him again. I think Mike looked for love and affection and some sort of home life in a way, and because he couldn't find it he ducked and dived around with different women and he didn't want to be serious with anyone. It wasn't until after meetings when we got a bit drunk that he really opened up. He was a bit insular. He didn't want to get involved or show his affections to people because of that fear of being hurt. He felt insecure and he had to prove himself on the track. That was his motivation, to prove himself to be the best to get friendship. That's how I felt about it. We only saw his step mum Pat occasionally at meetings. Stan was obviously a lot older." (Pat wore a considerable amount of make-up and had eyes so striking that, as someone has said, they preceded her into a room, but literally underneath the make-up she was a warm, natural and sweet person herself.)

Tired or not, Hailwood stormed the 500 Championship, winning five of the first six races. The only one he didn't was the first, at The Island, and thereby hangs a tale which demonstrates that his relationship with Hocking was strained, to say the least. Read again: "At MV, Hocking sort of invented the steering damper. It was hydraulic. They put one on and Hocking went out and broke the lap record. He was sharing the same garage as Mike, it was at the Douglas Bay Hotel. I was there. Mike came into the garage and Hocking went 'fantastic', and Mike went 'Right, I'll have one of those'. Hocking said 'Bloody hell, I've thought of the idea, I've worked on it'. Hocking was upset, that was Hocking resenting Mike, although why shouldn't anyone else see it and adapt it? I'd have slowed it off and not broken the lap record, I'd have said it was worse with the damper in some places – and then done it in the race ..."

Mike was not, as we have seen, a works rider in the accepted sense, more a works-backed privateer ("I think Stan bought a thousand MV scooters in exchange for Mike getting the racing bike", Read says, and surely he did. Surtees confirms it.)

"Mike came into my garage and by that time we knew one another although only casually", Sprayson says. "He asked 'Will you fit me a steering damper?'. With racing motorcycles you can get into a situation where they get what is called a tank slapper. The front wheel starts flapping, the handlebars start wobbling and to damp that out you had a damper. It was a friction damper that you screwed down, but in the more technical days it became hydraulic and you put it between the forks and the frame. I always concluded that they were not a cure to the problem but a camouflage of it. The primary objective should have been to get the steering right in the first place.

"I said to Mike 'What do you want one of those for?', and he said 'Hocking's got one, I want one'. This was typical of Mike Hailwood. Technically he hadn't got a clue, all he knew was that Hocking had this thing, Hocking was the opposition, and he had to have one. I fitted it, no problem, although really we were only on nodding aquaintance."

Redman describes the 350 on the Island, June 1962, thus: "Marlene and I went to catch the race from the bottom of Bray Hill, a steep fast stretch immediately after the start. There we saw the tingling, awe-inspiring sight of Gary Hocking leading Mike Hailwood and Tom Phillis by only a couple of feet. When they came hurtling down at the end of the first lap they were really going some, and the Honda, which did not handle as well as the MVs, was bucking and bouncing all over the place. He must have been pulling out all the stops on every part of the circuit."

Phillis crashed not far into the second lap and was killed. He had been doing what a brave man would have done, trying to stay with Hocking and Mike. He was 28. His wife Betty was in the grandstand with their son Braddan, named after a place on the course because he had been born on The Island during the TT the previous year. Phillis' daughter Debbie was playing in a nursery with Redman's son Jimmy. There is nothing else to say...

The race? Hocking did the first hundred mile an hour lap from a standing start, 100.90, which Mike promptly beat with 101.58. Hocking – now on the move and fast – did 101.49, but Mike won the race by five seconds. Those are the statistics. This is what really happened.

"It was perhaps the hardest decision we have ever had to make on tactics", Stan wrote in *Motor Cycle News*. "Mike started 10 seconds in front of Hocking, which is a definite disadvantage. We talked it over secretly and came to the conclusion that if Mike was to go flat-out from the very start he would probably blow up and the chances were that if Hocking was trying to catch him he would break down as well. Two blown-up MVs would not have pleased Count Agusta.

"We took a gamble. Mike was not to go flat-out all the way, but to let Hocking catch him on the first lap. We felt this would give Hocking confidence and make him think he had the edge on Mike. From then on Mike was to sit on his tail making no attempt to pass. This would also have the effect of saving their motors.

"The gamble was based on the assumption that both riders were roughly equal, but Mike had ridden in some 400 short-circuit races and Hocking in perhaps only 100, so I felt that Mike might have a slight edge on the drop down The Mountain, which is a short-circuit rider's dream. The plan worked beautifully. The two MVs screamed round the course as though tied with a 10ft rope. It must have been hair-raising for the spectators to see those two red 'fire engines' going past. And when they came into the pits together the excitement in the grandstand was tremendous.

"On the fifth lap, coming off The Mountain, Mike was to make his effort. I wanted to see him make at least five seconds down to the start and then throw everything into the last lap in an attempt to gain a further seven seconds, which would give him the race on corrected time by two seconds. The scheme worked as planned – until a few miles from home. Mike had gained five seconds at the grandstand (crossing the line into the last lap), at Ramsey on the other side of The Island it was eight seconds. Then came the blow. Hocking had cut it back to five seconds at The Mountain Box. I still had hopes, but I felt that something had gone wrong. It turned out Mike's engine started to miss going up The Mountain, but then Hocking's started misfiring. Which was the worst? Could Mike still outride Hocking through the tricky parts?"

Yes.

In this graphic and detailed description Stan did not mention Phillis. No, there was nothing to be said.

The 500? Hocking now did 103.76 from a standing start and then, on the move fast again, 105.75, and that gave him a 16-second lead over Mike. On lap three Mike's clutch began to slip and the repairs took 13 minutes. His race was completely destroyed. The mechanic who did the repairs (he had to change the clutch plates) was given a vast, heartfelt ovation from the grandstand facing the pits. Mike made a racer's gesture and set off as if the lead was at stake, although of course nothing at all was at stake. He clawed back enough to finish 12th, which one historian has described as "astonishing". It was.

"Mike started 30 seconds after Hocking", Stan wrote, "and here we had decided to let him go and Mike keep level on time. We told him where he was through signals. On the last lap he was going to make his effort. This worked on the first lap when there was only one second between them on corrected time, but eventually Mike had clutch trouble."

Hocking, distraught about the death of Phillis earlier in the week, announced his retirement with immediate effect, returned to Rhodesia and did not clamber onto a racing bike ever again.

There were smaller meetings, too, in 1962, the Mallorys and Oultons and Snettertons. "I was riding well, so Mike and I usually cleared off from the rest of the pack", Robb says. "We'd make a wonderful dice and then the bugger used to wait until the last lap, he'd look over and make a gesture as if to say *see you* and vanish. There was such a wonderful feeling with Mike. You weren't racing against opposition, you were racing against a real buddy.

"I remember once in practice for a Grand Prix in Ulster where there was a 105mph right-hander, and you really had to wrestle a bike round. Mike came swooping up to this Irish lad, went 'underneath' him (inside) in the middle of the corner, cranked the bike over at 45 degrees, took a hand off the handlebars and stuck a finger up this lad's bum! That sort of fun was typical of him and he was physically able to do it in a 105mph corner, but he just passed that sort of ability off."

7

The Sixties were beginning to swing now, although it must be said that Stan had always swung (the word didn't have the same meaning as it might now; then it meant only doing your own thing in an uninhibited way). "Stan lived a great deal of his immediate retirement in Nassau", Rous says, "and I know that he had a woman who lived in New York. At Monza, Stan and I were in the same hotel, he phones up New York and she was on the next flight. She arrived, a most delightful person, real top-level stuff if you like. You would not get any indication that she was a prostitute in any way, shape or form. Mike knew her, everybody knew her. When the race meeting was over there was a strike in Italy and we were all put on coaches to take us from Linate airport to the other one at Milan, Malpensa, to get a flight. She was on the same coach. That was the one and only time I had seen her, although others had seen her before. Without question she had come from New York to Monza at Stan's wish, and now she was going back gain. That assignment was over as far as she was concerned.

"I met two or three others, one not so young, two youngish, in their twenties. They didn't give the impression that they were anything but what they were. One came to Assen for the Dutch TT, another came to Daytona Beach. The journalists and a photographer had gone there early because it was cheaper that way, there was a cabaret that night in the hotel with two blokes playing piano and bass guitar. I remember them ever so well, they were called Easton and Gilston. We had a terrific evening and we went there every night. One evening I came down and Stan was sitting there all alone. I said 'come with us, we've found a place with music and food', and he did come with us, a party of, say, half a dozen blokes all connected with racing. We had a very good evening. It was very like the Continent; you don't pay for your drinks as you go along, you have a running tab. We were all going bloody barmy, you could say. Perhaps Stan went outside to the gents, but he never returned. When it came to paying the bill, the bill had been paid. The man said 'that *commander* guy paid on his way out.' Stan had also given an enormous tip because he did not know what the bill was going to come to (presumably he couldn't be bothered to wait while it was totted up), and that was Stan. Sometimes he liked to be like the Royal Family and walk around with no money in his pocket. I've often lent him £1 knowing I wouldn't get it back, but it was repaid in many, many other ways" (like at this bar in Daytona).

"His lady friend hadn't arrived the night he came out with us, then she did arrive and he was all fine. He didn't look around locally for anybody, he would call one and fly one in, and that is what he did all the time. She was down there and Mike knew, and I think in a way it might have affected his life from a very young age."

The paragraphs above are not, I hope, salacious, but relevant. I have used them because of the last few words and because, I repeat, Stan did not conceal what he was doing. In that sense Stan and Mike were very similar. Neither (if you'll excuse an awful pun) gave a stuff.

Stuart Graham was a young rider in those days, and when he first met Mike "I found him a terrific guy, friendly and very helpful, just generally natural. Yes, sure Mike could see that his father was becoming lonely, and obviously like a lot of old men who have a lot of money he had people around him trying to help him to get rid of it. Certainly latterly Mike realized what was happening, and was keen to try and stop it, try and protect his father from being ripped-off. Mike resented the fact that these people were exploiting his father when his father was least able to cope with it. Stan was not in the best of health, but people who lived his life style are not just going to drop out of it, they are going to buy their happiness. Stan was stubborn and wasn't going to listen to his son, anyway."

Stan's women were not the sole topic of conversation down the pit lane. Mike's were, too – as Murray Walker and so many others attest they made for him in large numbers. His sheer stamina won universal admiration from fellow males, although I must be careful neither to under nor overstate this. Listen to Ralph Bryans discussing the reality of the situation:

"There were a lot of times to be perfectly frank when I thought Mike was lonely. It might sound strange, but I did. You see, Mike was always very shy with people he didn't know. I'm the kind of individual who'll rabbit away to anybody, but Mike didn't do that, he didn't converse easily with total strangers. He just didn't.

"There was a lot of travel, a lot of hotels, we'd play cards or go to the cinema, go 10-pin bowling, whatever, because contrary to what you hear, while there were girls involved here, there and everywhere – there always are – it wasn't what a lot of people seem to think, a different girl every night or any of that nonsense. You just couldn't do it, man, particularly with the pressure Mike was under.

"If you take for example the low, which is the Monday after a Grand Prix. It's all finished, the paddock's deserted, everybody's gone home and then you've got the hassle of travelling to the next Grand Prix and you've got two practice sessions there. The first practice session you're getting the gearing right, you're getting the bike right and you find you're a second adrift here, half a second adrift there, or somebody's quicker. All this is going through your mind. The next day is the second session and you find OK, maybe you've carved a second, a second-and-a-bit off your lap times, but so has some other bugger, right? You're back under that pressure again, right? And then you've got the bloody race, right?

"Bang, you're away in the race, you're really on a high with that – so your life went in cycles, the build-up and then all the way down again and you can well imagine the logic of why, when you've arrived at the peak, the adrenalin is still flowing, right? You still feel light, *giddy* with the whole thing. So you start having a whale of a party afterwards and everybody would go out and get smashed, and then you wouldn't touch another drink until the prizegiving after the next race, which might be a week, might be two weeks later. It is a fact of life that that is the way things happened. Mind you, we did have some awful, awful good parties ..."

8

Mike had said to Brian Johnston "Yes, I think I might do a bit of motor racing". He'd had a dabble at Silverstone in 1960 in a Lotus-Climax, it was wet, he had no feel for a car's limits and spun, striking the barrier hard. He decided to postpone this other career.

"I first met him when he started in car racing, which would have been 1963", Brian Hart says. Hart was to become a noted builder of engines all the way up to Formula One. "It was in the Formula Junior, a get-the-youngsters-up-and-going formula which developed into 1,100cc production-based engines. The cars were Brabhams and Lotuses and I was driving in it.

"That first time was a windy and cold Snetterton and he was a larger-than-life character enjoying himself. He was quite good. He showed promise, but he didn't take it terribly seriously. I think he thought 'Let's have a go at cars, John Surtees did cars, I'll do cars'. He drove a Brabham (which had cost him £1,700, and he collected it direct from the factory). I met Stan, who was a rare character, and he, too, was larger than life, rushing about. Mike was professional, although don't forget this was club racing, it wasn't like going from the top of one to the top of the other. Sometimes in cars he was better than other times, maybe he hadn't had such a late night the night before.

"Socially you met at club dinners, which in those days were very good fun, at the British Racing Drivers' Club and places like that. I also met him at Mallory Park when he was riding 250s and 350s, and that was fun, too. He used to say 'Look at this, Harty, I've got three bloody bikes to ride and they're tuning them up for me. Go out to Shaw's hairpin'" (a very, very tight right-hander at the far side of the circuit) "'and watch me coming through the esses'. The bloke did things on a bike which...well, Mike could just handle a bike. He could ride the 250s and 350s with one hand.

"He had a sense of balance which was totally natural on a bike, and he was able to transfer a certain amount of that to a car. What he didn't have in a car in those early days was any idea of what to do with it (in the technical sense). A bike is pretty basic, they were very fundamental, it was a question of getting on and going for it. There weren't a great hotch-potch of different tyres and that kind of thing" – you didn't have to make choices based on technical calculations, you rode. "The tyres weren't terribly wide, but he could lay a bike over more than anybody else without getting out of the saddle. He didn't sit out of its side, he hung a leg out. It is a gift. Jimmy Clark, Fangio, they had that gift. Other people couldn't push it that far.

"Riders didn't have knee-supports and pads and footpads, and he'd take a bike so far over he'd wear his overalls out, he'd wear his knees slightly and wearing his boot out was no trouble to him at all. Maybe early on he wasn't taken seriously on the car side, but on a bike he was ... brilliant."

Rod Sawyer left school and went to work at Lotus in the early Sixties so had been involved in motor racing all his life. "I met Mike along with Roy James (one of the Great Train Robbers) and Co in Formula Junior." Sawyer didn't get close to Hailwood then and had no particular reason to, but on Saturday, March 21, 1981 Sawyer's phone rang and "we spoke for an hour and a half. Mike was contemplating getting out of the bike business in Birmingham. He was really down, terribly, terribly dejected. Because I knew him so well I detected that, and it's why I stayed on the telephone for so long."

But this is July 20, 1963. Mike and his car took their place on the fifth row of the grid for the Formula One British Grand Prix at Silverstone. Reg Parnell, a former driver and by then team owner, had persuaded him to have a go in one of three cars he was running, and Mike paid Parnell £5,000 for the privilege of joining the team; pay-drives are nothing new and endure to this day. Chris Amon, a promising 20-year-old New Zealander, and Masten Gregory, a 31-year-old American, were in the other cars, and all were strictured not to do any damage to them because the team simply had no spare parts.

The world then was radically different in its concepts and conceptions. Today, the very notion of an heroic and all-conquering bike rider suddenly appearing at Silverstone to race a Formula One car would provoke enormous curiosity if nothing else. In the whole of its edition before the Grand Prix, including a specific preview, *Autosport* mentioned Mike only once, in paragraph 23 of that preview. This is what it said: "Reg Parnell has discovered a most promising youngster in Chris Amon, who celebrates his 20th birthday tomorrow. He will be in a Lola-Climax, as will Mike Hailwood." Well, nearly right. Hailwood would be in a Lotus, not a Lola.

And that was the mention.

Mike always found the Formula One people stand-offish, and particularly so when measured against bike racing where pretentiousness and pseudo-pretentiousness were unknown and would have been mercilessly exorcized if discovered. Bike racing remained in many ways rough and ready but homely with it, very homely.

Practice was on Thursday and Friday, the Grand Prix being traditionally held on a Saturday to circumvent any Noise Abatement Society protests about disturbing the slumber of a Sunday in the same way that Stan had worried about it when Michael was using Highmoor Hall as a track. On the Friday, five drivers broke the 1,500cc record and another equalled it. Mike was not on this pace or anywhere near it, though he was considerably faster than Gregory. The grid, which wasn't two-by-two in those days, lined up like this:

J. Brabham	G. Hill	D. Gurney	J. Clark
Brabham-Climax	BRM	Brabham-Climax	Lotus-Climax
1m 35.0s	1m 34.8s	1m 34.6s	1m 34.4s

	A. Maggs	B. McLaren	J. Surtees
	Cooper-Climax	Cooper-Climax	Ferrari
	1m 36.0s	1m 35.4s	1m 35.2s

I. Ireland	T. Taylor	R. Ginther	L. Bandini
BRP-BRM	Lotus-Climax	BRM	BRM
1m 36.8s	1m 36.8s	1m 36.0s	1m 36.0s

	C. Amon	J. Hall	J. Bonnier
	Lola-Climax	Lotus-BRM	Cooper-Climax
	1m 37.2s	1m 37.0s	1m 36.8s

T. Settember	M. Hailwood	R. Anderson	J. Siffert
Scirocco-BRM	Lotus-Climax	Lola-Climax	Lotus-BRM
1m 40.8s	1m 39.8s	1m 39.0s	1m 38.4s

	C. de Beaufort	I. Burgess	I. Raby
	Porsche	Scirocco-BRM	Gilby-BRM
	1m 43.4s	1m 42.6s	1m 42.4s

	J. Campbell-Jones	M. Gregory	
	Lola-Climax	Lotus-BRM	
	1m 48.8s	1m 44.2s	

Quite how many of these people Mike knew, or had even spoken to, is impossible to gauge. Certainly Innes Ireland was there when Mike first tried a car at Silverstone in 1960. That day Ireland had taken the same car round a lot faster; obviously Mike knew Surtees, who had been in Formula One since 1960, the year he also won the 350cc and 500cc World Championships. The rest? He might, he might not, and whatever they thought of him he was vastly more famous and able than most of them. With no disrespect to any of them, who remembers Hall and Setterer and Burgess and Raby and Campbell-Jones?

Race day had a sombre beginning. In the Sports and GT car race a woman driver lost control of her Austin-Healey and spun into the pit area injuring a scrutineer. He subsequently died.

The Grand Prix was dominated by Clark, who led for 79 of the 82 laps, while further down the field *Autosport* said "Siffert and Hailwood were having a go, the latter driving extremely well and showing all the signs of making a career on four wheels". In a caption *Autosport* added: "First Formula 1 race for Mike Hailwood, in a Reg Parnell Lotus-Climax 24, resulted in eighth place after a steady drive. For most of that time Mike kept close company with Jo Siffert.[15] Hailwood stopped briefly for adjustment of his gearchange linkage." This is why he finished four laps behind Clark, although there was no particular shame in that. Clark was consummate in a car, always had been, and is arguably the greatest driver who ever lived, just as Mike is arguably the greatest bike rider who ever lived; nor is the analagy as obvious as it might seem. Both were shy until they'd had a little Dutch-courage from a pint, a glass of wine, or something stronger, both had natural gifts which were surely born into them. Clark could drive anything, Hailwood could drive and ride anything, and all who knew them are agreed that they would have hated the clawing, cloying full-blown cardboard-cutout PR-cum-public persona of today. It's scant consolation that they were both spared it. You have the full measure of Jimmy Clark that he is mourned as much as Mike Hailwood, and the full measure of Mike Hailwood that he is mourned as much as Jimmy Clark, each in their different ways and yet each in the same way. Mike judged Clark a nervous chap before a race, the greatest driver he ever saw during a race, and good company when he unwound after a race.

Iain Mackay recounts an interesting anecdote about that. In 1963 there was a non-Championship Formula One race at Solitude, near Stuttgart in Germany. "Jim Clark had the same sort of talent as Mike, he was the same sort of bloke as Mike." But surely Clark lived in a more discreet way? "Yes and no. After the race at Solitude we all went to a party and it was quite surprising because Clark was different to what he had been at the track, he was really wild. He became an extrovert and that was an eye-opener. 'Let's go here, let's go there', he was saying, and that was nice to see, actually."

Mike did one more Grand Prix that year, at Monza, where he qualified on the second last row of the grid and finished 10th, again four laps behind – well, behind Clark.

"There were", *Autosport* said, "the inevitable brushes with the Monza cops.[16] On Friday Innes Ireland was the victim and on Saturday Mike Hailwood had a near punch-up in the pits area. It became so bad that the Press photographers had to petition the organizers for better facilities and less interference by the constabulary. During the night someone pinched one of the Dunlop vans. It was

---

15. A Swiss, Jo Siffert drove in 97 Grands Prix, won twice and was killed in a non-Championship race at Brands Hatch.
16. Monza was notorious for its heavy-handed and chaotic officialdom as well as its enormous and chaotic crowds, called the tifosi – fans, in fact.

found next morning less 20 wet-weather tyres." The race? "There was a wonderful scrap between two-wheeler experts Bob Anderson[17] and Mike Hailwood, the verdict finally going to the latter." Mike was 10th, Anderson 12th. Who noticed that? Clark had won the first of three World Championships, Surtees – whose engine went on lap 17 – would have to wait another year before he could become the first man to do it on both four wheels and two.

---

17. Anderson was not a front-rank rider. He rode 500cc Nortons in 1958 and 1959 and would ride a 250cc Yamaha in 1966 in World Championship events, though he didn't win any. He drove in 25 car Grands Prix with a best place of third. He was killed during a private practice run at Silverstone in 1967.

MIKE AND THE BIKE

*"So I said to Stan 'I think you are a bloody fool. Have a go at the record'." –
Charlie Rous*

*"Count Agusta has often been regarded as a phantom ogre. Nothing can be
further from the truth." – Stan Hailwood*

*"Apparently Mike, who didn't know me from a bar of soap, heard I was going to
drive and stuck stickers all over the car: steering wheel, temperature gauge,
gear lever." – Dickie Attwood*

1

The office is medium-sized and functional. It mirrors its occupant. John Surtees
sits with his back to the window; his hair is white now but his handshake firm,
strong, secure. Another mirror of the man. Once upon a time, between 1956 and
1960, he won 22 500cc Grand Prix races on MV bikes. All these years later and in
quieter times who better to explore and explain the curious world of MV which
for the next four years would be the centrepiece of Mike's racing career? Each of
those years he was World Champion.

"Count Agusta could be described as autocratic. He was head of the family and
acknowledged that responsibility by looking after the interests of his brothers.
Mother was there when I joined, and would have been when Mike joined, too.
She was the Italian mother, they all respected her. Count Agusta was on a
massive ego trip, but he worked very long hours, the majority of them juggling
finances because they had partly built up the company on the aviation side.

"He wasn't an engineer, although he had been associated with engineering, so
he had some knowledge of what went on. Strangely enough, he didn't go along
the same path as other bike companies and try to employ the very best people
because he wanted to be totally and utterly dominant. That meant everything at
Agusta was trial and error, trying this, changing that. It was not planned
development, but in the end the whole thing was running along on the immense
amount of experience they had gained.

"In many ways the Count was similar to Enzo Ferrari, though not so totally
counter-productive as Ferrari could be at times. He had a twinkle in his eye and
a bit of humour. He'd get on a train, go to the races and become involved in

Mike came from solid stock. His grandfather, George Arthur Hailwood (seated behind the shield), taught gymnastics to the poor of Salford, his pupils including his sons George (next but one to his right) and Stan, Mike's father, behind his left shoulder. (*Picture courtesy Doug Hailwood.*)

Stan Hailwood, the proud gymnast, with a winning shield. (*Picture courtesy Doug Hailwood.*)

A severe leg injury didn't stop Stan Hailwood from keeping fit with a pair of Indian clubs. (*Picture courtesy Doug Hailwood.*)

George and his wife Elisabeth about to have a go on Doug's first bike, a Levis. (*Picture courtesy Doug Hailwood.*)

An early bike in the coalyard where Stan Hailwood began his 38 years with King's of Oxford. (*Picture courtesy Doug Hailwood.*)

Still in the coalyard, but a few years later. Stan had already made his mark and was beginning to drive around in style. (*Picture courtesy Doug Hailwood.*)

Mike might have been shy, but he was always photogenic! (*Picture courtesy Chris Buckler.*)

Mike was always close to his sister Chris. (*Picture courtesy Chris Buckler.*)

Stan and a camera-shy Mike on a BSA combination. (*Picture courtesy Chris Buckler.*)

The cheeky grin, which would never leave him. (*Picture courtesy Chris Buckler.*)

Growing up fast. A more serious Mike in the uniform of a Pangbourne naval cadet. (*Picture courtesy Chris Buckler.*)

Out of uniform and with a bike of his own. Mike with sister Chris in the garden of the elegant Hailwood home. (*Picture courtesy Chris Buckler.*)

Mike and Stan in the early days of a brilliant two-wheeled career. (*Picture courtesy Chris Buckler.*)

Getting down to it in 1957. Mike racing a 203cc MV at Oulton Park during his first season and fittingly carrying the message 'FOR LOVE OF THE SPORT' on the fairing. (*Picture courtesy Nick Nicholls.*)

The angle of lean is already greater than most. Aboard a 250 NSU at Mallory Park in 1958. (*Picture courtesy Nick Nicholls.*)

Port Elizabeth, South Africa, with an NSU on New Year's Day, 1958. Mike's wide-brimmed hat is covered with motorcycle club badges. (*Picture courtesy Chris Buckler.*)

Mike's trip to South Africa proved he had something special to offer. A celebratory picture after the Port Elizabeth meeting. (*Picture courtesy Chris Buckler.*)

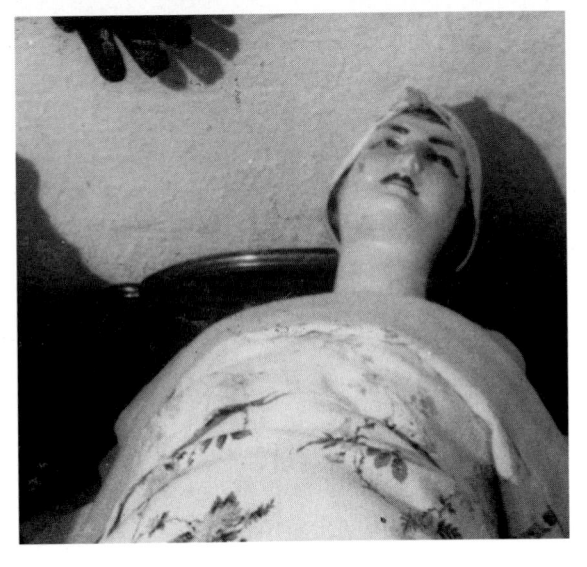

Mike had respect for but little fear of the stone walls lining the Clypse circuit on the Isle of Man when he raced his 125 Paton in the 1958 TT. (*Picture courtesy Nick Nicholls.*)

One of Mike's mechanics was terrified of women, and when he returned to his hotel room after a drinking session and found one already in his bed he fled and spent the night in the corridor! The following morning the plaster model was still waiting patiently. (*Picture courtesy Pam Lawton.*)

Mike about to test a 175cc twin Ducati at Brands Hatch early in 1959. (*Picture courtesy Mick Woollett.*)

Sporting a new line in unconventional headgear, Mike and his good friend Paddy Driver, from South Africa, with an experimental disc brake at the 1959 German Grand Prix at Hockenheim. (*Picture courtesy Mick Woollett.*)

Mike and his Ducati (No 4) lining up for the start of the 1959 Dutch TT alongside Horst Fugner (MZ) and Tarquinio Provini (MV). Mike finished third. (*Picture courtesy Mick Woollett.*)

Another start, another race, this time at Aberdare Park, Wales. Left to right, winner Hailwood, Alan Trow, Dan Shorey and Eric Hinton, all of them on Nortons. (*Picture courtesy Mick Woollett.*)

Ernst Degner and his MZ narrowly leading Mike's Ducati on the Clypse circuit during the 1959 125cc TT. (*Picture courtesy Mick Woollett.*)

Neatly tucked in behind the fairing, Mike swings the 125 Ducati through a left-hander during the 1959 Ulster GP. (*Picture courtesy Nick Nicholls.*)

Formation flying. Derek Minter and Mike wheel-to-wheel on their Nortons at Brands Hatch, the scene of so many of their close encounters. (*Picture courtesy Nick Nicholls.*)

Later the same 1960 season, Murray Walker asks Minter for his version of their latest confrontation while Mike enjoys the joke. (*Picture courtesy Nick Nicholls.*)

That ever-youthful grin, and in 1960 there were not too many stress lines to be seen. (*Picture courtesy Nick Nicholls.*)

Stan Hailwood, a proud father whose aggressive promotion of his son's achievements so often made life difficult for Mike. (*Picture courtesy Nick Nicholls.*)

With Bill Webster and Stan Hailwood in 1961 after Mike had collected both the 125 and 250 trophies during TT week on the Isle of Man. (*Picture courtesy Nick Nicholls.*)

Stirling Moss, having been voted the 1961 TV Sports Personality of the Year, gets the low-down on Mike's Norton. (*Picture courtesy Nick Nicholls.*)

Mike uses the shoulder of his tyres on the 250 Honda during the 1961 Ulster GP. (*Picture courtesy Nick Nicholls.*)

Beginning of a new era. Mike sits astride the four-cylinder works 500 MV Agusta for the first time at Monza in September 1961. Team manager Nello Pagani is on the left and Bill Webster on the right. (*Picture courtesy Mick Woollett.*)

them. It was all a bit like one feudal state against another, which is very common in Italy. He meant to use motorcycles to put the name of Agusta on the map rather like Enzo Ferrari used cars to put the name of Ferrari on the map. This was family honour, and that was what it was all about.

"It was very frustrating because all the time you were trying to achieve more than they apparently wanted. No, that's not strictly true. They wanted it, but at the same time, if they couldn't be totally involved in how it came about it didn't happen. This in turn appeared to be autocratic. Basically there was no delegation and you often got a lot of things done by accident or by persuading the lady secretary to get Mr Agusta to sign a paper agreeing that you could make a new type of brake or wheel so that to all appearances it was his idea. They took on mechanics who developed themselves through experience into superb race people, although it was painful for them on the way."

Stan saw this from an external perspective, from the receiving end. "First of all let me make one point absolutely clear. Count Agusta has often been regarded as a phantom ogre. Nothing can be further from the truth. I met him and corresponded with him quite a lot, and he was always the perfect gentleman and a real racing enthusiast. He could be absolutely charming. The Count was generous and fair in all his dealings.

"On one occasion we were passing through Italy on the way to Argentina for the Grand Prix. When we arrived at Linate airport, Milan, we faced the prospect of a coach trip across the city to Malpensa airport and a wait of about four hours. Instead we were greeted by a chauffeur-driven limousine with orders to go to the MV factory at Gallarate, over 40 miles away. We arrived at the Count's office at 10 in the evening, where he had a snack and champagne waiting for us. He wanted to fix up a contract for the following year and had kept his secretary behind. We agreed the terms, he dictated the contract. I was amazed at his fairness and generosity – like insuring Mike for £10,000 and other small points." (Small points!)

"The trouble with the Count was that he was unpredictable. One just did not know what he was going to do next. Whether this was the result of his Latin temperament or that he was such a busy man, I don't know. Busy he undoubtedly was, working well into the night every night running his huge business. Racing was just a hobby to him, and he was apt to overlook the rider's point of view. For instance, when Alan Shepherd wanted a talk with the Count he sat in the outer office for well over a day, actually it might have been two days. Mike once sat there over six hours and then went again the following morning."

Mike himself claimed he waited three days to get into that office, most untypically worked himself into a rage, said to hell with it, and left the factory pursued by mechanics on pushbikes calling for him to come back. He did, and still the Count made him wait. Mike judged that the Count wanted a psychological advantage over everyone – including Mike.

Always there is a gain and a loss, and the gain was enormous, although not financially in the beginning. (Mike signed for £1,200 for his first season. Four years later this had risen to £7,000.)

In 1962, after Hocking departed The Island and bike racing altogether, Mike won the next five races and the Championship. He won seven of the eight 500cc World Championship races in 1963, seven of the nine in 1964, eight of the 10 in 1965. Putting it more starkly, he failed to win only five in the span of three years, and of these five either the bike failed or he didn't compete. In no race was he beaten when the bike was running at the end.

"Mike broke away (from home) either deliberately or accidentally and around the time he went to MV the very strong influence of Stan had certainly been removed", Murray Walker judges in a careful, measured way. "That was when Mike started to blossom as an individual. The thing that never failed to amaze me was how his enormous success – think about it, he was a national figure, a World Champion, and everyone knew him everywhere he went – did not affect him at all. He was always the same Mike."

In 1963, Geoff Duke persuaded Gilera to send him 350cc and 500cc bikes, vintage 1957, for his own team. Bob McIntyre had set the world one-hour record at Monza in 1957 on just such a 350. On them Duke now fielded Minter and John Hartle and, says Rous, "the Gilera was the only thing which could offer a challenge to the MVs". Minter won three early non-Championship races and beat Mike at Imola (also non-Championship).

We've already had Minter's description of how Mike crashed into him at Brands Hatch. "Then we went to Imola", Minter says, "me on the Gilera, Mike on the MVs. That was the time I fell off the 350 Gilera because things were touching the deck. I told Duke it was happening and he said 'impossible, nothing touches the deck'. Come the race the footrest dug in and away I went. I'd never been to Imola before, the 500 race was afterwards and I beat Mike then. The newspapers said he was still recovering from his accident at Brands Hatch – but I'd just fallen off in the 350! However, it was only the newspapers saying this. Mike could have made all the excuses in the world – the bike wasn't right or whatever – but he never did. He could have said he was still suffering from Brands, but he'd never ever do that either.

Jerry Wood: "There was a race at Brands" – perhaps the Minter crash, perhaps not – "where Mike was beaten, and afterwards some Pressmen gathered round and said 'what was wrong with you, what was wrong with the bike?', and he rounded on them. 'Nothing. Weren't you watching what happened? I was beaten by a better man on the day. Why don't you give him some credit?'."

A bitter irony. Minter himself crashed a little while later at Brands, and the other rider involved was killed. As Rous says, "that more or less eliminated Minter from the entire season. In my opinion, until the time Minter broke his back, he was slightly better. If he had met Mike on equal terms 1963 could have had a very different outcome. Hartle was a good team rider, Phil Read, who replaced Minter, was not in the Hailwood class. Good as Hartle was, when he lapped the Isle of Man at 105mph Mike lapped it at 106. He was so nonchalant in the way he did it. He did it to bring down their morale: every single lap that he rode in practice or the race was at over 100mph, which in 1963 was still a feat. He'd take off without any flurry or anything like that, come back, say he was pulling up to check the plugs and it was still over 100. In the race Hartle went off in front, but Mike had a slight advantage in that he started late and all he really had to do was catch Hartle." *Motor Cycle News* allowed the statistics to tell the tale. They are eloquent enough. "Hailwood opened with a standing-start lap of 106.3mph and followed it with a new lap record of 106.41 before 'slowing down' to an average of 104.64 for the 226.4 miles distance. Second to Hailwood was Hartle at 103.67 with a fastest lap of 105.57mph."

"He acted very professionally", Rous says, "but he loved a laugh. He would go to the East German Grand Prix at the Sachsenring, which was the home of MZ.[1] Lord knows what they did to prepare their machines, but invariably Hailwood would ride for them. I don't believe he ever won (he didn't) but he was always leading the race when he fell off or the bike failed. He would put in phenomenal laps until he was toppled for whatever reason. They had crowds of upwards of half a million there and they loved to see Mike."

Rous found himself invited by Mike to accompany him to MV for some negotiations. "At London Airport there was a red carpet out up to the aircraft steps – it was the type of aircraft where you got in under the tail – and Mike couldn't resist joking about that. 'They couldn't have known I was coming!' It was the inaugural flight of a new plane, I think the Trident, in commerical service, and we had a wonderful time, champagne and everything else. We were coming down perfectly normally towards Linate.

"Subsequently I worked it out that the plane was automatically flown, but for the last 50 feet went back in the hands of the pilot. I am not being critical of the pilot, but for some reason as the plane was almost on the ground it suddenly went haywire, a tyre burst, the wheels seemed to be spinning. People started to scream. Mike turned to me and said very calmly *'I think we're going ...'* The wheels didn't collapse although the plane ran off the end of the runway before the pilot stopped it. We got off, away we went to MV and that was it."

The final race of 1963 was in Argentina, and Buenos Aires seemed to offer only one desirable commodity: the airport out. "There was a bus to transport us backwards and forwards from the hotel to the circuit", Redman says. "This one day we were driving down the highway in the bus and it was full of riders and mechanics, maybe 40 people.

"We were up to our eyes with Argentina. We had had all our valuables stolen – watches and cameras and money – from the garages while we were practising. You get so casual, you throw all your gear in a heap and go off, and then the mechanics follow you over to do a bit of timing. Somebody had watched this and scooped the lot. Before that we hadn't been able to start the practice properly because a rider went out and crashed and there was no first aid. The whole thing was a disaster and at the end of it you're all in a filthy mood.

"First of all we couldn't get in the bus because people thought it was a general bus and it was full of them. We had to wait for somebody to come and eject them. Then down the highway going back to the hotel two car-loads of locals positioned themselves in the fast lane and the slow lane. I don't know whether they were just doing it in front of any bus or doing it to us because it was us, but they crawled along and kept us behind them. We got our driver to go down a slip road at a flyover and come up the entry road at the other side so that we were in front of these two cars. We said 'right let's teach them a lesson, we'll pull them over and give them a thump'. We pulled them over, they stopped and we opened the door and poured out – well, the only ones were Mike, Luigi Taveri, myself and Alan Shepherd. The other 36 people just sat tight. We were going to give these guys a couple of sharp slaps, but there were two of them to every one of us. One guy was getting out of a car – I'd pulled the door open and grabbed him and given him a thump. I thought I could hit pretty hard and he would go down, but he didn't, he unfolded to about 6ft 2 and with plenty of reinforcements. We had

---

1. MZ made two-stroke bikes. The company had been called DKW – Das Kleine Wunder, the little wonder – before the war and was based at the town of Chemnitz which, when the Soviet Union assumed control of that part of Germany, became Karl-Marx-Stadt. Since the re-unification of Germany it has reverted to Chemnitz.

a scuffle and beat a hasty retreat. We all took off for the bus, but Luigi was the last into it and got clonked over the back of the head with a starting handle and had a big egg on his head. The bus driver was ready, and as we got on he hit the accelerator and the bus went *wooosh* and we were already moving ..."

You note that of the four who did get out Mike was one of them; and you note that Redman instantly adopted Mike's very own motto: Hit them as hard as you can and if they get up run like hell.

"What sort of a bloke was Hailwood?" Redman will muse (long pause). "Ahhhh" (long pause). "He was Mike, you know. It's hard to say because he was a one-off. He had various guises. One minute he wants to go out every night and raunch and rump, then he would come down to South Africa, say to Durban, and sit around and play cards and not want to go out, you know, sit around the pool. He always knew a few dollies so he could phone one up, or I could and have somebody come round for company and all that.

"Mike had too many moods and ...I don't know. Generally speaking he was much quieter than people think. His hell-raising was in bursts. Between, he was quiet. He and I, I'd go to England and we'd sit around and shoot the breeze and have a meal and do sod all. Another time in Durban he was at the Club Med[2] every night. They had a good comedian at the time who'd say to Mike to come down.

"And he'd always attract a load of hangers-on. He had a lot of patience with the hangers-on. I'd see them and I'd avoid them. Mike didn't bother, you know, *if they're there they're there, if they're not they're not*. You couldn't say he was like *this* or like *that* because he had so many different swings."

2

At eight o'clock that February evening a cable arrived at the Daytona racetrack, Florida. It contained one word: Yes.

Stan returned to the Holiday Inn where he was staying – it was handy, just across the road – and pondered and pondered. He estimated that the "terrible" decision facing him was "probably the most difficult I've ever had to make" in the context of Mike's career. It was now simple. To go for the world one-hour record or not go for it. "Should I let my son take this risk? I said nothing to anybody and went to bed for a long, cool think."

The record was held by McIntyre (as we have seen in Footnote 1 of the previous chapter). On a 350 Gilera McIntyre had lapped Monza at 143mph. McIntyre's record had been set on the old banked Monza, not the one you see today.[3] McIntyre was lamented and respected, and the record should perhaps have stood as a memorial to him, but there was a problem about that. Rous was at Daytona, as he thought, simply to cover the United States Grand Prix, first round of the 1964 Championship. "I wrote a piece saying there was no place left in the world for breaking the record except Daytona. Paris (Montlhéry) was too

---

2. Club Mediterranee, a French holiday organization which spread worldwide. It has camps, which are similar to hotels, is aimed at young people, and you're supposed to be a member to get in. (Naughty aside from Murray Walker: "And when you are, it's very easy to get your member in!")
3. The banking interlocked with the present circuit.

bumpy, Monza's banking was bumpy and not really being used, Brooklands was no more. What a pity that here we are at Daytona in this beautiful speed bowl where cars lap at 175mph and somebody cannot have a go at the speed record. This is ridiculous. I wrote it several times and Stan said to me 'let's have a go'."

Strands were coming together, and despite innocent appearances there was little innocent about it. Stan scarcely needed encouragement and the idea was firmly in his mind long before he flew to Daytona. The year before Mike had had a trial run on a Norton just to feel out the territory, just to see, and had lapped at 139.6mph. Stan estimated the 1964 MV was at least 10 miles an hour quicker and asked permission for another trial run one morning before official practice began. Mike lapped at 148.4mph.

First there was the matter of McIntyre's memory. McIntyre had been on a 350, Mike would be on the 500, and so in a very real sense McIntyre's record would still stand. Second, as Rous pointed out, "at the circuit was somebody or other, an American I think, with a very peculiar looking machine which I heard was expected to break the lap record. I said to Stan 'I think you are a bloody fool. Have a go at the record. If this bloke does it you are going to look stupid'." Rous had seen that this other bloke's bike looked "like the kind American speed cops have, big old twins and that sort of thing, although he was I understood only intent on breaking the lap record. I said 'If he breaks that, go for the hour and put him right in his place'."

In England, Stan had already broached the subject with Dickie Davies, Dunlop's competition manager, and "he told me it would take weeks to make special track tyres. He advised me against using 'ordinary' road racing tyres because of the risk due to the heat you get at 145mph coupled with the track heat under the burning Florida sun".

There was another problem, much bigger than all this: the distant, autocractic Count Agusta, whose family name and honour would be tarnished by failure, as would the name and honour of the company which, inescapably, was his own name, anyway. No attempt could be made without his permission. Count Agusta had a further problem. The attempt would have to be on the morning of the Grand Prix on the race bike, and if it broke down or was damaged Mike was effectively out of contention for eight Championship points. Count Agusta faced the prospect of an aborted attempt with all attendant publicity and an abort in the first round of the Championship. Only the practice bike would then be available for the Grand Prix; it had already been worked hard and surely even Mike couldn't win on that.

"What were we to do?", Stan mused to himself. "Mike was mad keen to have a go, but to be on the safe side I cabled Count Agusta asking his opinion. Back came the reply that in view of the lack of special preparations and the lack of spares plus the risk he did not approve. Reluctantly, but with a certain amount of relief, we packed the practice machine back into the crate ready for shipping. However, the organizers so badly wanted to see a record taken at their track that they sent an urgent cable to the Count begging him to let Mike try. The reply came back, and to my amazement the Count said 'Yes'."

Hmmm.

Rous says that "Count Agusta hated racing if there was any chance of something going wrong, and because they hadn't sent special machines they didn't feel Mike's would be good enough and they didn't want to blow up the Grand Prix bike. The Count said 'No', but..."

There can be little doubt that once the inital refusal arrived Stan betook himself to the organizers and pointed out what he knew all about: the publicity value of a successful attempt. Whether he cajoled them into sending a second request or they did it themselves hardly matters, although knowing Stan as we do he probably dictated it and got them to sign it and then dispatched it himself. Americans understand publicity too, none better.

Now Stan was having his long cool think up there in his room in the Holiday Inn. It was late evening, Saturday, February 1, 1964. He confirmed to himself the decision he had been making all along, and it was not really a terrible one except in its possible consequences – but if a man pushed his son to compete on the Isle of Man at 18 he wouldn't baulk at Daytona. In comparison Daytona was a bowl, a bowl of cherries.

Only the practical questions demanded answers. "I decided we must not use the race machine, but would the practice bike do it? What were we going to do about tyres? We had a brand new set on the race machine, but the tyres on the practice bike had done about 100 miles and that wear might make all the difference. My biggest headache was Mike himself. If he ever found out that I had the permission in my pocket and had not said anything about it I do not know what his reaction might have been, but I can well imagine. After a sleepless night I decided as dawn broke to take a chance. Who could help us prepare for the attempt in this short time? Charlie Rous had been a well-known sprinter and knew all about record-breaking. I went banging at his door."

Rous: "Stan came and got me out of bed about three or four in the morning. 'We're going for the record first thing. Would you help Vittorio (Mike's MV mechanic) get the bike ready?' I thought: this is incredible." Stan would remember Rous (now pulling his trousers on) saying "take this chance because if you don't Mike will never forgive you".

Exit Stan down the corridor to bang on the door of Vittorio, who was "equally enthusiastic". Stan "decided to let Mike sleep on in blissful ignorance while we rushed to the track, unwrapped the practice machine, swapped the tyres, refitted the fairing, put on the highest gear sprockets and generally prepared the machine. Vittorio was worrying and muttering away in Italian all the time. Perhaps it was a good thing I couldn't understand what he was saying. Never in the history of motorcycle racing can a machine have been got ready, or perhaps I should say thrown together, so quickly for a record. It was a record in itself. By nine o'clock we were practically finished."

Rous: "We got it out of the box, Vittorio and I, about five in the morning. It was beautiful sunshine. Earlier the Avon tyre people had said 'if he goes for the record pump the tyres up to 60lb pressure'." In the rush and the urgency of the attempt this statistic departed Rous' mind and would not return. "We had another problem which never ever came out. We didn't have enough tyres, so the bike had a Dunlop on the front and an Avon on the back. And I couldn't remember the pressure I'd been told. I said to Vittorio 'What pressure do you use in the races?', and he said '30lb'. I said 'We'll pump the tyres to 35lb'."

Stan dispatched Rous to organize the officials, who weren't far away – they'd all travelled for the Grand Prix – and agree to pay them their fee; oh, and actually hire the circuit. Stan phoned Mike at the Holiday Inn and told him to get down here sharp. It was on.

Rous had – *had* – to find a photographer. "Side views needed to be taken of the machine", Stan would say. "This was something new to us, but apparently it was to prove that the same machine was used for all of the attempt. It was a mystery to me how Mike could have come in, switched machines, set off again and still taken the record, but there we are, regulations are regulations."

An American who worked at the track whispered to Rous that at such an hour the prevailing wind usually favoured going round the bowl clockwise whereas all racing at Daytona went anti-clockwise. Of course, neither Mike (nor perhaps anybody else) had been round clockwise before. When Mike arrived there was a tactical talk; he was asked to go round the wrong way. Probably he just nodded. Clockwise or anti, he'd do either. If Stan had produced a real live camel he'd ride that instead. He was as good as that.

Stan, bustling under the urgency and no doubt loving it, had been on the phone to the local met office. They said "Fine weather, but rather cool". The British forces were deployed. Rous himself would time it, Stan would hold up a pit board to tell Mike how he was doing. The officials were gathering, the Press were gathering, radio and television people were coming in. The word had spread quickly. We cannot doubt who did the spreading: the white-haired man with the limp, who even now was borrowing a powerful pair of binoculars so that when he wasn't holding the pit board up he could monitor the tyres and their wear. That was the main concern. As a final task, as the sun moved higher and higher, Rous and Vittorio filled the petrol tank right to the brim.

A Major David Goode of the FIM dropped the Union Jack, Mike already had the engine running hard although it was a standing start. He pushed the bike off, eased himself so naturally onto the saddle and went for it.

Rous: "We had geared the bike high so he could keep it flat-out at near enough 10,000 revs."

Stan: "At the end of the first lap I realized to my horror that I had entirely overlooked the standing start. Mike's first lap was 136.5mph. I began to worry how many laps it would take to pull up to an average of 145mph, which was what we were aiming for. However, Rous said 'Not to worry, Stan, just let Mike go'. After 15 minutes he had pulled it up to 141mph overall by lapping consistently at 146.5mph."

It was done in a cunning way, too, playing to an obvious strength that Mike had. Rous: "If he kept low on the banking, say at 10 feet from the infield instead of 20 feet, he'd save yards and yards every lap" – the further up the bank you go the greater the distance you have to cover. "So Mike rode it like a road-racer, leaning into it the whole time." Mike made Daytona into the longest corner in the world.

Stan: "At 30 minutes the average was 142.9mph so we decided to give Mike the 'Hurry Up' sign, and at 45 minutes we had hoisted the average to 145.2mph, but then he started to lose a second or two per lap. This only added to my worries about the tyres. I was watching his rear tyre through the binoculars every time he passed by, searching for those telltale white patches of wear. I saw him looking round at his rear tyre – at 146mph. What he thought he might be able to see I don't know, but he seemed satisfied and I put the sign out to him 'Tyres OK'. We had agreed that if I saw any white he would stop immediately." (Rous thinks that at 30 minutes "Mike seemed to lose his concentration and that's why we had to give him the 'Hurry Up' sign".)

Mike went on and on and on, and it became a beautifully simple thing, a man, a bike, a bowl blending into a purity of movement and only Stan disturbed it by thrusting himself onto the rim of the infield from time to time with the enormous pit board which he brandished like a matador holding a cape.

A klaxon sounded 60 minutes, stopwatches were flicked, but Mike was allowed to complete the lap and, Rous says, "on that lap it ran out of petrol. He only just made it..."

Stanley Michael Bailey Hailwood had averaged 144.8mph, and you don't have to be a mathematician to know that that is 144.8 miles. Bob Mac had done 143, and that's a big difference, nearly two miles.

Stan: "He got off with a bad headache and cramp, but laughing as usual. I asked him what he had been looking round for, and he said he thought he had heard a bit of rubber flapping, but it must have been his imagination. I told him that his imagination had nearly given me a heart attack. We got a bill for 1,000 dollars (at that time £350) for the cost of hiring the track, officials and so on, and for taking the record we got exactly nothing except the glory." What else would Stan have wanted?

In the afternoon, in the United States Grand Prix, February 2, 1964, the results were:

1	M. Hailwood	MV Agusta	1h 16.09s
2	P. Read	Matchless	2 laps
3	J. Hartle	Norton	2 laps

Mike confessed to Rous afterwards that he'd been troubled by an Argentinian rider, Benedicto Caldarella, on a four-cylinder Gilera. "It was astonishing", Rous says. "The Gilera was faster than Mike's MV, the Gilera went away from it just like that and was miles quicker. Caldarella, however, had gearbox trouble. Mike said 'Christ, I was getting worn out trying to keep with him. This morning didn't do me any bloody good.' He'd covered more miles in an hour than anyone had done before, within an hour he'd gone straight into a Grand Prix which he won, but he maintained he only won because the other guy dropped out." Selfless honesty of the highest order.

When Mike returned to England, *Motor Cycle News* carried a strong letter from a Mr Murray who, while recognizing Mike's achievement, said that it was not to be compared to McIntyre's. "Mike and I couldn't have agreed more", Stan said. "Nobody will ever touch that record at Monza, and for once in his life Mike wrote a good letter in reply. He is a shocking writer, but this time he went to town and said just what he thought." To *Motor Cycle News* Mike wrote:

"I respect and appreciate the letter published from Mr Murray prompted by a spirit of loyalty to that greatest of all riders – my old friend Bob Mac. I will go further than Mr Murray and say that there never was a more magnificent ride than that made by Bob on the Monza track in 1957.

"Only riders who have attempted that circuit can truly appreciate the sheer guts and brilliant riding which made Bob's effort possible. I should hate my effort at Daytona to be even compared with it. There is just no comparison.

"I don't think I'm chicken, and believe me both myself and Count Agusta would have preferred to have made the record attempt at Monza, but after circulating there during practice for the Italian car Grand Prix in September I knew it was just impossible. In fact car drivers refused to race on the big circuit and the smaller one was used. Am I forgiven, Mr Murray? [4]

"I have hesitated to go for this record a long time because I would personally have liked it to remain a lasting tribute to the great sportsman who, both wittingly and unwittingly, taught me to ride – or tried to. His infectious grin of encouragement when I was a nervous beginner is a memory I shall always cherish. However, I knew that sooner of later someone would take the record

and I felt that Bob would like to think that at least one of his pupils was the man who did it. There are only a few of us still racing who had the pleasure and education of riding against the maestro – usually behind him.

"No, Mr Murray. Nobody can ever take away the glory of Bob Mac's epic ride. I hope it stays in the book as the 350cc record for ever. I do not want my record classed or compared with that of the greatest rider I was privileged to know as a pal – the immortal Bob McIntyre."

3

Faces in the mirror, faces in the mirror.

"I will tell you a nice little story. My ex-wife was a lovely girl, we were at the Ulster Grand Prix and I was having a cup of coffee. Mike was sitting with a crowd of people. My daughter was Miss Pears,[5] she was only two or three, and this woman walked past pushing a pram. Mike said 'Get a load of that', and I said 'Do you know what, the Irish girls are like that over here, Mike, they are all beauties'. He said 'That is a cracker, that is, come on, you must know all the women, give me an introduction.' I went to the door and said 'Doreen'. She looked round. 'Come here a minute, please. Doreen, I would like you to meet the famous Mike Hailwood. Mike, I would like you to meet my wife.' 'You bastard', Mike said in that lovely way he had, 'you rotten Irish bastard'."

You can see him smiling when he said it, the big open smile.

In the enclosed motorcycle community there lived a couple who were not, as Ralph Bryans says, "tremendous socializers. The man kept himself to himself. At Spa they had their caravan parked in the paddock. After the Grand Prix Ginger Malloy,[6] Mike and myself arrived back fairly late. Their caravan was parked on a hill with jacks to level it up. We decided it would be a good idea if I went and got my car and hooked this caravan up to the back because I had a towing ball and we'd take it for a lap of the circuit while the couple were still in it.

"We got spanners, Mike and I were round the back working on these jacks and I could hear from within the woman's voice saying 'there's somebody out there!'. We went quiet. The jacks hadn't been oiled and they were squeaking. The caravan brake wasn't on, the next thing I know the caravan took off down the paddock. We scattered.

"A week or two later we were staying at Limburg en route to another race. It was a camp site. I went to get some water. I walked round the corner on the way back holding a bucket in each hand, and who should I bump into but the woman from the caravan. She said 'You're a naughty boy, Ralph', and she bloody hit me round the side of the head and I couldn't do a thing about it."

---

4. This was the Italian Grand Prix of 1963 where the state of the concrete banking was so rough drivers were alarmed by it in practice and one narrowly avoided a serious crash. The banking was not used for the race because the police were unhappy about spectator protection on it.
5. A soap company.
6. A New Zealander who rode 250cc machines in the World Championship from 1965 to 1970.

Do you know Spa, incidentally? It has a very, very tight hairpin called La Source, which descends to a left–right kink and then the circuit rises as if up a mountainside. It is one of the great spectacles of car and bike racing to see all this taken at speed. The very thought of Bryans or Mike trying it towing a carvan with, no doubt, a screaming couple in it is not so much amusing as mind-boggling.

"I met this guy called Elvio Marconi, who had a little hotel in Balleria, Italy", Redman says. "Elvio arrived one day and was helping Tom Phillis and I at Imola, and then he said 'Come and stay with us'. The friendship built up over the years, he got to meet Mike and all the crowd. Around Imola time, around Monza time, we'd go and stay. It was a nice place right on the beach, we could water-ski and so on.

"Elvio knew everybody in car racing as well, and he worked his way in everywhere, and anyway we gave him tickets to get in. One day over conversation in the hotel Mike and I were discussing about getting Ferraris; Elvio had always talked about how he and Enzo Ferrari were friends. We never had any reason to doubt or challenge him, although it did seem... well, unlikely. Elvio said 'I'll get Enzo down for lunch' and we said 'yes, do that' but we thought: Enzo Ferrari coming to have lunch with us, not a prayer. Elvio said 'he'll be here at 11.30 or 12 o'clock, we'll have a drink and some lunch'.

"Suddenly this Ferrari turned into the drive and there he was. The hotel had quite a long drive and cars used to park to the left or right. This Ferrari came and parked directly outside the door and out stepped Enzo. We had lunch with him. First time I'd met him, I think the first time Mike had met him. He came down in the two-plus-two that we liked, it was a model which had just come out and we went and drove his car. We said 'Yes, we'll take two', and he said he'd give us a good price and we said 'No, no we don't want to pay anything' – not in those words, but that was our meaning. In the end we got two cars for the price of one. We wanted them in white and I did get a white one, Mike got a greeky one – which was what grey sounded like in Italian when Mike said it." [7]

Faces in the mirror...

Redman and Mike in a Mercedes showroom in London gazing at two very expensive pieces of machinery and Mike saying "I'll get these, you paid for lunch". Alas, it isn't true. "The words were a regular joke between us", Redman says. "Somebody must have overheard it and not realized."

"Mike fell off at the Sachsenring in Germany", Macauley says. "He landed on his head and he was unconscious for a while, but he wasn't badly hurt. I got a message from Stan. *Am flying out in private plane to pick Mike up*. It wasn't the thing then – people didn't have private planes. Nor would I have been absolutely certain that Stan couldn't have got a private plane behind the Iron Curtain because he was such a determined man. That's the way he was.

"Stan was very brash, but he had a great pride in Mike, which was a bit obsessive in some ways. One year at the TT Mike had 'flu and was very poorly, and it was touch and go whether he made the race. In fact he did. I'd been out on the track and I was walking along the back of the grandstand. It was a big grassy area. Stan was sitting on a bench with a portable radio to his ear listening to the course commentary and he had anxiety written all over his face because his lad was out there and could barely hold the bike up. It was the first time I'd seen Stan in that condition and it said a lot."

Count Agusta was present at the Nations Grand Prix at Monza on September 13, 1964, second last of the season. He watched with mounting appreciation as a young, slender Italian brought a Morini[8] into fourth place in the 250cc race behind Read, Mick Duff and Redman. Count Agusta decided to hire him. Whatever he had, he had one thing Mike could never have. He was Italian.

He was called Giacomo Agostini.

"When Agostini first came to prominence", Nobby Clark says, "he pitched up at a meeting with his helmet painted the same colour as Mike's. In a very tactful way Mike let it be known that everyone had his own design and colours, this was every rider's trademark, and would he please change his to something more original."

"When Mike was on the MV and I was on the Honda Mike would sometimes say to me 'What do you want – the last five laps to count?', and I'd say 'OK' with him because we'd do it properly, we'd ride together for 35 laps, look at each other when we were side-by-side, nod our heads and know this was it," Redman says. "Phil Read used to try and do it with us, but he'd try and steal four or five seconds when we were not looking, and if he did he would put his head down and go like buggery. We had to drag him back. If Phil said 'Last five to count' we'd say 'Not with you ...'"

Relations with Read were ambivalent. Redman and Mike devised a scheme at the Sachsenring once upon a time: Mike was in the 500 race and would walk up to Redman on the grid for the 350 and say in front of Read the opposite of the track surface conditions. "If it was slippy Mike would say grippy, if it was grippy he'd say slippy. If it was very slippy he'd say it was very grippy. What he said was 'it's expletive slippy'." So Redman knew there was plenty of grip and he pulled out seven seconds on Read in the first lap while Read was awaiting the slippy sections; and those seven seconds were the winning margin.

"Mike preferred to start from behind you. Rather than take a yard he'd give you a yard then with five laps to go he'd pull alongside on the straight and I'd say 'Yup, she's on', we'd brake into the next corner casually and from there the game *was* on.

"I think I beat Mike more than he beat me in 250 and 350s, but I did it by scheming, not by riding. The Honda was twitchy, you know, because it was shorter, lower, lighter, and I gave up on the handling because I needed to beat Hailwood. If I have a similar bike I have to outride him in the bends. My strategy was to sacrifice the handling and hang on to the speed, and during the course of the race I'd wear him down because I'd got used to the handling. I always had the legs[9] to pass him."

4

Count Agusta did not object in principle or practice to Mike continuing his Grand Prix car career with the proviso that he competed in the full 500cc calendar. Mike did nine of the 10 car races in 1964, Monaco in a Lotus-Climax and the rest in a Lotus-BRM, but at least once to accommodate both disciplines

---

7. Grey in Italian is grigio.
8. An Italian company.
9. An expression almost – but not quite – exclusive to motorsport. It means to go quicker than someone else.

he qualified for a car Grand Prix, flew off to race the 500 MV, then flew back for the car race (see below). Only a very strong man – in mind and body – could have done it, and indeed only one other man had ever tried to on this scale: Surtees.

The season can be embraced by simply looking at the calendar: February 2, US 500cc; May 10, Monaco GP; May 24, Dutch GP; June 12, the Isle of Man; June 27, Dutch 500cc; June 28, French GP; July 5, Belgian GP; July 11, British GP; July 19, West German 500cc; July 26, East German 500cc; August 2, German GP; August 8, Ulster 500cc; August 23, Austrian GP; August 30, Finnish 500cc; September 6, Italian GP; September 13, Nations 500cc; October 4, USA GP; October 25, Mexican GP; November 1, Japan 250cc.

At Monaco he was sixth in the Grand Prix, the first point he'd gained, although he was four laps behind the winner, Graham Hill. He would recount to John Thompson in *Racing and All That* how the 100 laps of the race took nearly three hours to complete; he was a "physical and mental wreck" at the end and needed three full days to recover. As he drew into the pits Tim Parnell said in a strong Derbyshire accent "eeh, lad, I thought you would have done better than that..."

It was Mike's only point of the season, and it proves a great Formula One truth which endures to this day. If you manipulate yourself into a front-running car you rack up points into mountains, but if you don't, each and every one is elusive, precious, rare. To place this squarely in a more modern context, Riccardo Patrese had a superb season with the Williams Renault team in 1991, and at one stage the Championship itself was not beyond him. Patrese, who had begun in 1977, spent the whole of the 1985 season literally pointless with Alfa Romeo, and he drove the full 16 races. I don't mention this to enhance Mike's single point, but rather to restate the great truth. Points come at you in profusion at one level, they are to be counted in singles at another.

One forgotten day in 1964 there would be a chance encounter at Parnell's factory at Hounslow and that encounter was "very casual. I ran across Mike, but I wasn't really taking much notice." The speaker is David Hobbs, then a young aspirant. Across the years to come he would take a great deal of notice, a very great deal.

Innes Ireland[10] was in a BRP that 1964 season and "I was giving up Grand Prix racing. I remember Mike as being a terrific guy with no side whatsoever, full of fun all the time. He was very good company, he'd play a banjo or ukelele or whatever the hell it was; he was a good chap to have at a party and a good man to have in a team. He hadn't realized his full potential in cars. In 1964 BP made a film called *The Time Between*. It was about four people, Graham Hill, Bruce McLaren, Mike Hailwood and myself. The film was centred on all of us and what we did from the French Grand Prix that year to the British Grand Prix. Mike raced at Spa in between (winning the 500cc) and the film of him going around the old circuit was amazing because he was bloody tanking on." Ireland, incidentally, is not an easy man to impress in these matters, and his words were couched in a depth approaching awe. "In the film there's a clip of him at a party playing the banjo. He also compared car racing to bike racing and said that 'at least a bike goes round a corner in a line, cars skitter about all over the place'."

---

10. A very experienced Scot who had first raced in Formula One in 1959, although he only won one Grand Prix.

Ireland was a good chap to have at a party, too, and Mike once recounted how he – Ireland – danced on tables after the Austrian Grand Prix wearing a kilt with nothing under it and Graham Hill did something unmentionable to him with a cactus.

To a man like Mike, who raced intuitively, by feel, by the instinct of feel, the transition would be a perennial problem. You could do it on a bike, but cars, inherently more complex and allowing endless, maddening variations in how they are set up, needed calculating.

Mike was pouring a fortune away on BRM engines, the car wasn't reliable, he suspected that the Grand Prix people were looking down on him, and he came to "dread" – his own word and a very strong one given his attitude to life – the Grands Prix.

5

"I met him in 1965 and I knew nothing really about the bikes", Dickie Attwood says. "It was at the time when Mike had invested a bit of money in Reg Parnell Racing. At the end of 1963 I was nominated the premier Grovewood Award winner[11] and BRM were interested to train up another driver – or get one under their wing – in case something happened to their establised drivers Richie Ginther and Graham Hill. In fact, through 1964 I did hardly any test driving for them, but I did one race that I remember, at Goodwood, where I finished fourth. They were very pleased with me, but they just didn't have enough time and cars to give me any drives. Tim Parnell (Reg's son) was running the Lotus 25 with BRM engines and BRM decided to supply Tim with an engine for me as long as they supplied me with a car. That was the way BRM could keep me in employment, as it were.

"The first race we did was Monaco in 1965. I know that by then Mike was getting fed up because obviously the cars were not up to scratch and he was spending a lot of money, I guess. He had decided he wasn't going to go on much longer anyway. I went down to Hounslow where Parnells were for a fitting for the car I was going to drive at Monaco. I'd never sat in it. Apparently Mike, who didn't know me from a bar of soap, had heard this poof[12] was going to drive this car and thought he'd take the mickey out of me. He stuck little stickers all over the car: steering wheel, temperature gauge, gear lever. That's the sort of humour he had. I didn't take on board what it really meant, I thought *bloody daft, of course this is a steering wheel*. I didn't know who'd done it.

"I can't remember exactly when we met and shook hands, but it was obviously at Monte Carlo and he was struggling with his car. I don't think he liked Monte Carlo particularly (as a circuit), but I did and I was getting better and better with every practice session. I ended up fifth on the grid in a privately entered car which, you know, was virtually unheard of. (Without being pedantic Attwood was sixth, relegated by Surtees, Ferrari, who did 1m 33.2s against Attwood's 1m 33.9s. Mike was 12th with 1m 36.5s.)

---

11. For promising young drivers.
12. Attwood is describing how Mike would have seen racing drivers, he is not describing himself!

"Mike was quite a deep sort of person" – at this point in the interview, given in 1991, Attwood moves subconsciously into the present tense – "If he thinks someone is a bit of a prat he doesn't bother with them. He doesn't suffer fools gladly." Then, equally unconsciously, to the past tense again: "In the race I was lying fifth, but at around half-distance a hub broke and I went straight off at Gasworks Hairpin.[13] Fortunately there were straw bales there and I didn't hurt myself." Mike had gone only as far as lap 12 when the gearbox broke. He would not line up on a Grand Prix grid again for six years – which was almost a different generation.

"After the race we had the typical Mike Hailwood event, if you like", Attwood says, "everything, the usual Monte Carlo scene and from that time on we were friends. That night we did the rounds, the Tip Top Bar[14] then a nightclub after that. He was with a girl, and I was, and we had a great evening. I gelled with him, he gelled with me. He was born two years earlier than me, but there were so many things I felt we were similar about – the way he was brought up and the way I was brought up. I didn't really know anything about him until I'd met him.[15] The car he was driving was too old, no matter what engine you'd got in it. He went back to bike racing and we lost contact."

The car career he was leaving behind is easily understood, comfortably digested, and can be set down in eight words: *12 Grands Prix and that single point, Monaco*, but you miss how goddamned dangerous it was then, and the cars were fast. The cars were also metal frames which under impact could pass through you. (As Redman said of bike racing, but circa the same era: The first thing was to survive the crash and the second thing was to survive the First Aid.) This career cost Mike many, many thousands of pounds, and this when £1,000 a year was a living wage. He had not enjoyed the experience, and persistent displeasure was entirely new to him. He simply went home to bikes.

Chris Barber caught the mood there. "At a bike meeting he could finish the race, come into the paddock, walk through it, and nobody would speak to him in the sense that nobody would bother him. 'That's just Mike, you know', they'd say. It wasn't the same in motor car racing where nine-tenths of the people were hangers-on wanting autographs or whatever and not anything to do with the racing. But the bikers thought 'It's just Mike'..."

6

Faces in the mirror...

The all-pervading influence of Stan had diminished and Mike had become a man, his own man.

"I was unemployed for a while, and then I drove an egg truck", Jerry Wood says. "Part of my round took me near his flat in Heston, so I parked it nearby one day. We went and had a few drinks, I was a bit tipsy and when we got back he said

---

13. The sharp right along the harbour leading to today's start-finish line.
14. Favourite drinking haunt for the motor racing fraternity and anybody else who can get in during the Grand Prix weekend.
15. The division between the car and bike communities is clearly demonstrated here.

'Hey, you never gave me any eggs'. I got a couple of trays of eggs and brought them into the room. He took two eggs and cracked them open on my head. Then we had an egg fight.

"He was a totally unspoilt man. On a bike he was so natural. Someone told me that when he was in South Africa he had been taken out in a dingy and an instructor said 'Ever been in one before?'. 'No.' 'Well, I'd better give you some tips.' At the end of the day they all had a race and Mike won by miles. That's the way he was. He could sit at a piano and play it, play the guitar, play tennis, he was good at whatever he did.

"I'd raced sidecars and given up, and I was invited to have another go. I'd sold my leathers so I called round and asked Mike if I could borrow a pair of his. 'Sure', he said, 'What for?' I explained. 'You're crazy, nothing would get me on a sidecar.' I admired him so much and I began to think that if Mike Hailwood thought it was crazy maybe it was and I shouldn't do it, but I had already committed myself ...

"He never got on with Phil Read and Read said to him once, pointing to his own backside, 'That's all you're going to see of me today' and straight away Mike said 'Yes, when I'm lapping you'."

"I can remember the first time I went to his flat", Nobby Clark says. "I had come over from Holland and was driving along the Great West Road. I stopped at a filling station near the Firestone factory and asked the pump attendant if he knew this address. He told me where it was, then he said there must be a party and he'd see me there later on!" (Anywhere in West London, just stop and ask for Hailwood, and yes, there would have been a party, and yes, lots of people would be there. Not so bad for someone who was shy.) "Mike was a very talented musician, I think a lot better than most people believed. He played the piano, guitar, clarinet and saxophone. Often he would play the clarinet or saxophone for hours in the flat.

"Normally I used to have about six cups of tea before I did anything. One day Mike got back with a box, all wrapped up, and he said it was for me. I opened it and there was an enormous mug. He'd worked out that the tea would stay warmer longer if I drank it that way. It held eight cups and needed one and a half teapots to fill!

"One day the TV started to play up and Mike liked to watch TV, not the serious stuff like Panorama, but Top of the Flops. He rang the hire firm and told them the problem and they said they'd send someone round in half an hour. That grew to 12 hours and still no-one had come. Mike rang again and got the usual stuff, we're very busy, we're understaffed. The next morning no-one had made an appearance so Mike picked up the TV and threw it over the balcony – nine floors up, mind you – and it landed heavily on the lawn. He rang and told the firm where it was. They collected it within half an hour: tyres squealing, a van roared up outside. They picked up the pieces and gave us another set while that one was being repaired. Would you believe it? In a week they brought the original back and it worked like a dream.

"In all the time I knew and worked with Mike we never once had an argument. We both respected each other. We had chaps come and stay at the flat from time to time from South Africa, Australia, New Zealand, the States. Most of them thought they had to make conversation from the moment they opened their eyes until they went to bed. Mike would tell them he didn't want to talk that particular day and they'd think he was a bit stand-offish – but that was Mike. He didn't mean to be abrupt, but he just wanted whoever it was to respect his wishes. He had a motto: if you don't have anything to say it's best to keep your mouth shut.

"Mike was an excellent skier and the first time he and Bill Ivy went skiing together they went up in a ski-lift. At every stop on the way up Mike said 'Don't you think you ought to get off here? You haven't skied before'. Bill said 'No' each time – he was going to the top. Mike said that when Bill set off it was like an avalanche coming down the mountain.

"Ivy lived in the same block, and a chap by the name of Paul Hawkins (an Australian sports car driver later killed) used to come around. When all three of them were together they got up to all kinds of mischief and could be quite naughty, but never in a malicious way. None of them trusted the other when it came to driving a car. Mike would say to me 'I must be crazy to get into a car with Bill'. They all drove really fast, but I always felt safe with any one of them driving.

"We were all at a party one night and Phil Read was there, too. A girl asked Phil who he was and he told her. He also told her that he rode bikes. She said she had never heard of him. Then he told her he had won three World Championships, and she said she'd only heard of Mike Hailwood..."

"I had a road manager, John Ryan, who had previously been road manager to a pop group", Barber says. "He was mostly engaged in what beds they'd been in the night before, getting them out of them, cleaning them up and getting them to work. He was a great motorbike enthusiast, had met Mike and introduced him to us having found out that Mike was a great fan of the band anyway. He hired the band a couple of times until he found out what it cost! (Barber was famous himself at the time, and to a certain generation, mine, still is.) He had a do at Mallory Park in the old clubhouse on the first floor and he sang. He sang the Sheik of Arabie... fairly well. Alright, he wasn't Frank Sinatra, but he could get away with a trad-type number because people who sing trad can't sing either! He was drunk enough to open the window behind the band and pee out of it. Lucky there wasn't a strong wind blowing that way. He was a tolerable clarinet player. I heard him playing, but without thinking 'how good is this chap?'. He had the idea what to do with it, you know. He wouldn't play with the band, although it wouldn't have mattered with us."

This performance at Mallory Park was a duet. The other 'singer'? John Cooper. "Mike wrote the words down for me on a bit of paper because I didn't know them. We'd had a few beers, we stood on the stage and sang. I can still hear it

> *Sheik of Arabie, Sheik of Arabie,*
> *Your love belongs to me ...*"

This was the night Bill Ivy[16] was so drunk he had to be carried to his car by four people, one at each corner, and the night Mike tried to drive, came to a fork in the road and went straight on. Some say his car went through a closed garden gate.

"Mike loved jazz. I spent an evening with him once in an hotel listening to Chris Barber. There were only about six of us in the room so Barber played for just us six", Cooper says.

---

16. Of Ivy, more later.

"Mike was a very good cook; there were cookery books in the flat, but they were never really used", Clark says. "Mike said cooking was exploring and improvizing. His dishes were always excellent and never the same, they had no names, and if anyone asked what they had eaten he told them some fancy French title.

"When we were in the flat Mike decided to have a new carpet fitted in the lounge. We rolled the old one up and put it on the balcony. About a week later Mike said 'Don't you think we should take the old one downstairs and put it in the garage?'. It had rained quite a bit in the meantime, the carpet was too heavy for us and anyway we didn't want to mess up the new one by dragging it across. We decided to toss it off the balcony wall. Mike said to me 'Go down and make sure no-one is underneath.' I'd give him a sign and he'd push it off. Down it came, made a hell of a bang and shook windows. People were looking out to see what on earth was going on. We got it into the garage, and next morning, when we were in the local shop, an old dear was asking the shopkeeper if he had heard the gas explosion the day before in Southall – telling him how bad it had been.

"One time at an America-versus-Britain team match Mike was the British team's non-riding captain and he was so disgusted with his riders' efforts that after the meeting he gave us mechanics a board with children's plastic tools fixed to it. He said the mechanics deserved a prize for our efforts and that he had bought knitting sets for his team.

"Mike, Jim Redman and I went to a party near Heathrow. It was supposed to be a pyjama party. We rocked up there with our supply of vodka and lemonade but the host said we weren't welcome because we weren't dressed for it. No trouble. We stripped off down to our underwear and all this time the vodka was being consumed to ward off the cold. Quite a few of the guests did not approve so off we went.

"Mike had a red BMW, Swiss-registered, and we ended up in Hounslow and went around a roundabout the wrong way. The cops were there and stopped us. When we'd left the party we'd thrown our gear in the back (so – Three Men In Underpants). The cops asked Mike who he was and he said 'Jim Redman' and they asked Jim and he said 'Mike Hailwood', and when they came to me and my accent they wanted to know where I was from. I said 'Sweden' because I had just been up there, but they wanted to see my passport. I kept feeling my chest and saying 'Officer, I must have mislaid it somewhere'.

"Eventually the cops said they would give us all a breath-test, but after much humming and hawing it was agreed that if I walked in a straight line for half a block we could go. I set off with Mike talking and coaxing me like I was a curling stone and he was one of those people who go along brushing ice in front of it. I made it and they let us go."

"I wanted to write a book, I wanted to get a book out of my system", Murray Walker says. "I wanted to call it *The Art of Motor Cycle Racing*, but not having done it to any great extent myself and certainly not having a name for it the book would not sell very well. I got this idea of doing it in concert with Mike, attaching Mike's name to it, using Mike's experience, getting Mike to talk about it, and that's what happened. Since his name was on the front it was a fair assumption that he'd want to know what was in it, check it very carefully, read the proofs and mark them.

"I'd go up to him at race meetings and ask about aspects of riding, lines in the corners, tactics, that sort of thing. You know what he was like, very, very easy to talk to. If you were in the media and particularly if riders knew you they were enormously easy and likeable, especially Mike. So I'd talk and then write.

"I'd take the stuff to Mike and say this is what I've written, and he'd say he didn't want to read it. I said 'But Mike, it has your name on it, it's your book, you should read it, there might be something wrong'. He said 'Are you happy with it?' I'd say 'Of course, I wrote it.' He'd say 'If you're happy with it, I'm happy with it.' I did get him to read one chapter, it was about clothing. I was talking about the crash helmet and what sort you should buy, and I'd said that apart from the fact that the rules require you to wear one it keeps your head warm, ha, ha. Mike looked at me and said 'You'd better take that out, it's bloody silly', and of course it was bloody silly ...

"If it had been me I'd have read it all because I'm vain, I am proud about my image, and if somebody had got something wrong which in my opinion reflected adversely on me I'd want it corrected. Now that may be the answer. He actually didn't care. Nelson Piquet is the same. Piquet never reads anything about himself. Piquet says: 'If I read something I may not like it, I am going to get agitated. The best thing to do is just not read it and then I can carry on in my own sweet way.' I think Mike was the same as that. He genuinely didn't care what people thought about him. If he had cared he certainly wouldn't have done a lot of the things he did do – although many were endearing." This could be construed as an oblique reference to the Hailwood Sex Appeal, and Murray Walker saw them arrive and depart. "Given the number of women he knew, he had all types from scrubbers to upmarket." No comment.

7

Carol and Lewis Young were in a sense people of that decade, Lewis a rider, Carol an extremely talented artist as you can judge for yourself by the drawing she did of Mike, which is reproduced on page 116.

What follows is unadorned, sincerely recording how they saw Mike, and presented in dialogue form because that's how my interview with them went.

Lewis: "I was a rider in the Sixties and I first met Mike in 1964. It was at Snetterton; he was in a 350 race. In the heats I was second and he was third – Minter was first – and in the final Mike was first, Minter second and I was third. This was racing in close company all the time, he was fair, but no quarter was given, none asked. He wouldn't do anything dirty. I wasn't a friend of his, but I did speak to him. Occasionally I'd ask him for a gear ratio or he'd say 'What's it like out there today?', as a fellow rider would. In those days the machines were the same and you had certain gear ratios for a certain machine on a certain track. You'd ask him what he was pulling and he'd tell you. It's what racing people did then, it was friendly and open, there was nothing guarded about it. He was a nice fellow rider and this was sport, it was fun and it was better than work (chuckle).

"Socially we came together a lot in 1966 and 1967 on the Continent and in England. After a meeting at Brands Hatch you went to the pub at night-time and you'd always have a good old drink and talk about the day. Everybody was there, all the top riders. Everybody enjoyed themselves. There were parties in Highgate at various people's houses. You'd bang on the front door and go in and there'd be one or two dim lights and a seething mass of bodies."

Carol: "A friend or ours who was with Yamaha, Jerry the Gnome, used to be up on the top of the wardrobe jumping down onto beds just for fun."

Lewis: "Bill Ivy was there once, and Mike had a Ferrari and Ivy had a Maserati outside. They were both jumping on the bonnets because they were so happy or drunk or whatever. Nobody else did it, obviously, because they weren't their cars."

Carol: "I met Mike through Bill. I went out with Bill Ivy for a little while. He was living in Heston with Mike, sharing a flat. I used to go round there, but I was so green and naive about some of the things they got up to."

Lewis: "In the mid-Sixties in the off-season there was a party every week in London or the suburbs, always on a Saturday night, and all the racing fraternity went there. The word would spread: there's a party at so-and-so's, are you coming? It was a normal thing, didn't matter who you were, it was one big family. This was the flower power, remember, people all loving each other and being nice to each other."

Carol: "I did paintings of the motorcyclists and that's how I got to know Bill. It was a hobby, really. Mike was in flat number 7, Bill moved in with him and they both shared number 7. They had different bedrooms. Bill had just come on the scene and Mike was the famous one, and Bill was in awe of Mike a bit, but they got on extremely well together. They were both as mad as each other, but they did have a few upsets and one of them was about a girl. She was Mike's girlfriend, she was lovely-looking and really nice to meet. She used to do adverts on TV. I'd never even drunk wine or gone to a restaurant in London, I was a novice, and she helped me along. Then Mike met Pauline, and that was sort of on-and-off, and this girl was a bit upset, so Bill used to take her out. She was irresistible, she was gorgeous, and Mike found out and it didn't go down too well. I think that was one of the reasons why Mike moved upstairs to number 37 and Bill stayed in number 7.

"Mike was very shy. I used to go round there, although we never actually went out together, but on a few occasions my phone would ring and it would be one of Mike's friends asking me to go out with him and Mike; he'd got the friend to ring me. He was either shy or embarrassed. I mean, I have seen Mike make bee-lines for women, but he was very reserved sometimes, very shy, really shy, especially if we were out and people recognized him.

"Do you remember that time we were out having a meal in a restaurant and there was a middle-aged couple looking over? They obviously recognized Mike and we were in the middle of our meal and the man came over and said 'Excuse me, Mr Hailwood, can I have your autograph please?' and Mike signed it. This man went back to his seat and later, as they got up to leave, the wife came over and butted in again. 'Mr Hailwood, I'd just like you to know that you've given my husband the greatest thrill of his life'. As they were leaving Mike turned to us and said 'Doesn't say much for you, dearie, does it?' The lady didn't hear ...

"He said it to make us laugh, but he did get embarrassed when people came up. I never saw him refuse an autograph. He was always uncomfortable, but he signed."

Lewis: "And sometimes he'd sit in the King's Road in a pub on his own to try and pick up a girl as a challenge because at, say, Brands Hatch all the girls knew who he was, but down the King's Road nobody knew him from Adam, he was just another bloke. He'd try his luck to pick up a girl and he failed half the time."

Carol: "When the girls knew that that was Mike Hailwood then they were all after him."

Lewis: "He'd try it as a challenge because he was sick and tired of the girls who knew him (by reputation). Those times on his own he'd nothing behind him but his shadow, as it were."

Carol: "He was very shy underneath it all, extremely shy."

Lewis: "A very homely bloke. I mean, in the winter time my phone would ring around eight in the evening; it would be Mike. He'd say 'You watching television?'. 'Yes.' 'You bored?' 'Yes.' 'Let's go down the pub.' He'd walk to the Rose and Crown in Heston and I'd meet him there, and this was a time when he was ultra-famous."

Carol: "I remember, funnily enough, talking about money. Honda weren't going to race the following season and they paid Mike £50,000 not to race. That seemed such a lot of money. I think Bill was on £25,000 with Yamaha. Mike was always pretty philosophical about things, wasn't he?"

Lewis: "He was doing a bit of car racing and testing, so the money didn't make much difference to him because he was into cars."

Carol: "I never really saw him upset about anything. He was very laid-back about things. I'm just trying to think if I ever saw him get upset about anything. I don't think we did. He was such an easy-going sort of person."

Lewis: "If he stopped in a race he wouldn't be upset, he wouldn't throw a tantrum like you see these days."

Carol: "He certainly wasn't ..."

Lewis: "... the Nigel Mansell sort."

Carol: "Mike used to cook, lots of women coming and going, of course."

Lewis: "Anybody in town used to stay at Mike's flat, any racing driver or mechanic. Nobby Clark stayed there for two years, was it?"

Carol: "Nobby was more like the housekeeper, doing the washing-up and the cooking."

Lewis: "We'd go out of a night to the pub and he'd say 'Let's go back to my place', and we played a fabulous game called lah-di-dah. He had about six who played and you had this little glass of whisky..."

Carol: "...vodka, usually..."

Lewis: "...and you'd pass it round..."

Carol: "...singing lah-di-dah, lah-di-dah lah-di-dah-di-dah, and if you ended up holding the glass on the last dah you had to drink it."

Lewis: "Six people and five glasses. After an hour of playing and you'd already been to a pub, everybody's drunk but happy. It was just part of growing up, I suppose, I don't know. Mind you, the drink-driving laws hardly existed in those days. He was often caught for drink-driving."

Carol: "Oh yes."

Lewis: "Most police, if they catch a well-known figure they normally book them, don't they? It's that attitude they have. Mike was often involved with the police for speeding."

Carol: "Well, there used to be some silly things. I remember coming back from Mallory Park. Mike was in his car and Bill was in – what was that car Bill had?"

Lewis: "A Stringray."

Carol: "We were coming down the M1 doing about 90 miles an hour side-by-side and they were lobbing sweets to each other through the windows, backwards and forwards. The M1 wasn't as busy in those days, but it was still a pretty silly thing to do."

Lewis: "But in recent years I was in with an Australian who was driving back from somewhere to where he lived doing 160 miles an hour in a Merc. That would pull on your brains."

Carol: "What about that time in South Africa when you were sleeping on top of the van?"

Lewis: "I went to South Africa in the winter racing. We took Mike's Honda-six in the van, we'd been in Rhodesia, we were transporting it and we were going from Johannesburg to Capetown, 1,000 miles. There were three of us in this van and it took us about three days. At night we used to sleep on top of it. This one time we were sleeping on top and it was a lovely morning."

Carol: "All the bikes were secure inside."

Lewis: "We were in a lay-by at the side of the road and we heard this boooom. It woke us up and we thought what the hell was that? Is it a car? No, can't be. But it was, I saw the rear lights. Turned out it was Mike Hailwood and Peter Gethin going to Capetown and they did the 1,000 miles in nine hours. There was very little traffic, but of course every hundred miles there was a town you went through. They must have been doing I don't know what speed. In South Africa Mike was the same man, only more so."

Carol: "There was a procession of girls. I mean, we didn't know how he could manage it (chuckle). He had one girl more or less living there and then all these other women used to arrive and disappear with him and come out smiling, then more would come."

Lewis: "He went to a party and met two Americans who'd never heard of Mike Hailwood, nice, funny Americans, and they had that ability to tell jokes which it takes two to tell, like Morecambe and Wise. They were like that, perfect, Mike loved them and they stayed the next two or three nights."

Carol: "Mike liked to have people around who..."

Lewis: "...made him laugh, who were way-out."

Carol: "...who were good comedians, and he also liked people who would say 'Oh, come on, let's go and do this or do that'. He liked to be led."

Lewis: "He liked people who were normal people. You could call him a bloody twit to his face..."

Carol: "...then he'd turn round and call you something, too, yes."

Lewis: "When I was racing and he was lapping me he'd hit me hard on the back as he went by. He had time to do that. I remember a race in Italy in the late Sixties and it was Hailwood and Agostini charging round, it was a 500cc road race and they lapped the slower riders because their bikes were better and they were better riders. As Mike came by he gave me a whack in the back (chuckle) and continued with a smile on his face. A fabulous person. But it was more friendly then, you see. You had time to be nice, I suppose."

Question from Hilton: "What did you make of this procession of women?"

Lewis: "Well, nobody cared because everybody was doing it."

Carol: "He was very highly-sexed."

Lewis: "He had the stamina of a bloody bull."

Carol: "I'm only saying it because I used to see the number of women he'd get through."

Lewis: "They'd all be sitting round the swimming pool and suddenly he'd disappear with a girl for about an hour, and two hours later he'd disappear with another girl."

Carol: "Yes."

Hilton: "I'm trying to do an honest portrait, and part of what he was was that, and part of what he was was the world's greatest bike racer, and part of what he was was a very British gentleman ..."

Carol: "Yes."

Lewis: "To put it bluntly, he could be the perfect gentleman when the need arose, and he could be the perfect bastard when the need arose. He could be anything. If all the people were posh and nice he would blend in, if they were like us, working-class people effing and blinding and drinking beer, he'd be just as much at home with those people."

Carol: "He could be very crude, very crude. I've heard him say terrible things to girls, and if he'd said them to me I'd have died. We were up at Donington Park or somewhere and there was a reporter who used to knock around with Mike. We had an Australian girlfriend who came to race meetings with us, a very attractive girl on her own and prey for all men.

"Well, on the Friday night this reporter was interested in her and she went off to the hotel and spent the night with him. The next night Mike appeared to be interested in her also; she went back to the hotel with Mike and she said they got into bed and Mike said: 'Humph, I can smell the reporter'. She felt so awful because in fact she wasn't the sort of girl to sleep around. Whether saying that was Mike's sense of humour ... well obviously it was."

Lewis: "He could say the most outrageous things just for a laugh."

Carol: "He did do some pretty naughty things in view of other people, like in cars at Donington."

Lewis: "Well, he didn't give a stuff didn't Mike. They were all looking for him and he was in the back of his Merc stuffing some girl. As a man he couldn't sit still, he'd pick up a guitar, whatever. He just lived hard and loved hard."

Carol: "In 1970, *Motor Cycle News* decided to have supergirls. They chose three girls to go to race meetings and promote them. I was one of the first. Well, there were the three of us and he had his hands up all our skirts, but because it was Mike and we all knew it was Mike we let him get away with it. If it had been somebody else we'd have turned around and said 'What do you think you're doing?', but he did it for a laugh. In fact we were quite chuffed to think that he'd done it."

Lewis: "Everyone accepted it because he was such a nice bloke. He proved on the track how good he was, he proved socially how generous, how kind he was. Do you remember when he was car racing at Brands Hatch in Formula One and we went to watch in the paddock and there was a big rope in a ring round the car and he was in the middle of this ring. We went there, but we didn't cross the rope. He spotted us, he immediately stopped talking to whoever he was talking to – probably Lord So-and-So – and came straight across and started talking to us."

Carol: "I don't think he ever felt really comfortable with the car types."

Lewis: "I've a photograph of a crash we had at Snetterton about 1965. They'd made a chicane, it was very, very wet, he was flung across and as he was getting up I arrived and knocked him down again. He'd got his bike up off the ground, I was sliding along and as he got his bike up again I hit him. It all happened very quickly.

Hilton: "What did he say afterwards?"

Lewis: "You bastard (chuckle)."

Hilton: "With a smile on his face?"

Lewis: "Oh yes. That's the sort of guy Mike was."

8

These mid-Sixties and quite by chance Mike met Pam at the London Boat Show. "I was working there", Pam says, "and I saw this guy walking towards me wearing a very long mack. When he got closer I saw it was Mike and he suggested we went out to lunch. It was a lunch I shall always remember because I learnt things that day I had not dared to even imagine before. We downed three bottles of wine between us, and with what I suppose was a little Dutch courage Mike told me for the first time how he felt about me.

"As I said before, he wasn't one to express his feelings in words, and I sat there looking across the table at this man I adored thinking to myself: I do not believe what this man is saying to me. He obviously had no idea how I felt about him. He said 'Well, you were always with some chinless wonder' – a great expression of Mike's – and I suppose he had thought I was not that interested in him. If only he'd known! Even then I couldn't find the courage to tell him!

"I'd always seen him with these stunning and sophisticated women, so how could he possibly like me? He asked me why I had never married him and I said 'Mike, you never asked me'. 'Oh yes I did.' 'Oh no you didn't.' He then reminded me that he'd asked me to go abroad with him and I'd said I had a job and my father wouldn't let me. He said 'Do you think I would have taken a little innocent girl like you away from home without putting a ring on your finger?' I said 'Well, you could have told me' and he said 'Well, I as good as did'."

Before we leave this luncheon table Pam Lawton needs to be heard on something else. I've mentioned to her that several people (particularly Carol Young, above) have stated how awkward Mike found it to ring and ask for a date.

"I find it hard to believe he was too shy to phone a girl up and say would she like to come out for a drink. People might say because he was a superstar if he rang a girl and was rejected it would have been more difficult for him, but Mike didn't perceive himself like that so I don't think it's got anything to do with it. You think that, but he didn't. I'm damned sure he didn't. To him he was Mike Hailwood, ordinary bloke."

MIKE AND THE BRONCO

"I came in and said 'Agostini's just fallen off', and Mike said 'Bloody good.' It wasn't the reaction I would have expected." – Ralph Bryans

Walker: "You are the first TT winner I have ever seen holding a bunch of flowers. How do you feel after that?"
Hailwood: "I feel a bit of a twit." – Interview, the Isle of Man

"If bloody Hailwood rides that bloody bike and bloody wins he deserves the VC."
– John Cooper

"When we saw him he didn't show any upset and disappointment. His face was just like as before, always smiling. We were very impressed." – Katsumasa Suzuki

1

In 1965 Mike won his fourth consecutive 500cc World Championship, which no man had done before. Surtees had four, but spread over five years, as had Duke. Mike was unimpressed by what he had done. The MV was intrinsically better than the opposition and he'd made it function properly but ... Agostini was on one, too. Hailwood 48 points, Agostini 38. Paddy Driver on a Matchless was next and the rest a lot further back, all the way down to Lewis Young with 1. The future at MV was young Agostini, also second to Jim Redman on the 350s.

Deep within the motorbike community the story is well known, but somebody has to say it and it might as well be Phil Read. "When Mike last rode for MV at Monza" – the Nations Grand Prix, September 5, the final 500 of the season – "and Ago was in the team, MV wouldn't let Mike have the best bike and he thought 'sod 'em' and went off."

Rous confirms this. "It was a well-known fact from years before that Agusta's ambition was to have an Italian World Champion. When Agostini arrived it was very, very clear to us in the Press Box that unquestionably he was getting favourable treatment. The three-cylinder 350 was brought out and it was Agostini who rode it. They did this sort of thing once or twice. Mike would never malign anybody. He would not say 'his bike is faster than mine', he'd say 'my goodness, my bike is not going as well as it usually does' – which is a way of saying his bike is quicker."

At Monza Honda arrived with a six-cylinder 250. "The reason we developed it", Shoichiro Irimajiri of Honda says, "was we had been struggling very much in races using the four-cylinder machine. Jim Redman had a big lead at Monza before a drop of oil pressure hampered him, so we put an oil-cooler on the machine." This paragraph is not the semi-technical interlude it might seem. This is another glimpse of the future.

"I'd tried to get Honda to sign him the year before", Redman says, "when they signed Alan Shepherd.[1] Alan Shepherd fell off at Suzuka, banged his head, and was never the same again, and that's what forced me not to go into Formula One cars. I had to stay with the bikes because Honda asked me to give it another year. Honda wouldn't sign Mike because of a little argument they had had previously." (I can find no details of this, but never mind.)

What Honda did do was provide him with a 250-six for the Japanese Grand Prix at Suzuka, a month after the Nations at Monza – there was no 500cc at Suzuka. Mike used all its power at the start and built up a 12-second lead by the end of the first lap. He won by 1m 32.8s, which is a lot.

Irimajiri first met Mike there. "My first impression when I saw him riding there with Jim Redman was: unbelievably fast! I got shocked. Why, I asked myself, can he ride so fast? I was impressed by his splendid physique, and that was why he was able to ride a machine putting power on at the corners. I had thought he might be a bit boorish, I felt afraid of meeting him that first time, but in fact he was not a rough man, I could communicate with him well. He was much gentler than he looked", and as he recounted it Mr Irimajiri was smiling, smiling broadly.

"At the end of the year I said to Honda 'Look, the only one to get is Mike. First of all, if you've got him you've got him, and you don't have to beat him as well. Racing is a double-edged sword, but it's only got a single edge if you have him", Redman says. There ought to be a thunder-clap, or at least a roll of drums, to accompany that statement, and for a particular reason. Honda were now poised to enter the 500cc Championship, a thunderous undertaking which would leave echoes some people can still hear to this day. Mike and *this* bike would stir admiration, anxiety, awe.

We have to look at the thinking before we look at the bike. "Honda started motorcycle racing with 125ccs", Irimajiri says. "Based on those, the company made 350 and 50cc machines and then we started to think about making 250 and 125s which were *much* faster than others. The lap times of our 350 were not so different from machines in the 500 class. We developed a machine based on a good 350cc to get the 350cc displacement bored-up in order to enter the 500 Championship. When we started development we thought it wouldn't be necessary to have more power, and we didn't introduce six cylinders. We thought about 80bhp would be enough – we were comparing that with the times Redman was getting on the 350-six. The first time we tested the 500 we did get 80bhp and I don't think we tried to raise the engine power afterwards. Our four-stroke engine was an advanced one in terms of engine power." You don't have to be a mechanic to appreciate what was going on. Honda were taking logical steps towards winning the big one, the 500, based on their own experience and the

---

1. An experienced Briton who rode 500cc World Championship races between 1960 and 1963 and 250s between 1961 and 1964.

only valid comparisons they could make. Wouldn't you? In these words you must single out *afterwards*. It means immediately afterwards. Later there would be more power – and more power.

The assumption was, and it became a highly contentious issue, that Redman, master of the 350 class which he had won for the last four years, would continue in that and the 500 bike would be prepared for Mike to challenge Agostini and MV, with Redman in a supporting role. The opening 500 race of the season was the West German at Hockenheim on May 22. Honda arrived with only one bike and Redman was to ride it. This has been widely attributed to Redman's strong position within Honda, where he had been riding and winning since 1960, and to his political skills. I asked him straight.

"That's the sort of way it came out, but it wasn't quite like that. The story has always been that Jim Redman exercised his authority as the team manager. Now you have to realize that the team manager's job I did was more taking care of negotiations for start money and entries and stuff like that. There was still a Japanese manager who controlled the team. If they wanted to sign up somebody like Mike, I made the approach.

"When it came to the bikes, when we were all in Japan together, I said to Mike 'I've won the 250 and 350 World titles plenty of times, you have those two and I'll have the one, the 500!' He said 'Yeah, OK'. That's how casual it was. For him the 500 was the same as the 350 for me. Supposing we'd only been competing in the 250 and 350 and he'd said 'I'll take the 350 because you've won it plenty of times and you take the 250'; I would have said 'Yes, OK'. Why not?

"Mike and I were sharing the spoils. We judged the opposition was going to be much fiercer in the 250 and 350s – from the Yamahas – and the 500 was supposed to be a cruise, the sort of cruise Mike had had on the MVs. I thought that being the older of the two I could have the easier run and also add the 500 to my list. (Interestingly, Mike would confirm that this was the arrangement, and he accepted it.)

"It turned out to be one of the toughest seasons when MV pulled their socks up. Ago was going quick, Mike used to say to me 'You know, Ago is seven years younger than I am', and I said 'You don't realize *you* are seven years younger than me. The three of us are racing. Imagine how *I* feel'."

Irimajiri charts the background. "Jim didn't complain about the chassis, but when Mike rode it he said 'I can't ride this!'. Our machine had a double-cradle frame layout and Mike said 'No way!'. That winter Mike took the machine to the United Kingdom and let an acquaintance of his make a frame, so Mike rode on his own chassis in 1966. That was exclusively for Mike. Jim and others rode conventional machines. At that time people couldn't understand why only Mike complained about the handling, but seeing him riding at Suzuka in 1965 I understood why. He had a technique which you would call slide-riding today, and it was different from Jim Redman and all the rest. At that time only Mike was using the technique. At a corner he opened the accelerator very fast and slid the rear wheel. The note from his exhaust was completely different to the others and the angles of his cornering were completely different, too.

"With what you can call a *grip*-riding technique the frame of a machine might not have a big problem, but with Mike's style a tyre keeps gripping *and* sliding. It's dangerous if a frame doesn't have enough rigidity. We learned later that frame rigidity should be the most critical point, and then we fully understood that only Mike had done slide-riding..."

"I rode the 500 at Hockenheim, the only bike they had there. Honda said 'At the moment we have only this one, but we'll have a spare for Mike soon', and, since we had already shared out the titles, if there had been two, Mike would have had the other one and would have come second to me, assuming that I could beat Ago. Once you get clear of the opposition you don't beat each other's brains out because you have made your team plan.

"And in the 350 if we'd got clear of everyone I would have tucked in behind him. In situations like that we used to make it look good for the crowd, too, passing each other on the corners and all that. When you ease off you can play the fool and you make it look tremendously exciting – as he puts the brakes on I go past and the next lap I brake a bit early in the same place and he does it to me, and the crowd love it, you know. You're only a second a lap off the full racing time, but it makes you so comfortable that you can do it all day."

When Redman first rode the 500 at Hockenheim he thought to himself: You'll never get to fling this around. It was a significant thought, as we shall see.

In the race he beat Agostini by 26.1 seconds, and young Stuart Graham finished fourth. Mike had already won the 250 in Spain, the first actual Championship meeting of the season, and he did it again at Hockenheim, adding the 350. Honda would also prosper with Ralph Bryans on the 50 and Luigi Taveri on the 125cc.

Graham, son of Les – World 500 Champion in 1949 and later killed in the Isle of Man – was a genuine privateer with a Matchless.[2] He had a van and a job and he took holidays to go to the races. He'd met Mike in 1961 or 1962 when he began. "He was one of the stars on the home scene then. I found him a terrific guy, friendly and very helpful and genuinely natural."

"At Assen" – the second race – "we had an extra bike so Honda could field the two of us", Redman says, "and as I've said, the plan was Jim'll win it with Mike second. I got away first at the start and halfway down the straight I nearly fell off the bike when Ago came steaming past me. I thought *Jesus, where did you come from? My bike's supposed to be best in the race*. Ago had a new MV and it was quicker than the Honda down the straight – I won't say outright quicker but quick enough to slipstream and pass. I tucked in and slipstreamed him and repassed, so overall the bikes must have been almost identical."

Redman won, Agostini 2.2 seconds behind. Mike lurked in third place early on, took the lead himself and hammered the lap record, which he'd set on the MV the season before, by more than two miles an hour. The next lap the gearbox failed, he reached for a gear but found neutral and he crashed.

"Ago passed me and I was second for a while, and then Mike came swishing past me behind the pits", Redman says. "He went round the outside of me and pulled in front to turn left. That was when he fell – as he peeled into the left-hander. I was slightly outside of him, I was in that little gap between his bike falling and the end of the road. By the time I slammed the brakes on and managed to extricate myself without crashing, and miss him and his bike, and looked round the corner, Ago was gone. I made a big *faux pas* in trying to catch it all up in one lap and I finished up going down the slip-road, which meant I lost my rhythm, and before I knew where I was I was 15 seconds behind. I thought 'Right, settle down, Redman' and on the following 20 laps I reeled in the 15 seconds.

2. A famous company who'd had 500cc bikes in the World Championship from 1954.

"I was quite proud, because I'd just had the conversation with Mike about ages, and Ago said to me after the race 'You – *multo forte*'. I'd worn him down mentally and also physically, but of course they were longer races then, at least twice the length of today, and you had time to wear people down." Graham brought his Matchless in fifth and was delighted. His whole world changed in the wet at Spa, the third race.

Spa was rightly notorious for the wet, this long, looping circuit[3] hemmed in by tall trees, and the Ardennes region of Belgium often unloaded not just drizzle, but heavy, remorseless, lashing rain. The trees seemed to hold the water in, dripping and condensing. A rider, any rider, faced two problems: staying on the bike and knowing where he was in the race. The problems also came at the rider in that order, survival then a result.

"The race started in a thunderstorm", Graham says, "and we were on the old, proper circuit, trees, houses, no armco, nothing. The wet never bothered me unduly. My father was well-known for being good in it, and I rode naturally in it, too, rode as I felt."

Redman: "We were on dry tyres, so I managed to get the start held up for a couple of minutes while we had the tyres deflated. If they'd have been pumped hard you'd have had no chance, no chance at all. I was thinking: I've won the first two races, and in conditions like this the thing is just to finish. Third place would do fine."

Graham: "The conditions were quite ridiculous, diabolical. Guys were falling off all over the place, and don't forget that when you were going slowly on the old course you were doing a hundred. I could hardly see the road."

One rider cascaded off and broke his thigh, another scudded off and broke his ribs and his bike finished in a river.

Redman: "I was third, just inches between Ago and Mike and myself, and I couldn't see in the spray. I pulled out and I must have been doing 150mph and I didn't know there was a lake at the other side of the track." Redman went down, instinctively put his left arm out and heard a crack. That's broken, he thought. "I was going along the road skittering over the wet tarmac at a hell of a speed facing backwards." He saw the bike coming at him and "lashed at it with both feet" and heard another crack. Leg broken, he thought. The bike spun away and smashed a small concrete milepost, Redman followed it over the milepost and descended into a ditch full of water. He looked up and saw a ragged hole in some wooden fencing and thought: Thank God the bike got there before I did to make the hole. "Then I saw another hole and I realized the bike had made that one, I'd made this one ..."

With four laps left Mike's gearbox went again, although he felt he could have nursed the bike to the end. He decided to pull in to the pits instead and walk away. He did not conceal that he had done this, and would say that it hadn't been a race but a struggle to survive physically. When he did get off the bike he felt more relieved than he had ever felt in his life before. More than a decade later he would

---

3. The original Spa circuit measured 14.10 kilometres, and after 1970 Formula One cars no longer raced there because it was considered too dangerous. The bikes, however, continued. The circuit was extensively remodelled, its distance cut to 6.949, kilometres and in 1983 the cars returned. The present circuit does retain the flavour and some of the impact of the old.

re-examine his decision – in one sense it violated a basic creed, that you have an obligation to go on to the end – and find that he had no regrets, no regrets at all. It underlines in a most graphic way how diabolical Spa was that day.

Graham, craning to see the pit signals held out by his fiance, deduced that he was in second place, although he had no idea who led. That was Ago, of course, who won it from Graham by 48.4 seconds. Graham was utterly delighted.

Bryans: "After the race we decided we'd go to the hospital to see how Jim was." The visitors to Jim's beside would be Mike, Bryans and Graham. "We found this huge old mansion type of a place made out of stone blocks. We inquired as to where Jim was, we went up a flight of stairs into a huge room, nobody was in there but Jim and Marlene. Jim was sat up in bed feeling sorry for himself, cursing and swearing a bit. Marlene looked across at Mike and said 'If you'd fallen off and landed on your head it wouldn't have hurt'. Mike didn't like that remark all that much. I thought Oh Jeez, here we go. We got over that, and discovered that Jim's injuries weren't as bad as we had initially heard, so we were very relieved."

Graham: "Jim said to Ralph, I assumed half-joking, 'We're buggered now, you'd better get young Stuart to give you a hand, it was bloody good finishing second'."

Bryans: "We were heading back out of the hospital and all the nurses we had seen were dressed in habits, so it must have been a convent hospital or a hospital run by the Catholic Church. Behind a big desk at the reception was a nun, and Mike said 'Hang on a minute, boys, I need to get something while I'm here'. He went over to the nun and said 'I need an injection'. I think the name was Streptomycin. The nun naturally inquired as to why. Mike replied that he was allergic to penicillin – of all things, imagine a rider being allergic to that – and of course she then inquires as to why he needed antibiotics in the first place. He replied 'Because I've got a dose of the clap'. I looked at Stuart and Stuart looked at me. I blushed, he blushed. Mike hadn't given us any prior warning, he hadn't mentioned that he'd got the clap or anything, he just came straight out with it like that, you know. The nun said 'Oh, just a moment please', went off and came back with a doctor, Mike got a jab in the ass in a little cubicle and we all headed back to the party."

Graham: "I always remember that quite innocent, quite typical Hailwood incident. Mike thought: Nothing wrong with it, just routine."

2

Faces in the mirror, faces in the mirror.

There had been another 'incident' – if that's the right word – at this same Spa, although Tommy Robb can't remember the year. It might have been 1966, but more likely was in the early Sixties. "We were going to the prizegiving, which we all enjoyed. You'd been living on a high flow of adrenalin, I suppose you never thought of being injured, but ... when it was over prizegiving was relaxing and Mike enjoyed his drink.

"He said 'Are you going down to Spa?', and I was on my own and I said 'Yes, sure.' He said 'Right, will we go in your car or mine?'. I can't remember if he had a Jag or a Ferrari. I said jokingly 'Let's go in yours!'. We got there early (Spa is three or four miles from the circuit, which is actually in the village of Francorchamps) and found a little bar and sat in it. That was when I felt closest to Mike. He said 'Look, you mix with the lads all week, every week. What do they think of me?' I suddenly realized here was a bloke who was World Champion, he was top of his world, money was no worry, he had charm, everything, and from deep inside him he came out with that question. I gave him the truthful answer. We thought he was what people said he was: The greatest in every way. He was embarrassed."

Robb saw the public face, too. "It was the parties at Mallory Park that he enjoyed most of all. We ended up on the bandstand one night. I think I was on drums, Mike was on base, John Cooper was on ...oh, I can't remember ..." A lot of people can't remember specific details of those parties and for the most obvious reason. (David Hobbs, who we'll be meeting again in a moment, isn't sure about *countries* he and Mike visited, they all vanished in the parties and the haze, but mind you Hobbs had a vast twinkle in his eye when he said that.)

"Mike was always a musician. Once when we were in Japan we went into a store and I heard this clunk-clunk-clunk sound. He was fiddling with all the knobs on a big machine which you could play as an organ or a piano or whatever, just by the switch of a button. They were unheard of in Britain and quite expensive."

Robb: "That is fantastic, that is."

Mike: "It's great, isn't it?"

Robb: "Are you going to buy it and take it home to improve your musical career?"

The machine: *bumpety-bumpety-bump.*

Mike: "My musical career? You've got to be joking. It's to improve my sex life."

"Mike was not terribly mechanically minded. He had an E-Type Jag which he regularly forgot to put oil in. If you asked where it was he'd say 'It's in the garage, the bloody thing's blown up again'. He was so casual and yet on a bike he'd come back after a race with his boot worn out and blood coming out of his toes. He always called me an Irish bastard or an Irish bugger – but affectionately. I never went over far enough to touch my boots, I was too afraid to touch my boots. Mike would say 'You Irish bastard, how come your toes are not worn away?' I'd say 'There are two reasons. The first is that I don't go as quick as you do, and the second is I'm not stupid enough. When you've got big feet like you have something's got to touch down!' Mike was like a night-rider, he felt his way round a corner, but it was also the angle he was at and he wouldn't lift his foot up. I don't know how many boots he went through in a season. I used to kid him. 'I couldn't afford your bloody boot bill and that's why I never touch my toes.'

"He got over to an incredible angle, and that is what makes a person great – being able to do things other people can't. You also have to remember it is the thrill. The further over you go – further than you have ever been before and you get away with it – gives you that feeling of being on a high, it makes your adrenalin pump. And when Mike was doing that he was running on tyres which were nothing like today's.

"You cannot evaluate brilliance, impossible. I have never seen any of your current stars go out and win on a 125, get on a 250 and win, get on a 350 and win, get on a 500 and win like Mike did, and these were machines of totally different contrasts. Maybe he'd been drunk the night before, the next day he'd still do performances nobody else could do in all those classes. I was a penniless Irishman and yet I could beat the bloke on occasions. I got more pride out of that, got more pride out of finishing in front of Mike Hailwood than anything else."

3

Redman, although he didn't know it, would not ride again. On the evening of July 3, 1966, as Jim lay in hospital, Mike was alone on the Honda 500 to challenge Agostini and with a crippling disadvantage. He hadn't ridden at Hockenheim, had crashed in Assen and now at Spa. Agostini already had 20 points and only six races remained, the next at the unlovely, unloved Sachsenring in the unlovely, unloved East Germany. There, Honda approached Graham and offered him 250cc bikes. That at least might lift some of the pressure from Mike who faced the 250, 350 and 500 Championships. Worse, at the Sachsenring, although Mike won the 250 (by 1m 4.3s from Read, Yamaha), his bikes blew up in the 350 and 500 races. The sole consolation was that Agostini got no points either.

Agostini surveys the unfolding of this duel with passion. "Of course, when Mike left MV and joined Honda we had a – how shall I say it? – battle each weekend which was wonderful, not only for the crowd but for the whole sport. We had been friends, and we remained friends. That's the sort of man Mike was. He was a very clever boy, but he remained nice."

What might save Mike in the 500 was the rule that only your five best results counted, which meant that he could keep whatever he got in the last five while at some stage – probably soon – Agostini would have to start dropping points. If Agostini finished second behind Mike in all these five he'd have to drop three of them and keep only 12 points, giving him a total of 32. Mike, racking up eight points each time he won, could total 40. So... mathematically it was possible.

"I always said I rode in the same race as Mike. I could not really ride against him because it was a no-contest situation." Graham is a sincere man as well as a perceptive one. "I was riding the 250 six-cylinder, Mike was riding the same machine, but of course he was very much the star, he was winning the World Championship. I was there in support, I was officially being groomed as I thought for the following year. Mike really took me under his wing in quite a lot of cases, and we chatted and talked about how best to go about certain things. He followed me a bit, I attempted to follow him so he could show me the lines. You have to remember at that stage Mike was head and shoulders above everybody else, and it was obviously good for me to follow somebody like that, watching and learning.

"Mike was not a very technical person. In general I'd get as much information from Jim Redman, who was more into how to conduct a bike. The whole thing to Mike was such a natural thing. He did not really think what he was doing, and if somebody asked 'Mike, how the hell can you get round that corner at that speed?', he would just shrug his shoulders and say 'I don't know'. If they asked 'What do you do here?', he'd say 'Blowed if I know'. He was very casual, almost flippant. Where he took a certain line it was just natural to him to take it. If he had to explain that he found it slightly difficult, but from my point of view to ride in the same races and talk about it was a great help."

Graham was having an uncomfortable time on the Honda 250 which was powerful, set up for Redman and extremely twitchy. "If you were getting a bit depressed because you couldn't cope with something Mike would help you out, build up your confidence ... but it didn't do a lot for it at places like the Isle of Man, where in practice I was struggling to break 100mph for a lap and Mike was cruising round doing 103, 104, and you got the impression he could have been reading a book at the same time.

"Inevitably, being in the team meant you were being compared, but no matter how good you may be you weren't going to be that good, so it didn't bother me in any particular way. He was deeply idolized. No way did he cause any resentment in me. It was a much harder task for the likes of Phil Read and Jim Redman, who theoretically were superstars in their own right and they still could not beat Mike."

Of the three Championships, Mike had no trouble in the 250 and won 10 of the 12 rounds, including Finland at Imatra. "I followed him round lap after lap", Graham says. "We didn't have any opposition when other riders dropped out. Mike rode at a pace I could keep up with. As far as Mike was concerned the 250 was just something else to ride, another title to win. To him the 250 was a great machine, it was only a toy, it was fabulous and he could win races with one arm tied behind his back. Mike certainly felt sorry for me." (This, of course, was the Honda-six with the oil cooler which Redman had ridden at Suzuka in 1965. As Irimajiri says, "Mike won and won and dominated 250cc racing in 1966".)

Mike had no trouble in the 350 with six wins and the title secure by the Ulster Grand Prix in mid-August. He'd done it with three races to spare. But the 500, ah the 500. He'd won Czechoslovakia from Agostini, Agostini took Finland from him, which gave a points total of 34–14, but now Agostini had used up all his five finishes and his lowest was second place. To increase his total he had to win, but it was more subtle than that. He had to win to stop Mike winning – because if Mike took the last three races he'd finish on 38 points and Agostini, coming in second place behind him each time, would gain nothing, so stay on 34.

The TT on The Island might be pivotal. It was held in early autumn – not June – because of a seamen's strike, and Mike embellished his own folklore. Every lap he did in the 500cc race on September 2 was faster than Agostini, and he took it by 2 minutes 37.8 seconds. Approaching the final race, the Nations at Monza, Agostini still led 34–30, but the permutations had all fled now. If Mike won he was Champion, if he finished second and Agostini anywhere behind him he was Champion.

You must imagine what effect this had on Monza, already a profound and palpitating epicentre of Italian nationalism and chauvinism annually stirred by those two feudal states Ferrari and MV. Ferrari had already played their part by finishing first and second in the Italian Grand Prix on September 4. The Italian Ludovico Scarfiotti won it from a Briton, Mike Parkes. Honda were now deep into Formula One themselves and were running an American, Richie Ginther, who retired on lap 17. This is a semi-official euphemism for a frightener. A rear tyre lost a tread and he plunged off into the trees. Ginther was unhurt.

Honda's bike team had been invited to come along and watch, no doubt because their race was at Monza only a week later. Mike had ridden the 125 on The Island, by now a rare thing for him to do, and was sixth.

Irimajiri says "We thought that 125 with its five cylinders was very fast. I asked Mike how it had been, and surprisingly he said 'Very slow. I will never ride that again!'. I still can't forget the way he said it (another smile). The 125 might have been just a toy to him, although if Luigi Taveri hears it described like this he'll be upset. Mike had all the talents: energy, quickness, power, flexibility. He may have been saying to me how could he ride a 125cc which never responded to *his* acceleration and didn't slide the rear wheel..."

Mike holds an informal press conference after winning the 1961 Senior TT. (*Picture courtesy Nick Nicholls.*)

Lightweight races, heavyweight trophies. Mike demonstrates his muscle power by holding aloft his 125 and 250 TT-winning trophies at the 1961 prize presentation. (*Picture courtesy Nick Nicholls.*)

Mike, Bill Lacey, Stan and Bob McIntyre after Mike had won the 1961 Senior TT, his third victory of the week. (*Picture courtesy Nick Nicholls.*)

Two months earlier, Stan had handed his son the symbolic key of the door to celebrate his 21st birthday. (*Picture courtesy Nick Nicholls.*)

Mike sets off on the 1962 Senior TT with his four-cylinder MV while Hugh Anderson waits his turn with his Matchless. (*Picture courtesy Nick Nicholls.*)

Mike flat-out on his 250 Benelli in the 1962 TT, a shot taken at Braddan Bridge that typifies his 'press-on' style; on this occasion, though, he would retire on the last lap. (*Picture courtesy Nick Nicholls.*)

A signed copy of the superb drawing of Mike on the six-cylinder Honda which Carol Young (formerly Carol Steed) drew in the mid-Sixties. Mike persuaded her to reproduce it at the time of his famous TT comeback in 1978. (*Drawing courtesy Carol Young.*)

Mike with Derek Minter and John Hartle on the occasion of the 1963 500cc Ulster GP. (*Picture courtesy Nick Nicholls.*)

An animated Stan Hailwood gives Mike the thumbs-up as he sets a new one hour speed record on his 500 MV Agusta at Daytona in 1964. (*Picture courtesy Nick Nicholls.*)

Later that morning Mike encountered tough opposition in the US GP from Benedicto Caldarella and his rapid Gilera until it broke down late in the race. (*Picture courtesy Nick Nicholls.*)

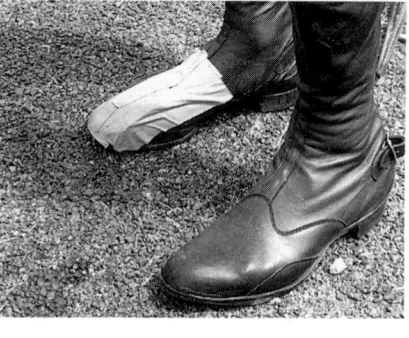

Mike would lean his bikes over so far that he was forever damaging his boots, not to mention his toes, and often required some emergency patchwork between races. (*Picture courtesy Mick Woollett.*)

A taped-up right boot is in evidence as Mike chats to Honda 'captain' Jim Redman before the 1966 German GP at Hockenheim. (*Picture courtesy Mick Woollett.*)

All the atmosphere of the TT as Mike tackles Creg-ny-Baa on the four-cylinder 350 MV in 1965. (*Picture courtesy Nick Nicholls.*)

Mike has time to acknowledge a signal as he takes the 250 Honda-six through Parliament Square, Ramsey, in 1966. (*Picture couresy Nick Nicholls.*)

Honda never did things in half-measures! A 16-strong group shot of the five 1966 team riders (from left to right, Jim Redman, Mike, Stuart Graham, Luigi Taveri and Ralph Bryans) and their supporting mechanics. (*Picture courtesy Nick Nicholls.*)

Mike at work in his 'office' at his Heston flat in February 1966. (*Picture courtesy Mick Woollett.*)

So – Monza was stirred by Ferrari and on the afternoon of September 11 here was the MV with an Italian upon it.

Mike took the lead, but tactically decided to let Agostini pass him. Mike followed, the predator as he had been behind other Italians, Provini and Ubbiali, so long ago. Mike followed and waited, followed and waited, and the immense crowd who might or might not have sensed his tactics howled and shrieked every time Agostini came by. And on lap six an exhaust valve buckled on the Honda. The Championship was gone.

There is a happier story about Monza, however. "The only time I found I was actually competitive with Mike was in the 250 race there", Graham says. "It was purely and simply because the machinery was good, the circuit was fairly straightforward and my weight against Mike's (Graham was almost two stone lighter) meant that my bike was quicker in a straight line. I had got my confidence on the machine and I was riding it a hell of a lot better.

"Mike had already won the 250 Championship, so there was no heat on. This race I actually had a chance of finishing ahead of him – I won't say beating him because it was only the weight-difference. But... did I dare finish in front of the great Mike Hailwood? I often wonder whether Mike would have let me win anyway if it had come down to it. You know the story of the British car Grand Prix at Aintree when Stirling Moss and Juan Manuel Fangio were driving for Mercedes. Did Fangio let Moss win? Mike was very much the same type. If he'd let me win and been asked about it he'd have said 'Oh, well', or something stupid like that, but he wouldn't have said he'd done it. I suppose everyone would have known perfectly well what had happened, but that's not the point. Mike never had to prove anything to anybody. He was in a position which very few are ever in: they can afford to do those sort of things and nobody thinks any the worse of it." Anyway, Graham's bike broke down...

4

Faces in the mirror ...

"I'd seen Mike race once or twice on bikes", Attwood says. "One time was at Mallory Park and he was just different to the rest. I don't know why. It was the sort of race where you had to run with your bike and jump on it. He was side-saddle nearly up to bloody Gerards[4] and then just casually cocked his leg over and off he went. Everybody else was in the tuck position going like hell. Mike was at one with the bike. I don't think anyone else I've ever seen looked like that."

"There was a Grand Prix at Suzuka", Jerry Wood says. "A few minutes before the start Mike had his leathers unzipped, he was holding his helmet like he was expecting people to put presents in it and he was walking up and down looking at the other bikes and he was psyching the riders. He'd kick somebody's front tyre and then gaze at them. He was getting them all wound up. The one-minute-to-go signal sounded, the Japanese mechanics were getting twitchy and he was still doing it. Then he zipped his leathers up, he didn't even bother to put a safety

4. Gerards Bend is about 250 yards from the starting line.

pin in as riders usually did to stop the zip sliding down, put his helmet on and at the start vanished into the distance."

There was one Japanese mechanic who got twitchy, and for a different reason altogether. He liked a drink, and on The Island, where practice began at dawn, he was particularly terrified that he'd oversleep. He found a convenient solution. He slept in the corridor outside Mike's bedroom and when Mike emerged to go to practice he patted the mechanic on the head to wake him.

Was it this same mechanic who, one of these mornings, made a lovely joke which itself has passed into folklore? Mike emerged, patted him and the mechanic said: *"You ... are ... a ... prisoner ... of ... the ... Japanese."*

Mike said something which is in the folklore alright, too, but at Suzuka, the track Honda own. Honda produced a brand new bike, he rode it round, came back in, and when he was asked what it was like replied "Bloody awful".

"I can remember one year at Imola", John Cooper says, "when it snowed and, typical Italians, they panicked and stopped the practice, no practice until tomorrow. Mike sent his mechanic out of the circuit in his car to fill it up with booze. We had a party in Mike's caravan, we were drinking vino in large amounts. The snow stopped, the sun came out and the secretary came across to the caravan and said 'Practice will go on as previously arranged'. Mike said 'You can't because we can't. We're all drunk now.'

"One time I went to see him at his flat in Hounslow. He was sitting there on his own strumming his guitar ..."

Another time Cooper was visiting a friend who had a farm near Mallory Park. Mike had already arrived. "There was a big scar on Mike's face and his face was bleeding. I said 'What happened?', and he said 'Oh, I parked my car on the wall on the way in'. He'd gone straight over a ditch and the car was on top of the wall rocking backwards and forwards. He'd smacked his face against the windscreen, been down to hospital to get it fixed, got back and left the car on the wall. He was giving out glasses half full of milk and half full of vodka and he was saying 'This'll settle your stomach'. He put a drop or two of vodka in the goldfish bowl and the goldfish were zooming round like the clappers.

"In Italy once I wasn't staying at the same hotel as Mike and he gave me a lift back. We were going down the road at some unholy speed like 120mph and we came to a crossroads; he put the brakes on, but couldn't stop. We went straight up on to a pile of stones. Mike left the car there and went back for it the next morning."

"I don't know whether the episode when he hit the cow in South Africa was his fault", Chris Barber says, "because I don't know who else was in the car and who was driving. But the car went under a cow at extreme speed on a small road and the roof of the car was taken off."

Pauline can offer enlightenment, although she wasn't in the car. Peter Gethin[5] was. "They were batting along through the night and a local farmer had left a gate open and black cows wandered across the road. Mike hit one at a rather high rate of knots and there was cow absolutely everywhere. Pete got out of the car and one of the horns had gone straight through the back of the seat where he'd been sitting. He'd managed to duck just in time. Pete went round

---

5. An Englisman who drove Formula One between 1970 and 1974 with a single win, Monza 1971. He now runs a driving school at the Goodwood circuit, Sussex.

and Mike was still in the driving seat blood all down his face. 'Come on, Pete,' Mike said, 'Stop messing around. We'll never get there at this rate'."

Barber treasures the folklore and recounts a delicious moment which happened in England. "Mike was driving up the A1 and he was stopped by a policeman for speeding. He had Italian plates on the car – probably Italian taxi plates, I expect. Mike started speaking to the policeman in Italian and the policeman said 'Mr Hailwood ...'"

And then there was Bill Ivy. I quote from *No Time To Lose* by Alan Peck. "Possibly because of their friendship the rivalry between them was particularly intense, but once the races were over, whoever won, there was never any bitterness over success and defeat. Both were sportsmen and neither went in for excuses, although they would laugh and pull each other's legs unmercifully.

"This spirit of competition was extended beyond the race tracks when they embarked on the long journeys from one venue to the next in their cars. 'We had quite a few burn-ups' Mike recalled. 'We had a fantastic dice from Zurich to Clermont-Ferrand once. Bill was in his Stingray and I had a Ferrari. We diced it up all the way and the cars were smoking, steaming wrecks by the time we got there – we did it in some fantastic time. There was another one from Barcelona to somewhere ... that was a bit hectic, too. Then there was that business in The Island.' The recollection of this was accompanied by an infectious Hailwood grin. 'There was a bird working in the Hawaiian Bar and she wanted to go for a ride in Bill's new Ferrari. So we all leapt aboard, with her in the middle, and went charging off down the TT course at about 140mph. As we came up to Greeba Castle I said 'Bill, you're going a bit too fast, you're never going to get round', and he said 'We'll be alright, we'll get through'. We got round the first bit, but arrived at the next corner in a great big broadside and he over-corrected it and went into the wall. We went along the wall for about 50 yards and tore the side out of the bloody car – and this bird was having kittens!'

"Mrs Lee (Ivy's landlady) remembers when Bill came back to the lodgings after the accident. 'He came creeping in and I knew he'd smashed his lovely new car up because a policeman had already brought one of the wheels here – it was all buckled up. Bill told me what had happened and said that they had a dolly-bird with them and afterwards she'd been leaning over the wall 'puking' with shock. 'I don't wonder at it,' I told him, 'it's a wonder you're all still alive. It's a good job you never killed the other fella because by God his Old Man Stan would have been up here and you'd have been for the high jump!'."

Ivy was fined £12 for dangerous driving, had to pay for repairs to the wall and discovered that because he'd bought the Ferrari in Italy he only had third-party cover in Britain. That repair bill was £1,000. It was a great deal of money in its time, and quite a lot now, too.

5

"I had terrible misgivings about the trip. I'd never been to Africa and for some reason or other I didn't like the thought of going to Africa, I didn't think I'd like it and I also didn't think I'd like Mike Hailwood. I had a predetermined disposition that I was not going to like this guy, and he had a predetermined disposition that he wasn't going to like me. He thought: This bloke's a car driver, he's a snob, he's an effete elitist pillock. *I* thought: This bloke's a bloody bikey, he's going to be a right berk, I can see this is going to be nine weeks of hell. I suppose it took us quite a long time to get to like each other ...25 or 30 seconds, by which time our feet had taken us to the bar. We just had an absolute ball."

The speaker is Hobbs, who had signed in the autumn of 1966 to drive the Springbok[6] series "for a chap called Bernard White, who was a bit of an eccentric. Mike had signed, too, and we went out there with two cars, a Ford GT40 and a Ferrari. The first race was the nine-hour at Kyalami, and neither of us I think finished it. To do the rest of the series Bernard assigned just Mike and I in the GT40. We went down to Cape Town to a track called Killarney, and if you look at it now you'd no more race there than fly to the moon – trees, no guardrails – people hit photographers standing at the apex. We were leading that, but we had a dumbo mechanic whose name escapes me. This bloke was all mouth, and Mike just couldn't take this bloke at all. The GT40 had a huge filler cap; we made a pit stop and the filler cap wasn't closed properly. Turn one at Killarney is a left-hander. Mike comes to turn one, brakes hard, turns in and the cap opens, fuel spills out and whoof the car went up. By the time Mike got out his face was all singed. By the time he got back to the pits he was hot in more ways than one. The car wasn't badly damaged.

"We spent most of our time partying, and we had a couple of really good ones in Cape Town which were very heavy work. We drove north to Bulawayo and won the three-hour race, and we had Christmas in Johannesburg, which was very interesting because it was the first time I'd spent it out of England. We went down to Pietermaritzburg and we won that. Our mechanic was sick in the lounge of the hotel, which caused a bit of a furore. It was a rather smart hotel, it was New Year, it was the middle of the day and I've never seen a bloke so sick in all my life. Mike and I looked and thought: Nothing to do with us!"

The South African Grand Prix was on January 2 and "I was going to drive this GT40 in the support race. As you know a Grand Prix is a very important showcase whatever you are driving. I thought this was a chance to show what a star I was in front of all those Grand Prix drivers and owners – I'd already done a couple of Formula One races and I was sorely trying to get in. As you go round Kyalami everything's a right-hand corner (Crowthorne, Barbeque Bend) although there is a fast left sweep (Jukskei) but it's flat-out, you don't brake. Then there's a sharp right-hander (Sunset Bend) before you get to Clubhouse, which is a sharp left-hander. Everyone in the Grand Prix world and his brother are standing watching there, and what happened? Same thing as Killarney some eight weeks before. The filler cap wasn't properly shut. I braked hard, there was fuel all over the windscreen, I pirouetted on it into the wall, boom, out.

"We went up to Lourenco Marques, which was in Portuguese East Africa (Mozambique), and we stayed at a little resort where there was a salt water lagoon and Mike taught me to water ski. The accommodation was very rustic, a bed and a bowl, but we'd go to a local restaurant and have wonderful prawns. We watched turtles lay eggs on the shore of the Indian Ocean and all sorts of esoteric things like that.

"We had a quick-lift jack and before the race at Lourenco Marques our

---

6. A sportscar series in South Africa which annually attracted an interesting variety of drivers.

mechanic decided he was going to change the rear wheels. Now the first thing you have to understand is that if there is already a jack on the front of the car you need someone standing on it when you put another jack on the rear – because the weight shifts forward and the one at the front folds up and jack-knifes. That's what happened. It jumped through the windscreen and the cars were getting ready to go onto the grid.

"Mike and I were on our way to the circuit and we passed our support truck going the other way. We thought that was bloody funny-peculiar. When we arrived our second mechanic said 'Aaah, he's gone into town to see if he can get a new windscreen,' which of course he couldn't. So we had a plastic sheet on the car and it rained, it rained like a son of a bitch. It was a race which started at dusk and finished in the dark, I started it, I came in for the first pit stop, jumped out of the car and there was Mike sitting in a corner in his ordinary clothes. I said 'Come on, Mike, you're driving' and he said 'It's raining, I'm not driving in the rain', so I had to get back in and do another stint. I can't even remember if I drove the whole race. The ironical aspect was that Mike was one of those guys who was rather special in the rain, he was incredibly quick in it. As drivers he and I were always on a pace with each other. That would have been fine for me, but he hadn't done much driving then and certainly hadn't driven big cars. He was on the pace straight away and in the wet he was very, very quick. He would have been in the top 10 drivers of the day."

6

This winter of 1966–67 Honda followed their creed and worked on giving their 500 even more power. The bike they made bucked and bounded so much Mike thought the frame had a 'hinge' in it. This was the famed, fabled and feared bronco, the bike a couple of experienced riders could not make go in a straight line; I know that is an astonishing statement, but it is true. Round the Isle of Man Mike would *average* more than 105mph on it, which is a much more astonishing statement. We are in legendary land, a land where a legend was made. Moreover – and here is the rub – it was a harsh, everchanging land: 10 rounds of the 500 Championship at successively Hockenheim, a concrete bowl of a place, the Isle of Man, custom-made Assen, the terrors of Spa and its micro-climate and horrendous speeds, the perils of broken-down Sachsenring, the perils of Brno which was a washing-board surface through villages, the trees of Imatra and no protection from them, the Ulster which punished error, the hyperhysteria of Monza, and the culmination at Mosport, Canada, itself no particularly friendly circuit.

The 1967 season began in a curious way. Honda did not offer Graham a contract and decided not to contest the 50 and 125cc classes at all. Mike would have to go for the 250, 350 and 500 with only Bryans, a 50cc specialist, giving whatever support he could. Curious? But yes. Mike needed a proven accomplice if only to finish behind him and keep the others at bay – variously Agostini, Read and Ivy.

"I'd first met Mike in the Isle of Man about 1963", Bryans says. "I joined Honda in 1964 and I didn't really get to know him until he came into the team and we were working together. There's no doubt about it, he was a hell of a guy.

"I was 5ft 7in and weighed around 9st 3 or 4, so my build was right for the smaller machines. I was not involved in the testing of the larger machines at all, but I did ride the 250s in 1967 when there were only two members of the team left, Mike and I. We travelled the world together and I got to know Mike better. The arrangement was that 1967 was a practice year for me, to keep my hand in, so to speak, not get rusty while Honda developed more competitive machinery for the 50 and 125 Championships in 1968. It didn't happen, which was a great disappointment to me.

"I think Honda were probably a little bit unfair on Mike in 1967. I am convinced they asked too much of him. It's no mean achievement winning a Grand Prix, but when you are expected to win three of them on the same day it's just not on. Undoubtedly that was the hardest year of Mike's life. I was told at the beginning 'OK, you've got one 250, it's a 1966 model and we haven't another. You've got to ride it and not break the thing'. That's a grand way to go off into a Grand Prix season, right? But I accepted the situation.

"It wasn't until midway through the season that I realized there were going to be no 50s and 125s for 1968 because I hadn't been asked to Japan to test. Then, and only then, when I started to query why, was I told there were certain difficulties. I suggested there was no point in having Mike battering his head against a brick wall – 250, 350, 500 – and I may as well move into the 350 as well as the 250 at certain Grands Prix. They agreed to that ..."

This is very important background, emphasizing as it does how alone Mike was. There is more background, too, around Easter-time. "He approached me at Oulton Park, where I was spectating more than anything. I was there as a trade rep for Reynolds", Ken Sprayson says. "Reynolds were experts on frames and frame design; we'd done frames for Geoff Duke, we'd done frames for John Surtees, all of which had had a lot of publicity. Reynolds were the obvious people Mike would approach." Mike asked "Could you make a frame for the Honda?".

Sprayson: "Well, I need time."

Quietly, privately, Mike had decided he'd have his own frame made. Sprayson explains that "People naively think you can make a frame and they can collect it tomorrow. I said 'Look here, this is going to take at least three months, even if I can get Reynolds to agree'."

Mike: "I cannot wait that long."

Mike approached another frame maker, Colin Lyster, who did manage to make one in what Sprayson estimates was "within a week. It was better than the Honda, but it was still a bit of a camel".[7] Mike raced this bike a couple of times before the Grand Prix season began, but Honda understandably forbade its use in the Grands Prix. Mike would have to ride Honda's Honda 500 and nobody else's.

"The stiffest competition from Honda's point of view was in the 500 against Agostini on the MV. The 500 Honda may have been fast, but it was not the easiest machine to ride, to put it diplomatically. I never rode it, no, never, ever, ever. Honda had two big problems in the 250, the Yamahas of Read and Ivy, and those things were fast. The Honda-six handled better, but with nothing like as much power, which meant that on fast circuits we were going to be third and fourth or thereabouts. On other circuits, where you could use the brakes and handling, we were in amongst them and could beat them", Bryans says.

"In the 350 class there was practically no opposition whatsoever. In hindsight, I probably should have dug my heels in or consulted with Mike more and said 'Listen, this is going to be a long, hard season, I've got a 250 and I'll do my best for you there, but I should be in more 350 races'. I'd have been taking points away from the others and easing the burden."

How much of a bronco was the Honda 500? First a judgment from Redman, now of course in retirement after his crash at Spa. "Hard to ride? But I rode them all the time, I grew up with them and I didn't mind that they were light and twitchy and short and all the rest of it because I was used to them jumping around. I liked the speed that they turned out. The lightness gave you the speed. The 1967 that Mike rode was virtually the same bike. It's very easy to build a frame for a Norton which is giving 50 horsepower, but when you had 120 horsepower in a similar frame it handled a whole lot differently."

It did.

Murray Walker once interviewed Redman after a TT win, incidentally, and saw that it had obviously been *very* hard work. Redman, however, wouldn't be drawn into any discussions like that.

Walker: "How did it go, Jim?"

Redman: "Like a dream."

Walker: "Any problems?"

Redman: "No, no. The engine ran like a clock and it handled beautifully!"

"One time we were testing at Zandvoort", Luigi Taveri says, "and we make a joke, Mike and me. Mike said 'You're on the 500 now so you can see what happens.' I got on and I did ride it and you needed a big heart to go at full speed on the straight, *ja, ja, ja*. The bikes now are so different. Even when you don't really know how to ride a bike they are perfect even in the corners, but with that Honda it was all ... enormous. On the straight it jumped from side to side.

"We were in Japan and one evening in the hotel we had a big discussion. John Cooper said 'When I ride it I will show people how fast I can go', and I said 'When you have it, it will make you look bad'. Cooper said 'No, it wouldn't', and gave me an example. 'At Monza in the Curva Grande[8] I go at full speed with the Norton.' Cooper didn't believe me, he was a little angry, so I tell him I hope that one day he can ride this Honda ..."

"When you say Mike Hailwood's bike taught me a thing or two, well it taught me that only Hailwood could ride it", Cooper himself says. "That bike was the worst bike that could possibly be steered. How Hailwood rode it I will never know. Holding it when I rode it made my wrists swell up half as big again. It was just so impossible to ride.

"I rang Mike up – I can't remember how it came about – and I said 'How about me having a ride on that 500?'. He said 'If you want to, come down and fetch it, it's in the garage at Heston'. He'd got it in his lockup there. I did go down. Mike said 'I shouldn't bother if I were you because it's so bad, but if you want to you can. Nobby Clark can come and look after it. You'll find it's pretty rough' – and it was true, by God. Before I left he said 'Wherever you fall off put a mark on the track and I'll know where it happened for when I race there ...'

"I took it to Snetterton for a 20-lap race. There were one or two BSAs,[9] they

---

7. A motor racing term used to denote a car or bike which doesn't handle well.
8. A right-hand sweeper about 500 metres beyond the chicane on the start-finish straight, it was the first major corner drivers reached on a lap.
9. A British company which enjoyed considerable success in 500cc races. They ceased production in 1963.

came past me on the bends and then I streaked past them on the Norwich straight just miles an hour faster. I got to a turn and it was just bloody impossible to steer round these corners. Rain was spotting, I opened it up crossing the start-finish line and it went bloody sideways. I stayed on it and finished and I thought I was unbelievably lucky I hadn't fallen off. I raced it at Oulton Park the following day, but the push-drive broke, so I only did a few laps. Next time I saw it it was locked up in the Donington museum and that's where it ought to stop. An Irishman said you couldn't keep that bike in a 10-acre field. You pointed it at a corner and it wobbled out of control. It was out of control permanently. I find it unbelievable, quite unbelievable, that he got it round The Island. I can't believe that he ever raced that bike and *I saw him do it*."

(There is a charming, innocent period-piece anecdote to accompany this. "I had a garage in Derby and I parked it on the forecourt – it was an era when people didn't steal things – and a Japanese tourist came by, recognized it and wondered where on earth I'd got it." The astonished tourist did what he was always going to do, out with camera, click, click, click.)

Several good men and true witnessed John Cooper's Epic Ride at Snetterton. One was Jerry Wood. "Cooper managed to hold on to it and I saw him afterwards. He was walking through the paddock, he looked at me and he said 'If bloody Hailwood rides that bloody bike and wins on it he deserves the bloody VC. I do not know how he does it.' And John Cooper was a strong man."

"I was on my Triumph 500," Percy Tait recounts with some relish, "and John Cooper said 'I'm really going to blow you off today'. I got into the lead and it was a little bit wet and at the start-finish Cooper suddenly decided to pass me up the straight. They say they've never seen anything like it. The bike went from one footrest on the floor to the other footrest on the floor and he held it, he didn't fall off and I don't think his bowels were particuarly good for the rest of the week. And John Cooper was good."

(A charming but not so innocent anecdote: "I have a friend who used to go down to see Mike at Acton, and they'd ride about on the Honda 500 in the back streets, which was a very hilarious thing to do, really", Chris Barber says. "Yes, yes, this was the racing bike, the non-handling awful one, the one Mike hated." The mind boggles again.)

"In 1967 I was riding for Suzuki", Graham says. "It was a rather strange little scene, a rather exclusive club of works riders, so we travelled together and parked our caravans together. There were probably six or eight of us, something like that. Mike was very much of the same little crowd. We spent an awful lot of time together and you could see the pressure Mike was under. There was no secret of the fact that Agostini was the young hot shot, he was the threat to Mike's crown in all respects. If anything he was better-looking, he was Italian, and his women tended to be even better than Mike's, and that didn't help, you know ..."

7

The 1967 season opened at Barcelona, although as usual there was no 500cc race there. "In the 250 Mike got a puncture and Phil Read won, I finished second. We went to Hockenheim, and after about two or three laps something went wrong with Mike's bike and I won. So he had no points", Bryans says. That 250 race followed the 125 where Ivy and Read crashed; in the 250 Ivy had to stop for plugs, but cut Bryans' lead from 40 seconds to four at the end. Later Ivy wandered over to Mike's caravan, but once inside it he collapsed and had to be taken to hospital with delayed shock. Hard men in hard races, you see.

The 500? "Mike could take the pressure if he was winning", Bryans says, "but he was let down by that Honda at Hockenheim. After the race I went in to see Mike and he was sitting in his caravan with the curtains drawn. I said 'Tough luck, Mike', and he gave me a stare as if he was looking straight through me, bitter disappointment written all over his face. He'd been out there riding his nuts off and the bloody thing stopped about two or three laps from the end, stuck in gear or something, and Agostini won it. It's a terrible thing to be under that amount of pressure and lose it through no fault of your own. Mike took losing hard, he wanted to win, he was a winner. When he gave me that stare I shrugged my shoulders and went out. He came out later when he'd got over it and he was back to his old self, everything's fine again. But when he got himself in a mood like that he was basically and completely unapproachable."

Agostini 8, Hailwood 0.

In a sense the 250cc Championship moved in the background of the 500. "After Hockenheim", Bryans says, "I had a first and a second and Mike had no points whatsoever. Then we went to Clermont-Ferrand for the French Grand Prix. I'd only been there once before and my machine had expired after only a couple of laps, so I was not familiar with the circuit and it was a difficult one to learn. Mike, Read and Ivy were ahead and I was holding on to a very secure fourth place. About halfway round the last lap I caught Mike. Obviously he had machine troubles – I discovered later that the gearbox had jammed in a particular gear – and I didn't pass him.

"I knew the situation, the effort was being put behind Mike. I had a 1966 machine, he had two 1967 models, he was the man who was supposed to win the races and, let's be frank, his talent was greater than mine. So all things being equal he should beat me anyway. I was there as back-up, I was there to take points off other people, but not off Mike. After the race Mike quizzed me. 'Why didn't you pass? You'd be leading the World Championship now.' I said 'Mike, at the end of the year you'll probably need those points more than me', and it transpired so, too ..."

Thereby hangs a tale of Clermont-Ferrand, recounted with some relish by Honda mechanic Katsumasa Suzuki. "Mike led at the start of the race, but by the middle of it his machine had transmission trouble and he couldn't change into fifth gear at all. Ivy and Read were coming closer and Ivy should have been able to pass him easily, but he didn't seem to try for a long time – I assumed because of their friendship! Of course the crowd didn't know about that and it looked normal to them, but we at Honda knew, and so of course did Yamaha, and both teams watched with great interest ..."

B. Ivy	1h 09m 14.4s
P. Read	1h 09m 22.7s
M. Hailwood	1h 09m 47.7s

Then – the Island, where Mike was so much, so very much at home. "I went to the casino with Mike", Cooper says. "We had a few drinks, we were talking and chatting to people, and it came to about four o'clock in the morning and we were still there. Bad news, really. We went straight out, back to the hotel for our leathers and did a couple of laps practice. You see practice started just after light."

Hard men, hard races. "Do you know, I've ridden in the Isle of Man and Hailwood rode in the Isle of Man in mist when you couldn't see in front of you. Bill Ivy, I remember, ran into a bloody bank, fell off his bike, got back on and did another lap. He couldn't see. Nowadays, if it looks like cloudy they say 'No practice', but those days, bloody hell, Hailwood used to go round at a hell of a lick in all sorts of weather, rain, hail."

Mike won the 250 and 350 easily, but the 500 has become a genuine historical event, Hailwood-versus-Agostini, Honda-versus-MV. "I liked to race at the Isle of Man", Agostini says, "although it's not the sort of place you can discuss in terms of safety. It was a racer's circuit. To beat Mike on The Island was almost impossible and to have done that was almost like winning the race of your life. So I had a dream..."

Mike went number four, feeding the power into the big Honda while he sat side-saddle on it, hoisted himself high and settled into the tuck position, and it all conveyed his sheer strength. Agostini went 30 seconds later. After a mile the gap was held at 30 seconds, but at Ballaugh Bridge it was down to 23. At Signpost Corner it was down to 19. Mike crossed the line to complete lap one at an average speed of 107.4mph, but Agostini averaged 108.4 and the gap was down to 18 seconds. Hailwood responded, lapped at 108.8 and cut Agostini's lead to 8.6 seconds. It meant that somewhere out there Mike had forced the gap back up to 23 seconds and he kept on forcing it up. It was almost an act of willpower, and to those who saw him in his life as laid-back, flippant, nonchalant – well, think about it. And think about this:

They stopped for fuel after three laps and Mike began to call for a hammer, a hammer, *get me a hammer!* The twist grip had worked loose and he beat it back on. He'd been averaging that 108 not knowing from moment to moment if the twist grip would come completely away in his hand and he would become essentially a passenger on the bike before he hit something like a stone wall or The Mountain itself.

At the pitstop Mike had forced the gap to merely two seconds. While he beat the twist-grip Agostini arrived for his stop. Mike was stationary for 47 seconds, Agostini away after 37 seconds. That opened the gap out to 12 seconds. Whatever Mike had found out there had melted before him as he stood astride the bike, motionless save for the arm doing the beating with the hammer.

He moved away fast, muscular again, vaulted over the bike and crouched and the echo of the Honda flattened and rose. Agostini sprinted away – a lighter step, a man more slender, but beautifully balanced and poised, almost feline; and he, too, strong. You couldn't do it at all if you weren't. No-one would know what these two men were doing to each other until it had settled and they were back into their grooves. Lap four would be refinding the grooves, lap five would be the race again.

By Kirkmichael on that fifth lap Mike had cut the gap to three seconds. At Sulby they were level. At Ramsey Mike led by a second. Up The Mountain Agostini – fluid, fluent, neat, eager – clawed that back and they were level again. A ripple of rumour passed urgently through the crowd strung out down the course because they all knew, all knew that when Mike passed them Ago should be coming exactly 30 seconds later. The rumour which rose from a whisper to a murmur to a babble of inquiry:

Where is Agostini? Where *is* Agostini?

He limped past them. The chain on the MV had broken. He reached the pits to deep, standing applause. This was no mocking applause, sardonic, gloating, taunting, this was the Great British Public standing aside from its emotions and responding to a brave man and a great racer and telling him that's what they judged he was. Mike came safely home. Murray Walker interviewed him immediately afterwards.

Walker: "You are the first TT winner that I have ever seen clutching a bunch of flowers and smelling them. How do you feel after that?"

Mike: "I feel a bit of a twit holding these things. I'm a bit tired naturally. It was a very, very hard race."

Walker: "Did you have a bad first lap?"

Mike: "Every lap was bad (chuckle) but actually I didn't expect to be in the lead, I didn't expect to win at all today actually."

Walker: "When you came into the pits you were hammering at something."

Mike: "Yes, well the throttle kept sliding off, so I thought that if I hit the end of it that would stop it sliding off. Apparently the bit I was hitting was all attached to the throttle anyway so it still kept coming off."

Walker: "And you still had this trouble all through the rest of the race?"

Mike: "It was only coming off slowly until the last lap, when it was so loose it fell off once. I couldn't do anything but hold it on. I was riding virtually one-handed."

Walker: "When did you know that Agostini was out of the race?"

Mike: "Somebody very kindly stuck out a signal at the Hawthorn Inn. I didn't know whether he was fooling me hoping I'd slow down so Ago could win or something (chuckle). I couldn't have done anything about it anyway. It was a relief to see another signal saying the same thing."

Mike gave another interview a little while later and expanded on the twist grip. "The throttle came right off in my hand, which was quite exciting, and I banged it back. All the wires had gone over the top and into the streamlining and I had to pull it off and start all over again ..."

This was a concentration of human drama, all eyes upon it, this was one context of what happened, but there are others. Cooper was fourth. "It's pretty boring on The Island, you just ride round and you don't know much about what's going on at the front. I can't remember anything about it because I wouldn't have been aware of it. With Hailwood and Agostini clearing off into the distance you never got a sight of them."

Mike sought Agostini out afterwards and said, as he remembers so well, "that I wasn't to worry about it. 'I'm very sorry', Mike said, 'it wasn't your fault.' That was typical of Mike. He understood that it was not his power which had won the race but my misfortune. I'd been leading when the chain broke and I had seen my dream coming true..."

Agostini 8, Hailwood 8.

Peter Carrick would write in *The Story of Honda* that "The Honda was probably the most famous 500cc machine of all time and became literally immortal. The brutal but magnificently elegant 16-valve bike which delivered 85bhp was still at the start of the TT races of 1976 – nine years later – holder of the 500cc TT lap record."

Mike and Agostini traded blows (metaphorically). Mike won Assen from Agostini and on that day took the 250 and 350 as well. In the 500, a 20-lap race, Agostini clung for the first nine laps, but Mike escaped through some tail-enders and smashed his own lap record by more than a second. The cumulative effort began to bear down on even him towards the end of the race, and he was so exhausted by forcing himself towards the finishing line that he nearly sank away off the bike. The ceremony on the podium had to be delayed while he recovered.

Agostini 14, Hailwood 16.

Agostini won Spa from Mike by 1 minute 2.76 seconds and that was 22-all. Agostini won at the Sachsenring. "That was another occasion when Mike surprised me", Bryans says. "Again something went wrong with Mike's 500. Agostini was leading right through to the last lap and lo and behold it was raining and he lost it in exactly the same place as Jimmy Guthrie[10] – who was killed at the Sachsenring in 1937. Agostini fell off at the same corner.

"I came into Mike's caravan and told him that. I said 'Christ Almighty, Agostini's just fallen off over there!'. Mike said 'Bloody good'. It wasn't the reaction I would have expected, not at all. I expected 'Oh God, is he alright?'. Mike was still in with a shout for the World Championship and that's the only thing he was caring about at that particular time; 1967 was bloody hard on Mike. All you've got to do is look at some of the photographs before the Grands Prix and look at photographs of him on the rostrum after three races. The man aged about 10 years in a day. Mike put everything into it." At the Sachsenring Agostini remounted and won.

Agostini 30, Hailwood 22.

Mike won Brno on a rebuilt machine, set a new lap record of 103.77mph and beat Agostini by 15.8 seconds, but he crashed into the trees at Imatra at nearly 100mph – a witness said he was draped *round* a tree – and Agostini made no mistake at all.

Agostini 44, Hailwood 30.

This year the number of finishes a rider could count had been increased to six, and Agostini had already filled his quota. Mike had only four and three races remained. These calculations were simplified after the Ulster Grand Prix where Agostini's clutch burned at the very start, leaving him 26th. Even Agostini couldn't do anything about that.

Agostini 44, Hailwood 38.

At the Ulster, Bryans took over a 350cc bike. "Mike concentrated on the 250 and 500 because he'd already won the 350. Mike was over two stone heavier than me and the Honda 350 was set up for that. I couldn't get them to change the suspension units from my 250 to the 350 because the mounting points were different. They just wouldn't fit. I finished with the rear tyre in shreds because the back was off the ground more than it was on it." Mike won the 250 from Bryans, Ivy third, but that Championship was tightening like a ratchet: Mike 46, Ivy 44, Read 42, Bryans 39 and the best seven finishes to count. Mike had scored in seven, Ivy in seven, Read in six, Bryans in nine. The supporting role of Ralph Bryans is easy to overlook, but he like Mike was riding his heart out.

At Monza Mike didn't get points in the 250 – Read won from Ivy, Bryans third – and Bryans took the 350, an event now irrelevant to Mike, of course. Mike needed to win the 500 to keep the Championship alive in Canada and

---

10. A Scot and a famous Norton works rider of the Thirties who in 1934 became only the third man to win the 350 and 500 races at the Isle of Man – he did both on a Norton. He is commemorated on The Island today by the Guthrie Memorial on the climb out of Ramsey.

magnificently he constructed a 17-second lead with a mere two laps to go. And the crankshaft buckled. Agostini went past him in front of the main grandstand to a roar which they probably heard in deepest Sicily, never mind all round the genteel parkland of Monza. Mike struggled over the line 13.2 seconds after Agostini. Macauley wrote that the crowd were "literally weeping with joy. Mike pulled in at the end of the straight and pushed the Honda roughly against a wall. He strode off close to tears." Agostini had averaged more than 200kph, and that had never been done before.

The mechanic Suzuki remembers Monza, will never forget it. Honda assumed that "MV would be in perfect winning condition since Italy was their home ground. Mike was leading at the beginning – a good lead – but he had a shift problem again. He was locked in fourth or fifth gear and the drum wouldn't open. Mike was trying so hard to stay in front but there was no way he could win the race. Agostini passed him, there was a huge crowd and they were all cheering Agostini. Mike did not stop, he continued, finished and just after he crossed the line he stopped his machine and got off.

"We expected and understood that he didn't want to talk to anybody. He'd lost a race he was going to win due to sudden machine trouble, he'd been passed by Agostini in front of the stand. However, when we saw him walking towards us he didn't show any upset and disappointment. His face was just like as before, always smiling. We were very impressed." Between parking the bike and striding back Mike had done what he was always going to do at supreme moments: composed himself, returned to his real self.

Mosport remained, but a second place was all Agostini needed and he got it, 37.7 seconds behind Mike. It gave the most tantalizing final table. Agostini had 58 points, but could count only 46, Mike had 52, but could count only...46. Both had five wins, so it went down to second places and Agostini won that 3–2. It was September 30, 1967. Mike never did become World 500cc Champion on a Honda. Nor was there much consolation in taking the 250 – he won that at Mosport from Read and Bryans, there was another dead-heat with Mike and Read both on 50, but Mike had it 5–4 on wins.

No, Mike never would win the 500 on a Honda. Without warning they summoned he and Bryans to Tokyo and announced that they were withdrawing from racing. They made Mike an amazing offer, however; £50,000 not to race in the 1968 World Championship. "It left me", he would say, "in a bit of a void." He could have Honda bikes for non-Championship events, but that remained a void.

We cannot leave it there, cannot consign the bronco to memory so quickly and carelessly. Some witnesses who reveal almost unconsciously that the years have gone by, the years have gone by:

Derek Minter: "I saw him riding it, although I'd finished by then. It was ideal watching because you know how the things behave and handle. For the general public it might have looked hair-raising, but to me it just wobbled and wriggled a bit."

Percy Tait: "He was so natural on The Island. I know things are different today and The Island has changed a lot. There's not so many bumps and Quarry Bends, for instance, are virtually flat-out. It was quite sharp in those days. And, of course, the Mountain is all altered now, and the lap times are quicker, but that's due to the fact that the course has got much better. The big Honda wobbled. I watched him riding that on The Island and it was terrific. He didn't mind if it jumped around a bit. He used to get the wheels off the ground, it was so powerful. Was it frightening to watch? Well, it wasn't good to watch, but knowing Mike it gave me a lot of pleasure."

Geoff Duke: "The rather remarkable thing about Mike was that mechanically he was limited. He wasn't all that good at sorting a bike out from the handling point of view. He could just ride them and he could ride anything. Oh yes, I remember the 500 and it was a handful. He coped with it without too much trouble. I can't think of anyone else who could have done as much justice to it. That bike was very potent. It was frightening to watch him on it."

Stuart Graham: "At the time it was considered a real monster, and Mike the only one who could ride it. He freely admitted it scared the daylights out of him. I didn't ride it until the Eighties and then not in a race. It had been in the Donington museum. John Surtees had checked it over and prepared it. Pauline asked me if I would ride it. I distinctly remember walking up to the bike in the pits and thinking: That's not the 500! It looked so small, so insignificant compared to my ardent memories of it when it did look a real monster. Mind you, it demanded respect just looking at it. At the time it was a big bike. Now, these old bikes seem quite small, don't they? So I looked at it and I did think *is that really the fearsome 500 we were all so terrified of?*

"I rode it round Donington, but I didn't ride it that hard. The bike was far too valuable and it would have been far too risky to have done that. Literally it felt like a 250. It was only when Surtees came up later on – he had been on a 500 MV – and said 'God, that thing flies, I've been scatching like mad trying to catch up with you' that I realized. I hadn't realized before. It showed how quick the bike actually was. I remember Brno. The mechanics were lying in a ditch down the side of the road opposite the pits. There was a bit of a rise in the circuits at that point. The mechanics were down at ground level watching ..."

John Surtees: "We did a track test. I put some tyres and things on it and got it running. We'd taken the engine out and checked it over. The bike had enormous potential, but it was twitchy. It seemed a very small, compact bike, but that's how things went, because MV-fours went very small."

Nobby Clark: "If Honda had spent more time listening to Mike and doing what he wanted – especially in design – instead of welding bits and pieces on here, there and everywhere, plus rushing along with heaps of unusable horsepower in frames which were more like rubber bands, they could have won many more races and Mike would have won many more World Championships."

Katsumasa Suzuki: "In 1967 Yamaha had improved in the 250 so that sometimes Honda won, sometimes Yamaha won. Honda also had a hard time against MV in the 500. Mike never showed his disappointment or became upset if he lost. Some riders would say bad things about their machines if they lost, but I never remember him doing that. He never complained. What did we in the Honda team think when we saw him riding the big 500? We thought he would win easily."

Soichiro Irimajiri: "What surprised us in 1966 was that Jim Redman, our ace rider, was no match for Mike. We wondered why such a big difference happened. Few machines had enough power to allow Mike's slide-riding technique, although I believe the later Honda did. MV might have been close to that level with around 70bhp or even bhp in the upper 60s, but apparently they were underpowered compared to the Honda, so I'm not sure they reached a point where they had the frame problem. We gained engine power significantly and rapidly and sometimes the frame didn't fit with it. Unfortunately, nobody could understand the balance. I drafted engines for five Honda machines and we didn't know how the frame should be. We were simply trying to gain engine power. However, the problem was not just Honda's. No-one in the motorcycle racing field knew. We knew later. We started to know in the Seventies.

"As far as the engine power was concerned Mike didn't complain at all. The concern was the response caused by the carburettor, and we worked on that many times. There was an engine which had a valve-system driven by pistons and we introduced it to give a rise in rpm, but this gave a poor response in the low rpm area, although overall it had higher power, as Mike pointed out. We changed his machine back to the way it had been before."

This is a classically simple exposition of one branch of technology moving more quickly than another. Harmony in technology is difficult to achieve when the branches are all going as fast as they can; harmony is trying to hold a balance, but with the nagging thought that the balance will slow the process if you can strike it at all, and the moment you do strike it and hold to it the balance will be disturbed because all the branches are still going as fast as they can. This is as true today as it was then, perhaps more so as the pace quickens and quickens. The evidence of the disharmony is contained in the Latin dictum *Si monumentum requiris, circumspice* – if you want evidence of it, look around.

It was only one man and one bike, only races which went round and round, only an activity which some might see as esoteric, egotistical, elitist and exclusive; only one aspect of one sport among so many sports that people play year after year on all places on the earth. I accept the premise and endorse it with but a single proviso. Only one man accepted this disharmony of technology which had pushed speed to the point where it could kill like an aeroplane crash, but had not yet found the means of harnessing it, took it to the most feared place on earth, leant and urged and flung it within a foot of raw-ragged stone walls and ravines and escarpments and spectators and telegraph poles and memorials to those who had died trying to do this; and covered 37.75 miles at an average speed of 108.77mph.

Stanley Michael Bailey Hailwood.

8

"At the end of the year Mike approached me again", Sprayson says. "It was at the Earls Court motor show. Mike said 'You wanted time. We now have all winter. Can you do something for the beginning of the 1968 season?'." Sprayson said "Yes". "Mike let me have the Lyster bike with the Honda engine." Which Honda engine remains a mystery; Sprayson thinks it might have been the 1967 version, or perhaps another which had been planned for 1968, but "Where it came from I have no idea. Mike brought it to Birmingham, the two of us carried it from his car and plonked it on my desk. I actually drew drawings of it from the engine itself.

"I put it on a service table, levelled it all up and then measured all the bigger points. You measure the engine and the points where it is joined to this, that and the other on the frame, then you have to wrap the frame around it. The engine I worked on was producing 98bhp, and that was a lot in those days. Horsepower is a funny thing. The Nortons were only producing 58bhp, but as soon as you touched the throttle it shot straight up to the top, it didn't feed the power in.

"That was the trouble with the Honda engine. It peaked immediately, just kicked straight in and, of course, if you leant over on it all that power was going straight to the rear wheel and it kicked the back out."

Mike needed to be able to lean over to his usual 57 degrees without scraping the ground. Sprayson now examined the overall problem: to set the engine low Honda had dispensed with the bottom supporting tubes and consequently the wheels were only held in line by the two tubes at the top. They were of one-inch diameter.

As Sprayson pondered he understood why the bike was flexible to the point of terror. The Lyster frame in front of him had been a brave and logical attempt to correct that by raising the engine to get the two tubes underneath, but inescapably the whole bike became much too high. Sprayson's knowing eye fell upon the four-inch oil sump running along the bottom. To get the engine out of the frame enough clearance was needed to get the sump out, too. Sprayson's dilemma was simple: to get the tubes underneath. He decided on a radical step and placed a single tube there, 1.75 inches in diameter. There were inevitably complications, but it worked. Sprayson completed the design by mid-October, but needed detailed information from Mike, who was in South Africa. All Mike really wanted was the bike to resemble the original Honda so that they wouldn't be too upset – and that it would go where he pointed it.

Construction took only a couple of weeks and Nobby Clark was pressed into service. Mike wanted to race it at Rimini on March 24. The week before, Mike and Clark journeyed to Reynolds for the final preparations. He was due to give the bike its shake down [11] at Brands Hatch on the Wednesday. Mike stayed until two in the morning and departed for Brands to try and get some sleep. Clark and Sprayson worked on until four, hoisted the bike into a van and Clark drove it away. That morning Sprayson, too, set off for Brands, "But when I got there the gate was locked and they said nothing was happening on the track, so I came straight home again." Brands was being resurfaced.

Mike took the bike to Rimini untested. "The thing was never developed at all. Mike rode it exactly as he took it away from Reynolds, although he could cope with things like that. At Brands I'd wanted the Girling people to help sort out the suspension – that is highly critical – but Brands never happened."

At Rimini Mike led Agostini for 10 of the 28 laps, but crashed on a corner – rider error, as he freely confessed – remounted and finished second, breaking the lap record. He moved on to Imola, but the engine gave trouble and Clark spent the whole night bolting in the previous year's spare. Mike beat Agositini and then departed for Modena, Ferrari's test track, to drive their Formula Two car. *Motor Cycle News* reported that "At the moment Ferrari are short of drivers, but no decision as to whether he will join the team has been reached". This is no more and no less than an extremely intriguing footnote about what might have been. Mike never drove a Ferrari in a race.

"I contacted Mike early on in this", Sprayson says, "and said we must get down to sorting this thing out. He arranged to go to Snetterton, but at the last minute he couldn't make it, so what he was actually riding was a bike whose only changes were made by Nobby Clark altering a few dampers. It was never technically got into at all."

---

11. A motor racing term denoting a new bike or car's very first run.

And that was the Bike that Never Really Was. Honda said "No" to it contesting the World Championship, and the rest drifts into the realms of surmise, conjecture, daydreams and a much bigger historical footnote. Could Mike have beaten Agostini on it across a whole 500cc season? Those sort of daydreams.

9

Rimini, ah lovely, sun-kissed Rimini, where foreign visitors are warmly embraced. Aren't they? Mike was staying at an hotel with Clark. "We were sitting outside having breakfast when someone passing by saw Mike. The news that he was staying in the hotel spread like wildfire and by lunch time there was a crowd outside just looking at him. He really went crazy. He jumped into his car and drove off to find somewhere quiet where he could read a book."

Rimini, ah lovely, sun-kissed Rimini, or more properly Cesenatico, which was "just along the road, it was not actually in Rimini", Bryans says. "Luigi and Tilde Taveri were on holiday because although Luigi had retired in 1966 he used to come down."

Graham was there, too. "Our works rides with the Japanese teams all stopped at the same time, so Mike, Ralph and I – Ralph had the small Honda, Mike had whatever (the Reynolds 500) and I had a Suzuki – did the pre-season Italian races on works bikes, but not as part of works teams. In fact those Italian races were our big earners for the season."

Phil Read was there, too. "There were a whole series of meetings round those parts where you earned a lot of money, and obviously these meetings pulled a lot of people down to the coastal resorts. I think the locals resented us because we were rich and famous. The Italians are lovely people, but if they can take an extra five or 10 per cent off you they will."

Yes.

"We found this nice nightclub", Bryans says, "and we went in and at the end of the evening we were presented with a mammoth bill. We decided it wasn't on, but we paid it. We also decided the nightclub was good, the party was good, and we would go back. The deal was: Listen, boys, when we go this time – I think it was me who thought it up – everybody who orders a round pays for it there and then and at the end we are not going to be presented with another mammoth bill. Ah, but we got another mammoth bill, didn't we? I was in like a flash to this manager. We should have walked out of the place, but we got involved in an argy-bargy ..."

Graham: "One or two had had a drink and it all started to turn nasty. The next thing people are blowing whistles calling the police ..."

Bryans: "Someone phoned the local hoods. The place was in a cellar, you had to go up a flight of stairs onto a landing and turn and go up again to get out onto the street. When we decided to leave all the hoods were at the top ..."

Read: "I forget how many people I hit. Everyone was hitting everyone else. Luigi is a fiery fellow when he gets angry and Tilde was screaming and shouting ..."

Graham: "People were taking swings at all sorts of people, and our main concern was to try and get Mike out of the place because you can imagine the trouble it would have caused if Hailwood was locked up in jail the night before the race. It would have been an international incident ..."

Bryans: "It was a good row, that was. We managed to get out. Lots of people got hit. I hit a few myself, aye. One of our chaps came off worst because somebody hit him when he hadn't got his eyes shut and he had a bloodshot eye for months. Mike hit a guy so hard he broke his own finger. Phil Read was in the thick of it. There were one or two there who could handle themselves, you're young and you're so fit and you could take care of yourself ..."

Graham's wife Margaret: "When we got back to the caravan site where we were staying I did a head count to make sure everybody was back safely ..."

Bryans: "Do you know who had the last laugh? Phil Read. When it had all settled down and everyone had gone home you know what he did? He got himself a nice big brick, he drove off in his Jaguar, hopped out and heaved the brick straight through the nightclub front window .."

Three postscripts.

Bryans: "Mike was supposed to be racing at Brands Hatch the next week and couldn't because of the broken finger ..."

Graham: "Mike got himself fired up the same as everybody else, but generally his tendency was to shoulder pretty well anything because he did not need the aggravation. What's another £20? But when you know you shouldn't be paying it ..."

Clark: "At the end of the 1968 season MV asked Mike if he would like to ride at Monza in the Italian Grand Prix. He tested the bikes and was very pleased with them. He was also very pleased with his lap times. The next day Agostini was there testing and so was Mike, but Mike couldn't get down to the times he'd set before. He asked what had been done to the bikes and he was told they were the same as the previous day. Mike just upped and walked out. He honestly believed the MV personnel had given them to Agostini."

10

Mike was now seeing Pauline regularly. She'd been married before and her divorce came through in 1968. Mike stressed, however, that he wouldn't marry. "I think it was something he had in his mind that he wouldn't while he was racing.

"He fell out with Bill Ivy, it was only a minor falling-out, but I did notice Mike's knuckles go white. I'd started seeing Mike, but he had had a girlfriend, one particular girlfriend, for a couple of years. Mike and I had gone to a pub, Bill came in and intimated that he'd been seeing this old girlfriend. Mike was furious. He had this loyalty thing. He had these various girlfriends, but if he found out they'd been unfaithful to him – well, he was allowed to have other relationships, but they weren't! *Then* Bill started seeing another of his ex-girlfriends and it seemed Bill was going round picking them up, because I'd come on the scene quite heavily by then. Bill thought he could pick up where Mike had left off with the others. I saw Mike get a bit peeved about that.

"I played it as quietly as I could with Mike. Mike was someone you had to give an awful lot of rope to. I knew that, and if I wanted him – I'd known I wanted him straight off – the only way was to give him as much rope as he needed. I used to say to him 'When you ring me I want it to be because you want to speak to me'. If he was with me it was because he wanted to be, not because I'd pestered him.

"I gave him enough rope. It was the only way I was going to keep him. I'd rather have had him on those terms than not at all. I was prepared to do that. When he went away for two or three months to do the Springbok series I'd say 'I don't mind you keeping in practice as long as you don't wear yourself out!'. (Long laughter.) I think I scored a few points there. (More laughter.) If I saw him chatting somebody up I'd try not to get the hump about it, I'd just smile sweetly at him and go and talk to someone else and in about 10 minutes he'd be back."

However inevitable the nature of their arrangement was, Pauline handled it in a most mature, realistic and sympathetic way. She remains a striking woman and not just visually. I repeat what I said in the very first chapter of this book. You can see why they fell for each other, lived with each other. Mike had stature. So did Pauline.

MIKE AND THE CAR

'My arm was totally encased in plaster and his leg was totally encased in plaster. He said 'You can press the accelerator and I'll steer the wheel'." – Guy Edwards

"He had this bloody awful big American thing. He opened the door and said 'Why don't you lot eff off', and they were all chanting in their Italian accents 'Mike, Mike, Mike'." – Derek Bell

"There was debris flying all over the place. I'm standing there hyper-ventilating and he's calming me, not me calming him." – Pauline Hailwood

1

"Mike had been at Le Mans, but we didn't really do anything except have a laugh and a joke and that was it. During the 5000 series it was such a big party time it was unbelievable. I don't think anyone appreciated how skilful the guys were because the cars were big unwieldly beasts." Rod Sawyer treasured every moment, the same Rod Sawyer who had worked for Lotus in the Sixties and had met Mike in Formula Junior.

"Formula 5000 was designed to be a big, gut-rumbling formula for people who enjoyed lots of noise. It was something John Webb[1] devised through Brands Hatch. It was a matter of getting together a bunch of people who could afford to build cars. Lola had agreed a cheap spaceframe chassis and you bolted in a big Chevy engine. It started off in 1969 with Hobbs, Hailwood, Trevor Taylor, Peter Gethin – there were a lot of good names in it – mainly guys who couldn't quite crack Formula One. Surtees put together his team and built the Surtees cars.

"We got onto the Continent and raced at Hockenheim, the Salzburgring, we went to funny places likes Nivelles, in Belgium, frequently to Zolder. We always stayed in the very, very best hotels, we ate exceptionally well, we drank very, very heavily. Ireland was mayhem. To go over there and try and do a motor race with all that Guinness was a waste of time.

"I remember one particularly profound night when Mike and I were sat at a

---

1. The moving force behind the development of Brands Hatch.

prizegiving. It was Irish and very local, and at an hotel on an incredibly foggy night. Mike and I were deep in conversation head-to-head across the table and we were ignoring the rest of the proceedings. A guy came over and in a broad accent said to Mike 'I used to be your greatest fan, but now I think you're the biggest (expletive) on the face of the earth'. Mike looked up and said 'What's the matter?'. It turned out that they had been playing the Irish national anthem and we didn't know. I said 'You'd better stay sitting down because if you stand up the guy's going to try and hit you'. Somebody saw the predicament we were in and ushered us out into this real pea-souper fog. We could hear all these Micks screaming after us. Mike faced a lot of that sort of thing."

Yes, Mike faced a lot of that sort of thing. Celebrities cope as best they can, and each in their own way. Mike never escaped it because however shy he might remain, however diffident, however lonely in private moments, he could never be reclusive. He disliked strangers invading his space, but every day of his life the invaders would be there with their fists or their pencils and papers; and it remained so even now, when he had essentially left bike racing. Honda had withdrawn, and anyway he was 29 going on 30, time to go back to racing cars. This was no leisurely retirement, but it was less stark than 500cc machines on the Isle of Man. Arguably anything else on earth was, too.

The fame you cope with because you have no viable alternative outside a monastery. "I remember once driving up the Champs Elysees when we were going somewhere. We stopped at the traffic lights and someone yelled out 'Hey Mike, Mike!'. Mike didn't know who the hell it was. It must have been a fan. On the whole he took things like that OK, but on the odd occasion when he was trying to have a quiet piece of anonymity and someone came up it got on his nerves", Pauline says.

"During the 5000 period we started driving around a lot together", Sawyer says. "We had a lot of common interests – food and girls and clubs – and I was very active and alive in London, having an apartment in Mayfair, which was quite a notorious apartment. I used to socialize with Terry Wogan and Mike got on very well with him, too, Terry was always popping in, Barry Sheene was always going in next door[2] – I won't name-drop, but there were a lot of people who went through both doorways, there was always a little *paparazzi* hanging around outside at night when everything got a bit more fresh.

"At the time I got close to him I wasn't sure what went on in Mike. I think he went through a transitional period when he felt that he didn't really trust a lot of people, and a lot of people took advantage of him. We socialized a lot, we were hanging out in Tramps and Annabels, all the places that the playboys would do at that time. I'd never seen Mike race bikes, all I knew about was his cars and that was through Formula 5000. It was fun. In hindsight we weren't taking our motor racing anywhere near as seriously as it should have been. When you work for a bloke like Norinder,[3] whose total existence was one great laugh from the moment he got up to the moment he went to bed – and who never really knew where he went to bed or when because he was always too drunk anyway, and he'd climb out of bed and go and race a car – it had to be a lot of fun.

2. This was the office of CSS, a promotional company started by Barrie Gill and run by journalists. Sheene was looked after by one of them, Andy Marriott.
3. Ulf Norinder, bearded Swede and bon viveur.

"Was Mike lonely? Mike was no fool, he had this lovely character, but he genuinely lacked confidence when it came to business, certainly when it came to pulling girls. The funny thing was he was great once the introduction had been made, but he couldn't cold-call a girl, he couldn't go up to a girl point-blank, or if he did it was a really rare occasion.

"In London, if I rang Mike socially at night – I had a permanent table at one of London's popular Italian restaurants – and invited him to dinner he was always free, he would always come. Socially I think he was possibly lonely. Additionally, my friends were not motor racing-orientated, they were not star-spotters, but successful people in their own right. I used to sign the bill for dinner. I got through a fortune. But this was a difference: Mike had found somebody who was prepared to pay bills just the way he was always prepared to pay them himself – someone who did not expect him to pay. (Of Mike's generosity, and an example of how hurt he was when it was abused, there will be a pertinent example later in the book.)

"He had a close relationship to people like Bill Ivy, he was very close to him because Bill was a tearaway, he was part of the flower-power Sixties – long hair, velvet bell-bottom trousers – Bill was fun to be around and he made Mike laugh. Mike liked to be entertained. That's why he got on well with Ted Macauley."

You know the score in motorsport, everybody knows the score. The good times are as good as you can get, the bad times you are never able to forget.

Bill Ivy was killed on July 12, 1969 after his 350 Jawa seized and struck an unprotected wall at the Sachsenring. Of him in *No Time to Lose* Mike wrote: "We were friends – close pals, in fact – despite the fact that professionally we represented different works teams and on the circuits we had to be the deadliest of rivals. That never impinged on our association as two bachelors hell-bent on getting the best out of life when the races were over and done with. He was a way-out character, anxious to be involved in whatever was fashionable at the time, and that meant long flowing hair and flared trousers, garish shirts and a blinding line in neckware. His body was a criss-cross of stitch marks from some fearsome crashes, but even though he lived on the limit he never backed off a single challenge. I would not say he was fearless – no man is that – but I would offer the opinion that his margins of safety were narrower than most."

2

In 1969 Mike was third in the 5000 series in his Lola and competed concurrently in the World Sportscar Championship. "We did the whole season", Hobbs says. "We went to Daytona and we were leading there, we led Sebring. I only met Stan once. Mike, Richard Attwood and I went to Nassau after Sebring. I'd always had a distant but loving relationship with my parents, it was very middle-class, you never ever swore in front of my parents, never thought of telling a dirty joke.

"I was amazed. We got off the plane and Stan was there to meet us. Straight away they were effing and blinding and started to swop tales of their latest conquests. 'You dirty old bugger', Mike said to Stan and they went off arm-in-arm.

"Back in Europe we didn't lead Monza, then we went to Le Mans. It was a two-car team of GT40s, Mike and I in one, Jacky Ickx and Jackie Oliver[4] in the other. Both cars qualified very low down. David Yorke[5] was the team manager, and John Wyer[6] the owner-director. Yorke was a real tactician who also wanted things done by the book. He set us a lap time of 4 minutes 14 seconds, which was a long, long way slower than we had done in practice.[7]

"It was the last year of the Le Mans start[8] and the year Ickx strolled across the track to do that start. I have to tell you that Mike didn't like Jacky at all. He found him a pain in the backside, as I did, because he was a spoilt little brat. Ickx was pretty quick and David Yorke thought the sun shone out of his rear end. Ickx was definitely the number-one man. At Daytona earlier in the season we'd had a motorhome. It was just an enlarged caravan, but at least we had somewhere to go. A butterfly got in there, Ickx is chasing round showing off to David Yorke how clever he is to be able to catch the butterfly. As usual Mike is hunched in a corner immersed in a book. Acrobatic Mr Ickx was dancing round and he used his knee or shoulder as a launching pad to try and grab the butterfly. He trod on Mike. Mike went absolutely into orbit. 'I don't give an expletive who you think you are, if you do that again I'll break every bone in your body.' Ickx shrugged his shoulders and smiled and walked out.

"Then at Le Mans I took first stint and made a terrific start while Ickx strolled across. From about 14th I was in the top six or seven and Ickx was one of the last people to leave. There was a big crash at White House[9] although I had already gone by. Ickx arrived on the scene and the road was nearly blocked. There was no pace car then[10] and you slowed or stopped if you came up to an accident. Ickx was stopped and, bingo, in two laps I am now a lap up because I came round again while Ickx was stopped. Our car was leading their car, and that's the way it stayed for hours and hours and hours. Gradually Mike and I moved up.

"In the middle of the night a couple of Porsches had passed me really *duking* it out together and they slowly drew away because we were stuck on this limit of 4 minutes 14 seconds, so it wasn't a case of racing. There were four tail-lights going away down the Mulsanne Straight[11] half a mile in front of me. They came

---

4. Jackie Oliver, an Englishman who won at Le Mans and drove Formula One for 10 years and subsequently ran the Arrows (now called Footwork) team.
5. David Yorke, a long-time team manager in motorsport.
6. John Wyer, a well-known figure in the sport who as team manager of Aston Martin in 1956 signed Stirling Moss to drive for them for £50! Wyer was also an expert on Le Mans and wrote extensively about it.
7. Le Mans being spread over 24 hours, the trick is to run at a pace which you and your car can sustain. You cannot, of course, race for 24 hours in the accepted sense.
8. The Le Mans start was an extremely famous and dramatic thing. The cars were lined up to one side of the track, the drivers at the other, and at the signal the drivers sprinted over, leapt in and got away as fast as they could.
9. White House (ethnically Maison Blanche) is a right-left before the Ford chicane and the pits.
10. The Pace Car is normally a saloon car which emerges and takes the whole field slowly round behind it in race order until an obstruction has been cleared. It can also be used in wet weather – until heavy rain eases or stops.
11. The Mulsanne Straight is the long, flat-out section running along the back of the circuit, now made slower by two chicanes.

to the kink which was flat-out, and these four tail-lights went round it and suddenly there was a flash of light – a headlamp light – which went all across the sky and then a huge ball of orange fire. I stood hard on the brakes, whistled round the kink slowing down, but I was still probably doing 150 miles an hour and the road was completely covered in smoke and dust and fire.

"There was no point in swerving because I had no idea where to swerve to. I zoomed through and emerged and I could see a fire burning on one side of the track, and in front of the fire was a bit of one of the Porsches bouncing down the road end-over-end. I was still slowing, I did swerve to miss this thing, and out from the cabin pops the driver and he starts to bounce down the road as well. It happened to be my 'in' lap. As Mike was getting in I said 'There's been a hell of a crash, there's a bloke been killed and, oh God, they're going to be ages clearing that up. Be careful.' Off goes Mike.

"It was a bloke called Udo Schutz, and he was a bit on the overweight side and he didn't have a mark on him. Hans Herrmann was in the other Porsche, and he was totally unharmed too, and just carried on.

"We were still leading the Ickx car and it came round to my turn again. Going down to the Mulsanne hairpin the brakes completely went away, I had no brakes. I went shooting along the escape road, turned round, returned to the pits and I said to David Yorke 'We've got a severe brake problem'. He said 'We knew you'd be ready for a pad change about now'. I said 'No, no, it's more than pads', but I sat there and they changed them. I nearly ran over the marshal at the end of the pit lane with a little red flag because this bloody car still won't stop, will it? And now, of course, I've got eight and a half miles to trudge with no brakes to get all the way back to the pits.

"A wheel weight had come off and clipped a hole in a little brake pipe, so they changed the pipe, put more fluid in and I set off again and everything's hunky-dory except in the meanwhile Ickx has passed us. That was the race which came down to an incredible shoot-out between Herrmann, who'd had the crash in the middle of the night right in front of me, and got away with it, and Jacky Ickx."

The Automobile Club de l'Ouest which runs the event described that finish thus. "After three hours of struggle wheel-to-wheel the Ford of Ickx-Oliver beat the Porsche of Herrmann-Larrousse [12] by a *breath*."

"Even David Yorke said we should have won that race. Ickx and Oliver were no threat to us at all, they were always between eight and 15 miles behind us until that brake pipe incident. We never missed a beat the whole 24 hours except for that."

In 1970 Mike did a further season of Formula 5000 in the Lola competing against, among others, Hobbs, who was driving for Surtees. Thereby hangs one of Hobbs' very best tales.

"It was a race in the spring at Brands Hatch. It was a three-by-two grid, Mike was on the front row and I was in the middle of the second row." Pauline was a spectator positioned on the inside of the circuit just after the end of the pit lane exit. Hobbs made what he describes as a "demon start. Unfortunately I leapt over the back of Mike's Lola. There is a photograph of me like a praying mantis right

---

12. Gerard Larrousse, later to jointly own the Formula One team which bears his name. It was he who, when he was working for Renault, took them and turbo engines into Formula One.

over his head as we moved towards Paddock with cars crashing and spinning and bashing. I took out the entire Surtees team because Andrea de Adamich and Trevor Taylor were in his other two cars."

"Mike knew where I was because he'd waved to me from the grid. The crash happened slap bang in front of me" – ("it was entirely *his* fault", Hobbs says, stirring laughter from Pauline, himself and myself) – "and afterwards there was still debris flying about all over the place. I was standing there and Mike came running to see if I was alright. I'm hyper-ventilating and he's calming me, not me calming him. He'd just got out of a written-off car and he was worried about *me*. Because he saw then how it affected me he didn't really want to take me to the races again", Pauline says.

"It happened right in front of Pauline", Hobbs says, "and she must have thought *my old mate Dave has just done in my other old mate Mike*. It took half an hour to clear it all up. The Surtees team were out, so Mike and I repaired to the bar and guffawed about it, and John Surtees was highly dechuffed."

At the end of 1970 Hobbs left the Surtees team and Mike joined it. The actual joining has given rise to another of those anecdotes which just has to be true. The night before there had been a bender of a party at Mike's flat, someone had been sick in the hall and the offending area had simply been covered in talcum powder. Enter Mike and John Surtees to talk over the deal, Surtees known as a martinet. We must assume that Mike struggled hard to keep a straight face.

Mike agreed to drive and it was settled on a handshake. That was more binding to Mike than a 50-page legal document is to some Formula One drivers now, and in the years to come when he'd have been better off leaving the team (there is some unanimity about this) he remained. The handshake was not negotiable. Mike knew that motorsport watchers would see he and John Surtees as "an unholy alliance" because their temperaments were so different.

"I think you have a certain degree of motion-and-tension in some drivers", Surtees says. "You had it with Mike, you have it with Nigel Mansell today, although they are totally different people. In Mansell there is a degree of competitiveness which this type – such as Mike – had.

"I first got involved running some cars as a team in F5000 and we had David Hobbs and an ex-Lotus driver. Hobbs raced against Mike, and Mike was having a great big tussle with his car, which was very much an interim Lola, parts of the sports car, using all sorts of odd bits up. People were talking about Mike crashing all the time and spinning and things like this. I said 'Mike, we need each other, come along', and he came along. Immediately he started to get himself all together and he did very well."

Back to Le Mans. "In 1970 Mike and I drove the third Gulf Porsche 917", Hobbs says. "We had one of the 4½-litre flat-twelves. Most of the top teams had 5 litres but that was relatively new and they all bust in no time. I started the race again and it was a nice sunny evening. We were doing alright, we were up to fifth or sixth in no time at all, and I gave the car to Mike. It started to rain, and in that he was absolutely the demon, he was up to third and flashing along at a great rate of knots looking incredibly good, but he was unfortunate enough to run into a car which had already crashed at the Dunlop Curve. It had been there a couple of laps, but I guess Mike was in spray and hadn't seen it. He clipped it and the next thing they are hoisting our car over the guardrail to safety on a crane. That was the end of that. John Wyer is reputed to have said 'Don't call us, we'll call you...'"

At the end of 1970 Mike set off to do the Tasman series and a venerable, venerated British gentleman, Rob Walker, flew to New Zealand, too.[13] "I'd met him around the circuits, but I didn't seriously get to know him until he drove for John Surtees and we went out to do the Tasman. I was a partner of Surtees then, so he was virtually driving for me as well. I took him out to dinner one night – it was the eve of a race – and we had a few bottles of champagne, we told a few stories and then he buggered off – he had something else to do. He told me afterwards he thought me a stuffy old bastard ..." This is an understandable but hilariously inaccurate judgment, as we and Mike will see.

"We got close during the Tasman series because you drive thousands of miles. The Tasman was four races in Australia, four in New Zealand. Mike drove the car which was Surtees' Formula One car for the following year, but with this big Chevy stuff bolted in the back", Sawyer says.

"The last race in New Zealand was at Invercargill, the lowest part of civilization in the Southern Hemisphere, and you knew it. We'd never been there before and went to do some pre-testing. There was a corrugated tin hut outside which was the loo, and if you tried to get the door open it wouldn't, and of course what had happened was a sheep had wandered in there and died something like 12 months previously. There was a dreadful smell. The place was that remote, it really was.

"We'd got pole position, we'd pulled a master-stroke and bought every single Firestone wet tyre there was in existence in the Southern Hemisphere to make sure nobody else could beat us on our practice times; it was a wet race and Mike went off full of confidence. He was going to drive away from everybody. He got into the first corner, lost it and went careering across a field completely out of control, water and spray everywhere, towards an ambulance. The ambulance driver jumped out and tried to run away and, of course, the car changed direction and started chasing after him. Mike missed him, landed in a ditch and the car was totally destroyed."

Faces in the mirror, faces in the mirror, circa 1970.

"He'd have a stock of paperbacks, six or seven of them, and he'd lie in bed in the morning and he'd open one up, start his day off by reading. He'd get 10 pages through and suddenly this book would hit the ceiling and he'd say 'I've read that'. Maybe he'd read it three or four years previously and it would refresh his mind after just 10 pages, and he'd throw it up in the air. Then he'd start reading another one. He read so much that it was really quite a job for him to find anything he hadn't read. He read anything, absolutely anything. It wasn't as if he concentrated on horror, or romances, or war books; didn't make a ha'p'orth of difference, but it was always fiction. When he had nothing left he read the Collins Dictionary from cover to cover. You never played scrabble with Hailwood. That was just suicide." And those are the happy days Rod Sawyer treasures still.

---

13. Rob Walker, born rich – which wasn't his fault and something he scarcely regretted – fell in love with motor racing early (he was given a car when he was 10), drove Le Mans in 1939, became a fighter pilot, then ran his own team whose drivers included Moss. Rob Walker rightly accords with every foreigner's notion of a British gentleman.

3

In 1971 Mike made a farewell appearance, as they say, on bikes. "I was working for Rod Gould, who was riding for Yamaha, Holland, the European importers", Nobby Clark says. "During the early part of the season I asked Mike if he would like to ride a 350 at Silverstone. He said 'Yes', so I got one for him, took it out of the crate, changed the tyres, filled it up with oil and fuel. Mike was second in practice behind Agostini and he hadn't sat on the bike before then! After practice we were all standing around talking about the bike. Rod came up and asked Mike why his boots were worn through and couldn't he afford new ones? In turn, Mike asked Rod how old his boots were, and Rod said they were new at the beginning of the season. Mike told him he wasn't trying hard enough. That ended the conversation."

Chris Barber was there. "I remember him practising. When the riders came back you could see grey marks on their knees and their leathers – bits of scrapes – and Mike came in with his boot worn right through and the flesh worn off his foot. He said 'That's how you win', and in fact that's how he won, that's why they all let him go and watched him win. You look at films of the races, you can see them actually watching him go, actually letting him go because they weren't going to do the same kind of thing. You could argue he had them all psyched out, but it wasn't a deliberate process, that's just the way he was; but he had them psyched out, yes."

At Silverstone there was one unpsyched rider, Yorkshireman Mick Grant, who had never raced against Mike, never spoken to him and had only seen him once before all those years ago when he'd been in the crowd at a meeting at Scarborough.

"I'd started racing in 1966, 1967, and Mike was at his peak, I was just coming out of club races to national level and, of course, he was away at the Grands Prix. At Silverstone, obviously I'd have recognized him if I'd walked past him in the paddock, but no more than that. It was a 350cc race and I'd read in the newspapers that he was in it, but I thought so what? I hadn't seen him in practice or anything. In the race there were a bunch of us scrapping together around seventh place, he'd obviously made a fairly bad start, and this bloke shot through the middle of us like a scalded cat. He'd got black leathers and a blue helmet and I thought who the hell's that? I put it down to some foreigner having an on day. I got back after the race and asked who it was and they said 'Hailwood' ...

"I didn't speak to him, no, not at all. I'm very old-fashioned, I'm from the old school. Today maybe youngsters have a better attitude, they see someone in brackets famous and go up and talk to them. I would revere them from a distance, I'd think you really shouldn't go and talk to such people. It's just the way you've been brought up, isn't it? Even if I had had the opportunity I'd have found it very hard to go and talk to him."

Grant would speak to Mike, but that was four years away; would ride against him again and at Mike's invitation try and show him the way round The Island, but that was eight years away.

Jerry Wood was at Silverstone. "Mike said he'd like the bike's seat moving back to give him a bit more room because it was uncomfortable. I tried, but it would have meant a major job on the frame so I had to say sorry, it couldn't be done. 'That's OK', he said. He never complained. Mike made a terrible start, but at the end of the first lap he had caught the pack and started picking them off – and it was a strong field, Agostini, Saarinen,[14] Cooper. When he'd finished third he said 'Sorry, I made a mess of it'. He'd ridden a fantastic race, he didn't give up, he wouldn't give up and then he apologized to us."

Mike and Surtees both gave long interviews to *Motor Cycle News* in July 1971 about safety on the Isle of Man, which was then becoming a point of keen concern. This is what Mike said:

"I don't know what all the fuss is about. Courses are there to be ridden and the TT is still the finest in the world. Most of the chaps who are screaming about the dangers aren't going fast enough for it to matter anyway. Even Agostini doesn't have to ride as fast as he could.

"I think one of the reasons for the ballyhoo is some people don't realize that smoothing out the course does not remove the stone walls and the other hard scenery. It is all dangerous, particularly the Glen Helen section and the top of Cronk-y-Voddy, but I see no necessity to change these or any other part of the circuit.

"I find it incredible that a works rider should refuse to ride in the TT because he considers it too dangerous or that a World Champion should give up because it was wet. In my opinion such riders are not worth their salt. If I were a team manager I would not stand for it.

"As a spectacle I agree the TT has deteriorated. I spent a couple of days over there this year and the atmosphere was sadly lacking. I can't pin down the reason. Perhaps the disappearance of fast works bikes has something to do with it. The lovely noises have gone ..."

4

Mike came back to Grand Prix racing in 1971, driving the Surtees-Ford at Monza and Watkins Glen. He noted immediately how Formula One had changed, how sombre it seemed, how alien he felt it was to him. He found most of the drivers "stern" and "quite withdrawn". As he looked around he found only one kindred spirit: James Hunt. Mike couldn't quite understand why these drivers vanished into their motorhomes and stayed there. He was overtly lonely and was forced to a lifestyle remote from him: a return to the hotel alone, a read of a book, dinner and bed. Mike was now a father, too. Michelle was born on June 10.

The passage of time is sharply illustrated by the 23 drivers who lined up at Monza on September 5. Only five had been at Silverstone on July 20, 1963 when Mike drove his first Grand Prix: Amon, Siffert, Surtees, Graham Hill, Bonnier. The 1971 grid:

C. Amon	J. Ickx
Matra Simca	Ferrari
1m 22.40s	1m 22.82s

14. Jarno Saarinen, a Finn with the most rare gifts on a motorbike. In only four years of 250cc World Championship racing he won eight times and was Champion in 1972. In 1973 he was killed at Monza.

J. Siffert
BRM
1m 23.03s

H. Ganley
BRM
1m 23.15s

F. Cevert
Tyrrell-Ford
1m 23.41s

R. Peterson
March-Ford
1m 23.46s

J. Stewart
Tyrrell-Ford
1m 23.49s

C. Regazzoni
Ferrari
1m 23.69s

T. Schenken
Brabham-Ford
1m 23.73s

H. Pescarolo
March-Ford
1m 23.77s

P. Gethin
BRM
1m 23.88s

H. Marko
BRM
1m 23.96s

J. Oliver
McLaren-Ford
1m 24.09s

G. Hill
Brabham-Ford
1m 24.27s

J. Surtees
Surtees-Ford
1m 24.45s

M. Beuttler
March-Ford
1m 25.01s

M. Hailwood
Surtees-Ford
1m 25.17s

E. Fittipaldi
Lotus-Pratt & Witney
1m 25.18s

N. Galli
March-Ford
1m 25.19s

A. de Adamich
March-Alfa Romeo
1m 25.78s

J. Bonnier
McLaren-Ford
1m 26.14s

S. Moser
Bellasi-Ford
1m 26.54s

J.-P. Jarier
March-Ford
1m 28.19s

Monza was a curious circuit then, famed for mass and continuous slipstreaming. The driver of one car tucked in behind another, got the 'tow' and would slingshot by. The car he'd just overtaken then did the same to him. Cars swopped and swopped again, and it was deeply intoxicating for the crowd who liked and understood intoxication. These were races within the race and they carried within them an echo of Mike and Redman on bikes and the 'last five laps to count'.

No arrangements existed amongst the car drivers, but that was not the point. The swop-swopping of places might last the whole race, and it was the last corner of the last lap which counted, and maybe even the surge to the finishing line after the last corner.

In the morning warm-up Mike's engine misfired and it had to be replaced. That can be curious, too. In theory it has to be risky, in practice it often works magnificently. You can never tell.

Nobody truly knows how many drivers led the Italian Grand Prix or for how long. The calculations were done then, as now, on how many laps – not yards – a driver was in the lead, and across 55 laps seven men were recorded as doing that. Others, darting like a shoal of fish, may have had their noses in front for fleeting moments. Sometime around lap four a single second covered the first eight cars. Mike was among them. On lap 16 he went up to fourth with the slipstreaming pack front and rear of him. On lap 25 he pressed past Francois Cevert and Ronnie Peterson and took the lead in a Grand Prix for the first time in his life. It lasted three laps before Siffert, charging, sucked himself past all three of them and took the lead.

Siffert's BRM stuck in fourth gear. Cevert and Peterson fought for the lead, Mike lurked behind and retook it on lap 35 "really enjoying himself leaning heavily on the two young 'aces' in the corners" (*Motor Sport*). Amon now made his move, going from fourth to the lead in the space of a single lap, Peterson attacked – and failed – on lap 40, Mike attacked and succeeded on lap 42. This time his lead was very brief indeed. Amon went by and pulled away, but not by much. Gethin had been running a steady race, always in touch.

With five laps left Amon tugged at his dirt-encrusted face visor to fling it away. He had another visor underneath and it would be clean: perfect visiblity for the run-in. Both came away together and Amon's face was unprotected. He slowed. Peterson was in the lead, Cevert and Mike hounding him and still the slipstreaming went on, furious now. Mike led on lap 51, but Gethin came clean through, judging his race beautifully. Behind him Mike, Cevert and Peterson probed each other, rehearsing what would be a chess game on the last lap: who could slipstream who, and where to steal out and grasp the race?

Lap 54: Gethin, Peterson, Cevert, Mike.

Lap 55: They ran hard and headlong down the short straight into the Parabolica curve, shaped like a horseshoe and which flung them round to the full-power rush to the line. Cevert led, Peterson outbraked him into the Parabolica, Gethin elbowed through and the rush was on. Four cars crossed that line so close together that the result stands almost as a freak.

P. Gethin	1hr 18m 12.60s
R. Peterson	1hr 18m 12.61s
F. Cevert	1hr 18m 12.69s
M. Hailwood	1hr 18m 12.78s
and in its context *much* further behind	
H. Ganley	1hr 18m 13.21s

There is an amazing and delightful postscript to this race from Rob Walker. "They started with about eight or nine towing each other round and round, and on the last corner they were down to four and Mike was one of them. He said 'Rob, I just don't know what all this slipstreaming is about. I haven't done it before.' I don't think he did know, and I don't think he cared. He just drove for the joy of it."

In one distinct aspect driving wasn't either easy or natural to him. He needed a long time to accept that a car drifts, and once confessed that in the early days when a car did drift "I used to get into a bit of a panic". Even in these early Seventies it troubled him still because old, instinctive "memories and reactions" remained. "I think", he said, "that my earlier motorcycle experience probably explains why I'm rather prone to wear out the front tyres when I'm racing cars. I can't get rid of the habit of throwing a car into a corner instead of trying to float it in and then use a combination of throttle and steering wheel to get it round in the shortest possible time.

"Steering a bike is a combination of balance and very little arm movement, something like controlling a horse. In a car your arms seem to be thrashing around like windmills. It's much more tiring mentally because everything is happening that much quicker than on a bike."

Mike didn't go to the race after Monza, in Canada (the German Rolf Stommelen, then known as rent-a-driver, took over) but he did go to the last one of 1971, at Watkins Glen. The car wasn't on the pace and he thumped a guardrail – he had a slow puncture – with five laps left.

5

In 1972 Mike did virtually a full Formula One and Formula Two season. Formula Two was a nice balance between drivers coming up and drivers going down, while others no doubt just drove because that was what they did in life: drive. Surtees himself and Graham Hill made brief appearances, Gethin was at times a strong competitor, but there is a much more accurate and revealing guide to the quality of those Formula Two grids. They contained three future World Champions – Niki Lauda, Jody Scheckter and James Hunt – and half a dozen other men who would form the backbone of Formula One across the mid- and late Seventies (and in some cases beyond): Patrick Depailler, Carlos Reutemann, Wilson Fittipaldi, Jean-Pierre Jabouille, Carlos Pace, John Watson, Jochen Mass.

There is an irony. Jean-Pierre Jaussaud, who won three races and finished second in the table, made no impact on Formula One at all. He moved into sportscars and won Le Mans twice, in 1978 and 1980. The Formula Two Championship included at differing times during the season 'graded' drivers – men already established in Formula One – and their results were not counted in the final table. Their presence did, however, enable a proper evaluation of those who were up-and-coming against them. This is how Emerson Fittipaldi, then with Lotus, dabbled to the extent of winning three races and is not in that final table. The races, incidentally, tended to be over a two-heat aggregate.

"In 1971 John Surtees decided to build Formula Two cars for 1972", Brian Hart says. "He approached us and said 'I'm running Mike Hailwood, we're having a proper go at the European Championship'. We said 'Fine'. Formula Two was very popular in the late Sixties and continued right the way through, Jack Brabham, Denny Hulme, Jochen Rindt, the whole bit. They all did their racing every other weekend in Formula Two. We'd produced the engine for Ronnie Peterson in 1971, which was a 1.6-litre. Then the Formula went out to 2 litres. John had a good little car and we embarked on a season of racing.

"Mike took it much more seriously now because he was going back to a slightly lesser formula (than Formula One, of course), but he was still competing against top drivers and new drivers coming along. He thought he'd never go back to bikes. The calendar took us around quite a bit from Sweden right the way down to Enna in Italy, and Mike got very serious. John helped him a lot in setting up the car. That aspect of it was becoming more sophisticated."

In the Surtees Formula One car Mike had as a team-mate an Australian, Tim Schenken. Sawyer explains their respective merits. "Mike was very much like John Watson, quick on the day, but not so good in qualifying. Schenken was doing a lot of the testing. Mike would turn up at a circuit after Schenken had been there for a week, drive the car quicker and blow Schenken into the weeds.[15] Mike actually drove his Citroen-Maserati round Jarama in the dry as quickly as Schenken drove the Formula One Surtees in the wet..."

Mike didn't go to the first Formula One race of the season, in Argentina, but in the second, South Africa, he seemed to have broken open a real career. He qualified on the second row and on lap 20 he set what would remain the fastest lap of the race as he attacked Fittipaldi for second place. On lap 23 he powered past Fittipaldi and went after Stewart in the lead. He caught him in two laps and began to search for a place to overtake – then a bolt in the rear wishbone mounting broke. He had to struggle hard to control the car while he was bringing it to rest.

"He had Stewart totally fixed", Surtees says, "and then that happened. It was bad for the team. I suppose the failure was in some ways human error ..."

In the end, of course, they all are.

Mike finished fifth in the opening Championship F2 race at Mallory Park. In Formula One at Jarama the electrics went on lap 20. At this meeting he made an interesting discovery about Rob Walker. "Mike came and had dinner with me at my hotel, we had a really good dinner and drinks. I was telling him a few stories, some of my wartime recollections of flying and that sort of thing, and suddenly Mike realized I was not a stuffy old bastard after all. From that moment on we were kindred spirits. We both did the same dreadful things, but in different eras. We became bosom pals. In Formula One he didn't like the people at first, he hated them because he thought that they were so snooty and considered a *bikey* beneath their dignity. In fact he had been to a far better school than any of them. He was the son of a millionaire, he had been to a naval college."

In F2 Mike got no points at Thruxton or Hockenheim. Just before the Monaco Grand Prix he was captured wonderfully in Marlboro's film of the year. It was a vignette. There he was beside the harbour, his hair had begun to recede, but the smile was the same and the smile was broad. Clouds were gathering over Monte Carlo and a wet race loomed. A wet race there – the 'circuit' is hemmed by armco and studded by corners – was the equivalent of water-skiing without the comfort of the sea beneath you. He was asked for his considered opinion. "Well, I don't know, it depends on the weather, I guess. If it rains I don't think I'll bother to go out", and the words buried themselves deep into gurgling laughter. "In the rain I'm absolutely hopeless. I'm the best crasher there is in the rain." And yes, the big smile to accompany that. No Formula One driver says those things today. Only Mike said them even then. In the race he and Ganley crashed, his oil pipe was damaged and he dropped out.

---

15. Motorsport expression for blowing or being blown away.

Preparing to tackle The Island. Mike and the 125 Paton with Bill Lacey and Giuseppe Pattoni before the start of the 1958 TT. (*Picture courtesy Mick Woollett.*)

Talented trio. Tarquinio Provini, Carlo Ubbiali and newcomer Mike Hailwood, who finished in the order 2-1-3 in the 1958 250cc TT. (*Picture courtesy Mick Woollett.*)

Mike rounding the hairpin at Brands Hatch on his 250 Honda-six in 1967, giving a perfect demonstration of speed and balance. (*Picture courtesy Nick Nicholls.*)

Getting down to it. Mike astride his 500cc Honda during a non-championship race in Italy in 1968. (*Picture courtesy Mick Woollett.*)

Silverstone, 1971. Although he always shunned publicity, Mike was invariably co-operative with autograph hunters, with whom he was inundated throughout his career. (*Picture courtesy Mick Woollett.*)

Daytona, 1971, and this time Mike was competing with a 750cc BSA along with team-mate Jim Rice. (*Picture courtesy Mick Woollett.*)

Even Stan Hailwood found time to relax now and again. (*Picture courtesy Chris Buckler.*)

Mike and his son David taking it easy in South Africa. (*Picture courtesy John Cooper.*)

Mike wasn't the first single-seater driver to discover the hard way that the rear wheels of a racing car are invariably wider than the fronts. It was the front bumper of the Ford Transit that came off worst in this tangle in the Silverstone paddock, but understandably John Surtees was more concerned about the state of the Formula One car's left rear tyre. (*Pictures courtesy Martyn Pass.*)

Mike about to put his Yardley McLaren on the second row of the grid at Silverstone for the 1974 *Daily Express* Trophy race. Four months later, when running fifth in the German GP, his car took off over one of Nurburgring's notorious humps, landed badly and left the track, Mike's serious leg injuries bringing his driving career to an end. (*Picture courtesy Martyn Pass.*)

Relaxing with Phil Read before the start of one of his 1978 Isle of Man TT 'comeback' races. (*Picture courtesy Mick Woollett.*)

Mike on the start line for the 1978 Formula One race with his Ducati. Ted Macauley had arranged for him the start number 12, his score of past TT victories. In a little over two hours he would have added another. (*Picture courtesy Mick Woollett.*)

Another nostalgic ride. Mike aboard the Ducati during his return to Mallory Park in June 1978. (*Picture courtesy Nick Nicholls.*)

A hotel sign on the TT course in 1978 that says it all. Mike's return to The Island brought visitors from the mainland in their droves. (*Picture courtesy Nick Nicholls.*)

Shortly before his death, Mike paid a return visit to Daytona, the scene of many happy memories. Here he is with Ted Macauley, Trevor Tilbury and Nobby Clark. (*Picture courtesy Nobby Clark.*)

Two weeks later Mike ought to have won his first F2 victory at Crystal Palace. "Maybe I'd seen him riding at the Ulster Grand Prix years before", John Watson says, "but if I had it didn't register clearly because I am not a big motorcycle enthusiast. I first met him at Crystal Palace. I found him very friendly, very helpful, unlike a lot of other people who are competitors. Very often competitors don't want to give something to somebody who may turn round and beat them. Mike always seemed to be more than willing to give advice and assistance, and genuinely. He was nice, easy company to be in and probably a better driver than he himself believed."

The race was won by Jody Scheckter, who remembered Mike from the Springbok series – Scheckter was South African – and equally remembers that "I was really competitive at Crystal Palace. Mike was leading, but I couldn't get past him and it became a stalemate. I caught and passed him right towards the end because his rear rollbar broke free of one of its mountings."

That mid-season was turn and turn about. On June 4, in the Belgian Grand Prix at Nivelles, he held off a determined thrust from Pace and was fourth. On June 11 he got no points in F2 at Hockenheim, then finished second to Fittipaldi (a graded driver) at Rouen on June 25. "Mike did particularly well there", Hart says, "and it became obvious about that time that he was in with a chance of winning the Championship. You could see him getting more and more serious. It meant quite a bit to be European Champion." In the French Grand Prix at Clermont-Ferrand on July 2 he was sixth. In F2 at the Osterreichring on July 9 he was second behind Fittipaldi again. The gearbox failed in the British Grand Prix at Brands Hatch on July 15, and he got no F2 points at Imola on July 23.

The front suspension failed in the German Grand Prix at the Nurburgring. Rob Walker remembers nothing of that, but he does remember The Ring. They were staying at the Sporthotel at the circuit, and the night before the race "four women turned up, and each one came from a different country and he had had no idea whatsoever they were coming. He was trying to farm them out amongst his friends. At my age I had to lock my bedroom door."

Between the Nurburgring and the next Grand Prix, Austria, he won a Formula Two race at Mantorp Park in Sweden, although only because Gethin had a puncture. The Championship table read: Hailwood 37, Jassaud 27, Reutemann 24, Lauda 21, David Morgan 19, Bob Wollek 17. He was fourth in that Austrian Grand Prix, won the first heat of the Formula Two race at Enna, Sicily, but the car broke down in the second. Jassaud could only finish sixth, and that was 37–28. Mike won at the Salzburgring, Jassaud's engine let go, and that was 46–28. *Autosport* reported that "at the front Hailwood never looked like losing his lead, although Pace was right behind. The former motorcycle champion was happy in the knowledge that his team-mate would not deprive him of the important overall win. The gap between them was 0.52s." It had evidently been an "incredibly exciting slipstreamer".

There would be none of that at Monza, the next Formula One race. Gethin's average winning speed in 1971 represented an alarming peak, the culmination of an inexorable rise since 1962 when the old banking circuit had finally been abandoned – the same banking on which Bob McIntyre had set his world record on the 350 Gilera in 1957. Without the banked section the average speed had been cut from 213.776kph in 1961 to 202.346 in 1962, but under the impetus of racing car technology every year after it rose, going back up past 213kph in 1965, and it kept on going, breaking 240kph in 1969. The organizers might have been delighted to have the fastest circuit in the world, but what if something happened at these speeds? They adopted the traditional remedy: chicanes. These chicanes are two of the ones you see today, the first at the end of the start-finish straight, the second at the Curva del Vialone, before the pump-and-push to the Parabolica.

The Italian Grand Prix of September 10, 1972 could decide the World Championship. Fittipaldi needed only three points, and if he didn't get them it was theoretically possible for either Stewart (Tyrrell) or Ickx (Ferrari) to catch him over the last two races, Canada and Watkins Glen.

When Fittipaldi checked into his hotel the receptionist said that there had been a terrible accident to the Lotus transporter. Fittipaldi went for an uneasy dinner with Frank Williams, and Pace, who happened to be around, returned to the hotel. Lotus team manager Peter Warr had arrived and he ticked off the extent of it. A tyre had burst, the transporter was wrecked, there were injuries, Fittipaldi's car was damaged.

Fortunately, Colin Chapman had a spare car in the Lotus Formula Two transporter just over the French border in Chamonix. It was there as a precaution. Twice Lotus had been in court proceedings at Monza: Jim Clark was involved in the crash which killed Wolfgang von Trips in 1961, and Rindt had died during qualifying in 1969.

In Italy, you could never tell if the repercussions of this were continuing, and the spare was in France where it couldn't be impounded. Fittipaldi would have to race this spare. He put it on the third row of the grid (Ickx was on pole). Mike was on the fifth row.

At the start, Stewart's clutch failed and virtually the whole field weaved past him. Mike, coming hard, flicked sharp left and almost put two wheels on the grass, but he missed Stewart and so did everybody else. Lap one: Ickx, Regazzoni, Fittipaldi, Andretti, Amon, Mike. By lap five Amon and Mike were attacking Fittipaldi – Andretti had fallen back – and Fittipaldi was moving on Ickx and Regazzoni.

Regazzoni took the lead on lap 14 and now the first five cars had bunched. There were still 41 laps left. Regazzoni touched Pace, who'd spun, a wheel was torn off, the Ferrari struck the barrier and burst into flames. Regazzoni got out and moved to safety. Fittipaldi was only one and a half seconds behind Ickx, and Amon and Mike were clinging to Fittipaldi. Midway through the race Fittipaldi did attack Ickx, Amon and Mike still clinging – "despite the fact that the latter had lost his airbox, which flew into the air and nearly hit Schenken, who had just been lapped by the leaders" (*Autosport*).

With 20 laps to go Amon fell away – brake wear – and with 10 laps to go Ickx suddenly felt the Ferrari's engine cut out. Electronics. Fittipaldi saw Ickx's arm go up – the traditional gesture meaning *I'm in trouble, miss me* – and the World Championship was spread before him; but he wanted to take it in the style of a Champion, wanted to win the race. Mike had been losing a second a lap for some time with a fuel leak, and Fittipaldi, anxious to save fuel himself, brought his braking points forward, smoothed the way he approached each corner. He could see from the pit board signals that Mike was gaining, but he calculated that even reducing his speed the gap would be big enough. That last lap was a long one and as Fittipaldi reached the Parabolica he took the car in fast, a great flurry of speed, so that if it did run out he'd have enough momentum to coast to the line. The car made it anyway, and he won it by 14.5 seconds.

Never before had Mike finished second in a Grand Prix. He never would again.

"That fault at Monza", Surtees muses. "A bit of solder fell off. It never happens ..."

Two weeks later Jaussaud won the Formula Two race at Albi, France. Mike's car failed in the first heat, although he won the second and set fastest lap. That was 46–37. Mike and Brian Hart went quietly off for a meal. It left Hockenheim, and that was anti-climactic. Jaussaud's drive-shaft broke and Mike came home second to Schenken. "We did Hockenheim, which was a hell of a party", Hart says. "Afterwards we all had a meal then a real good party. Mike said 'Right, come on, we'll go home now'. It was 4.30 in the morning. He had his Citroen-Maserati and we drove to England through the night. He was alright on the roads, he wasn't a lunatic on the roads. We slept in a lay-by for a bit and when we woke we wandered back.

"In those days the races were double heats and the result calculated on aggregate, so you had to be fairly sensible to get that right. He didn't show colossal emotion when he'd won it, he didn't go absolutely over the top, but he was very happy to be European Champion. I think then he realized he'd got a future on four wheels.

"He was quietly spoken, bordering on the shy, a nice bloke. He wasn't a totally outgoing personality, but once you got to know him he was very likable. He could be very serious. He thought seriously about his future and he wanted to do well in cars. He didn't necessarily take the rest of life so seriously. Superficially he was prepared to party, and then there were the women and what-not." Well, yes, the habits of a lifetime.

Final European points:

1.	Mike Hailwood	55
2.	Jean-Pierre Jaussaud	37
3.	Patrick Depailler	27
4.	Carlos Reutemann	26
5.	Niki Lauda	25
6.	David Morgan	23
7.	Bob Wollek	21
8.	Jody Scheckter	15
9.	Peter Gethin	10
10.	Mike Beuttler	10

Between them Lauda and Scheckter would win four World Championships; between them Depailler, Reutemann, Lauda, Scheckter and Gethin would win 50 Grands Prix. Mike might have joined them, but he'd always be that 14.5 seconds short, Monza, September 10, 1972.

Ian Phillips, reviewing the season for *Autosport*, said: "Hailwood's determined driving was a joy to watch." It was.

6

"And there was another time at the Swedish Grand Prix. A girl came down from Stockholm the night before practice and she didn't arrive until two in the morning. I said to Mike 'Did you do her?', and he said 'She'd come all that way you know, Rob, I couldn't really let her down'." This is Rob Walker again, and the story is instructive for another reason altogether. "Mike was definitely a bit off for practice, but he said 'For God's sake don't tell John Surtees'."

Mike's approach to the matter of being alive was very different from that of Surtees. Some speak of Mike sneaking about the pits unshaven on the morning after the night before so that Surtees couldn't see what condition he was in, but Surtees was, if he'll forgive me, a wise old bird and Surtees knew, Surtees knew.

"One of the good things I found working with Mike in cars was that on and off the track he was absolutely honest. He was the only one I could rely on to keep to what he said. He was trusting and that is probably why he got taken for a ride by a number of his ex-friends in business. The only time Mike became cold and calculating and decisive was when the flag fell for a race.

"In the immediate period before that, the practice days and nights, Mike was so wound up, and this explains in my mind his lifestyle. Mike couldn't keep to the pattern which champions often do or pretend they do: early to bed, deep sleep in order to get up in the morning all super fresh. I don't think that if Mike had gone to bed early he would have slept, he'd have needed all sorts of sleeping pills and God knows what else. We had a friendly relationship. Friends would go out with him on the town and this is the way he kept himself calm, this is the way that the nervous edge which is very important for a competitor didn't become dominant.

"In one sense he'd be tired and weary, but in fact the competitive side of him was still relatively fresh because it hadn't gone through a hell of a night of worrying about it. Of course we made certain he didn't get into too much trouble, and overall the important thing was we could sit down and talk." Mike knew that Surtees knew he couldn't corral him, and in fact felt that he influenced Surtees to relax and enjoy himself. Mike found a lovely word for that. John Surtees had *mellowed*.

"We won the Formula Two Championship and we didn't have the full 2-litre size engine, we had to make do with an 1,850. Brian Hart worked very nicely with us, it helped to put Brian on the map and helped us, too. We had a nice relationship with Brian. He adored Mike.

"I had been schooling Mike to take over from me. I was not driving all the time. The team had no real budget, we had a bit of sponsorship here and there, which just about built the cars, and we had to rely on drivers to have money of their own. We would, however, be able to support one and I wanted that to be Mike. We did Formula 5000, Formula Two, we brought Mike into Formula One with a development car. I drove it to get a good feel of it because that helped me to relate to what was happening in it when he came along and said 'the car's doing this or the car's doing that'. I could say 'Fine'. Mike would say 'Oh, if you set the thing up as you like it, that is how I like it'. And that is how he liked the cars.

"Too many drivers considered that they could set this up, set that up and virtually none of them could. Working with Mike the important thing was that he was honest. He would say 'I went into this corner and it did this'. He didn't say 'I'll change a bar, I'll alter this or that'. He just gave you the message of what the car had done. I understood what was happening and we'd change it. That is why we made a good team: because I understood the car, because I had been behind the design of it and I'd driven it. When he left my team (for Yardley McLaren) it was more difficult because they did not understand him as much as

I did. We come back to his basic honesty. He did not pretend to know what parts should be changed.

"As a driver he was good, very good. At one period he was partnering Carlos Pace – Pace was an incredibly good driver early in his career, although he made mistakes and he was a bit temperamental. Mike and he did not clash at all. Pace would go out and do a time, Mike would get a bit dispirited, and then go out and have a go at it, and that was good."

"I remember speaking to Mike and I asked him why Carlos Pace was faster than he was", Nobby Clark says. "I wondered if there was a difference in the two cars. 'No', Mike said, 'he is just so much faster than I am!'"

"John had quite an influence on Mike", Hart says. "They had a few rows, but Mike knew he had to rely on someone to get it all going and set it up. John knew a lot about that, and the cars were nice little cars. But there were a few humdingers. Mike was a natural driver, just as he was with bikes. Sometimes he'd say 'Leave the car alone and I'll drive it'. John would not agree and try and get him to flog round and do 10 more test laps, but Mike would say 'No, no, no, I'll just drive it'.

"Mike had this strong personality, but it didn't come over because you thought he was a little bit shy. The strength of the personality wasn't apparent to you, but when you considered what he'd achieved he clearly had it. He had to have it. I personally never saw him lose his temper.

"Then, at the end of 1972, he did a series in Brazil. It was just a Brazilian Formula Two series, it was at Interlagos and he was a riot out there ..."

Yes, Mike was a riot out there. The tournament was over three races, he was third in the second of them and won the third, and it was a good field, Emerson Fittipaldi, Pace, Hunt, Jaussaud *et al*. The riot? He arrived at one circuit after a monster night of convivial boozing and two hours sleep, strapped himself in the car, set off, and in the heat and humidity sweated it out. He was very sober when the race ended. The riot? A lady of easy virtue was caught in his room concealing money in a very strange place when the police burst in and the audience tried to scatter (one journalist hid in a closet and escaped). Another journalist fell deeply and desperately in love with a dusky lady – the kind which abound in Brazil – and over dinner was stroking the beads round her neck in an act of great affection. "Bet he wouldn't be doing that," Mike whispered, "if he knew where those beads were half an hour ago ..."

7

There's a true story that before the start of the Grand Prix races in 1973 Mike would tuck a paperback into his driving overalls so that "I'll have something to read when the car breaks down". He favoured detective stories and claimed he did a *lot* of reading during the Austrian Grand Prix.

The Surtees, a car which would evolve during the season, did break down. The driveshaft went on lap 11 in Argentina, the gearbox on lap seven in Brazil. And they went to South Africa. For once Pauline went to the race. She and Mike stayed with Paddy Driver, who lived some five or six miles from Kyalami. They commuted to and from the circuit on a motorbike which, if you can't get a helicopter, is the best way. Mike qualified on the fifth row and "Paddy and some others said to me 'Come on down to this particular bend, it's great watching from there'." The bend was called Crowthorne. "I thought no, no, I'll go to the pits, and that's where I went."

Mike ran eighth across the first two laps. Denny Hulme was leading, Scheckter second, Fittipaldi third, Peter Revson fourth, Peterson fifth, Reutemann sixth, Dave Charlton, an experienced South African in a Lotus seventh, then Mike. They flowed down the long, long start-finish straight into the right-hander at the end. Crowthorne.

Charlton pulled over and tried to take Reutemann on the outside as they were going in. Charlton lost control but Reutemann made it safely through on the inside. Mike couldn't avoid the front of Charlton's Lotus, smacked into it and spun away round Crowthorne. Charlton was beached on the kerbing pointing the right way, but out of the race. Stewart flicked out to miss Charlton, Mike was spinning in front of him, Stewart flicked back inside and Stewart made it safely through.

Regazzoni, close behind Stewart, may well have been able to see virtually nothing. Of it he has no memory. He struck Mike's Surtees and began to spin himself. Ickx, following, brushed against Regazzoni who slid away towards the exit of the corner, slid across the run-off area and Mike slid there, too. "Charlton lost it", Mike would say, "I hit him, and consequently spun and stalled in the middle of the track. Regazzoni came round and hit my car. The whole lot burst into flames and we disappeared off the edge of the track. I pressed my fire extinguisher, put my fire out, looked across and Regga was unconscious in the car."

The side of Regazzoni's car was torn out and the car burst into flames. A ball of yellowing fire gushed and belched from it perhaps eight, perhaps 10 feet high. Regazzoni, unconscious, was trapped.

The Surtees had come to rest almost interlocked with it. Mike levered himself up in his cockpit, his arms working as urgently as pistons to do that, was close enough to reach into the flames standing in his cockpit, but wasn't close enough to reach Regazzoni. He sprang full out of the Surtees, dipped full into the flames, unbuckled Regazzoni's seat belt and began hauling at him. "I was trying to pull him out by one arm, which was all I could get at. The car's left side was stoved in. I just couldn't pull him out by the one arm. His legs were trapped because the car was squashed." A marshal sprinted up and now the fire belched from the bottom of the BRM. Mike's feet were in flames. Both hands were plumes of flame. For an instant the intensity of the inferno forced him to twist his head away. He turned back, hauled again, but the flames were licking up his legs. He was going to burn to death himself. As Mike put it, "I burst into flames".

He sprinted across the track through the debris of the crash to where he could see a grassy, sandy area. He flung himself down and rolled over and over to quench the fire on him. "I'd been involved in the accident", Ickx says, "and parked my car some distance away. I was running back as Mike was running across the track. He was on fire. I tried to smother it as best I could." Ickx dived on Mike to do it. By now the BRM was only smouldering because the marshal had been spraying it with foam. Other marshals were hauling at Regazzoni. The car burst into flames again. Mike sprinted back across the track and dipped in again. Standing on the car he gripped Regazzoni under the armpits and hauled him out.

Pauline knew nothing of this. What she did know was that the Surtees had not come round past the pits to complete another lap as it ought to have done. "When Mike returned his face was totally ashen. He jerked his thumb to say

'Come on, we're getting out of here', we grabbed our crash helmets and that was it, we were off, off and gone. At Paddy's he had a vodka and tonic and he didn't want to talk. I knew something had happened, but I thought he would tell me when he was ready. I didn't know about it until I saw it in the newspapers the following morning."

Mike was given a special award, a *Prix Rouge et Blanc Jo Siffert* named after the Swiss driver killed in a fiery car at Brands Hatch in 1971. Mike was later awarded the George Medal, the highest in Britain for civilian bravery. He went to Buckingham Palace to receive it and looked extremely smart in a morning suit, posed for photographers – that smile again – and sincerely wondered what all the fuss was about.

When he could be persuaded to discuss what he had done he said "If you sat back and thought about it coolly and calmly you'd certainly run the other way (little laugh) but when you're in a race you've got the adrenalin going anyway so you're pretty het up. Of course I was in a situation where the car was burning, but I had all the fireproof overalls and helmet and breathing apparatus. I really wasn't in any danger. It was just one of those things you do on the spur of the moment." He was sure anyone would have done the same...

Regazzoni had only minor burns, something barely believable. Regazzoni would say simply: "Mike saved my life".

The rest of 1973 was hard, it was frustrating, it was depressing on the track. In Spain the oil pipe went on lap 25. At Zolder he crashed on lap five, although socially, as Rob Walker attests (if it needs any attesting) "we had a jolly good time and Mike was Mike. I said to him after the race 'Where are you going now?' and he said 'Oh, I don't know. I might go to Paris, I might go to the South of France, I might go and see someone in Germany.' 'Are you alright for money?' 'Well, I've got £5 on me.' 'How the hell are you going to get on with only £5?' 'If you haven't got any more you can't spend it, can you?' In fact he ran out of petrol somewhere on the way to Le Mans. I can't remember what he did to get some ..."

At Monaco he battled to the end, eighth, but three laps behind the winner, Stewart; in Sweden he stopped with tyre vibrations; in France he stopped with an oil leak; at Silverstone he was embroiled in the famous (or infamous) multiple crash on lap one. It was all somehow the pattern of a season. He stopped in Holland with an electrical failure, finished 14th at the Nurburgring. "He was the last of the great amateur drivers", Rob Walker says. "I remember so well after the Nurburgring. There was Mike in the paddock sitting on a seat with a girl on his lap, his leg up the girl's thigh and drinking a bottle of wine with one hand. They don't do that sort of thing now. You wouldn't even get the other chaps of that era to do it, either. Well, you might possibly get Graham Hill."

He was 10th in Austria, but five laps off the pace, seventh at Monza, ninth in Canada, the rear suspension failed at Watkins Glen. It meant he had not secured a single point all season, and anyway Surtees couldn't keep him.

"It was very unfortunate he did not win three or four Grands Prix with us", Surtees says. "That would have been the spark, that would have given him the confidence. In the end he did the deal with McLaren, but I had a great sadness because Mike was my best chance of the team staying together and progressing. I only wish I could have done it financially. If you look at the competitiveness of our cars on a minute budget it was bloody good. What made me upset was that so often we had the tail wagging the dog (lack of money). We had a ridiculous budget. To win the Formula Two Championship it was less than £25,000.

"The first decent budget we were ever going to get was when we did a deal with Bang and Olufsen, that was going to be £105,000 for 1974. They were the people who insisted upon Mike going. I had to tell him in America. I'd warned him beforehand and then down at the Watkins Glen Motel I said 'Sorry, Mike, they won't have it. They insist that Germany is a very important market and they need a German, so I have to put Jochen Mass in the car.' Frankly the deal was my only chance for developing the company. We designed and built everything from scratch, you see.

"He was disappointed, I was disappointed, I was angry about the whole thing, but financially we were already up to here, we did not have any other chance. As it turned out it was the beginning of the end because we never did get the money.

"As a driver he was bloody good. At that stage, and particularly on reflection, he needed us and we needed him. He needed us because of our similar backgrounds which enabled us to communicate and understand each other when it came to the nitty-gritty. There was mutual trust between us."

Mike also drove sportscars this year of 1973, partnering Watson. "I got involved with John Wyer and the Gulf Mirage programme. Mike and I were in one car, Derek Bell and Howden Ganley in the other. Our first race was, I think, at Daytona. Mike had a very scary moment on the banking during the night. Daytona is black, no moonlight, and something failed on the car, something came off, and although I didn't see it, it must have been a very frightening experience. He took it in a light-hearted, phlegmatic, understated way."

Mike joined McLaren, who paid him £10,000 and would run three cars – his under the banner of Yardley, a previous team sponsor, the other two for Hulme and Emerson Fittipaldi under the banner of Texaco – for 1974. The wisdom of running three cars has always been questioned, which is why today every Formula One team is restricted to two. A third can stretch resources mercilessly and inevitably stretches the management, too.

"I used to travel to some of the races", Hart says. "It is extremely difficult for a team to run three cars. Denny was very much in his prime, he'd been World Champion with Brabham and he was an experienced campaigner. Mike and he got on well together. It's difficult to see in a way where Mike would have gone if he hadn't joined McLaren. It was a fairly logical conclusion. What was interesting was that even in Formula One everyone had an enormously high regard for the bloke. Formula One was better in those days from that point of view (human contact) but still a bit of a closed shop.

"It may well be that because of his shyness and because he was Mike Hailwood people didn't go up to him and he took that as stand-offishness, and it certainly wasn't like that in bikes. There you all mucked in and the rapport between them was phenomenal. In the end he was accepted in Formula One. He had a very strong determination, but not the dedication to allow your whole life to be swallowed by it. As a generalization Formula One didn't take itself as seriously as it does now, and that suited Mike fine. He'd quietened down a bit, too, although he was the last of them before the world got serious."

It started well enough with a strong fourth in Argentina, a fifth in Brazil – though that was a hard one because the car developed a vibration which made it "murder" to steer, and by race's end he felt his arms were almost wrenched out of their sockets – then a third in South Africa. Leo Wybrott worked for McLaren then. "I went to the first three races. Mike was a very happy-go-lucky person, very serious about what he was doing, but only to a point. There was an element in Mike which always enjoyed itself. When the racing came along and we started the practice and so on he had an ability to switch on and off to the job in hand. I sometimes think he wasn't quite the sort of animal that he needed to be for Formula One. He was committed, but there was a lot more to life. The car was very much equal to the works cars, it wasn't second string at all, and in fact we had two cars for him (one race, one spare) from as early as Holland, which was mid-June."

This 1974 season Mike also contested the World Sportscar Championship, this time with Derek Bell, who would become one of the best exponents of wielding the big cars and winning in them. "He could abuse himself to all kinds of lengths and still do a brilliant race. He had the most amazing physique, slim hips, broad shoulders, strong arms, he was such a fit-looking bastard. He drank and ate and screwed, everything a driver shouldn't do. I was never that capable and there aren't many who are.

"I never knew him when he rode bikes. I first got to know him when he was doing Formula 5000. I turned down the drive at Surtees – and he took it – because I didn't want to go back from being a Grand Prix driver in 1970 to 5000 in 1971. I should have done because apart from having a good time Mike won the Championship and went into Formula One in the Surtees.

"These days guys get out of a car and sit there gaping at the back of it hoping some thought is going to hit them in the face and say 'This will make the car a second quicker'. Mike was the same as me, the car was there to be driven and afterwards he'd say 'Let's get the hell out of here'. We'd go and sup wine or something.

"He didn't get drunk at the races, he looked after himself. Strong, fit people can take a lot more than anybody else, although the odd thing is I'm fit and I hope strong, but I can't take it. To Mike it was something very natural in that he didn't have to work to keep fit.

"We drove thousands of miles together to races across Europe in his Citroen-Maserati, this bloody great thumping thing. He'd have the stereo on full-blast, he floored it and we just drove. He didn't talk too much. He didn't suffer fools. I was surprised I got on with him because at the start I had difficulty finding common ground. I couldn't find out whether he really liked me, then ultimately I realized that he did. At the time I was never really sure. He appeared to like me, but I thought: *Why? I don't understand this. What does he see in me as a friend?* (Bell was not yet famous, and perhaps assumed that a man of Mike's stature would be more comfortable among the famous – an error as easy to make as assuming Rob Walker was a stuffy old bastard, and equally hilariously wrong.)

"I think it was because I wasn't pushing or, in his opinion, trying to play a Jacky Ickx. He always hated Jacky. 'I'll have the (expletive) off today', he'd say. Basically Jacky and I got on terribly well towards the end (the Eighties), and particularly now, but in those days Ickx always got it right for himself, he was the most selfish man you've ever met. That was why he was such a star: because he made sure that Ickx got the best.

"Mike thought Ickx was a real little (expletive) because Ickx was too much of a star, Ickx played the part, Mike just played Mike. Mike was the Steve McQueen of motor racing, Mike didn't like all the glamour, he just liked getting on and doing it. He was really an unwilling hero, and sometimes he was terribly lonely. He was surrounded by sycophantic people, but that's what happens so much to guys who are that talented.

"We were at Monza driving together. You can imagine at Monza the fans didn't come for the sportscars, they came to see Hailwood, the king of bikes. The paddock was as full as it is for a Grand Prix today and there was no control. People used to· walk around the motorhomes – it was the early days of motorhomes. Mike had this bloody awful big American thing. He opened the door and said 'Why don't you lot eff off?' and they were all saying in their Italian accents 'Mike, Mike, Mike!'. The driver of the motorhome said something and Mike said 'I'm not effing walking out here, let me drive.' So he gets in the seat and drives the motorhome out of the paddock, almost grinding little Italians into pulp.

"It disturbed me. I thought how could anybody treat his fans like that, because without them you're nobody, but Mike didn't need them, Mike didn't thrive on anything like that, Mike had had a lifetime of it and Italians are particuarly over the top, anyway."

His Formula One season stuttered, ninth in Spain, seventh in Belgium, slid off on oil at Monaco, fuel leak in Sweden.

Guy Edwards was a young man driving a Lola-Ford: "After the race at Monaco we were in the Tip Top Bar having a beer or two or three (chuckle), and a chap wandered up, a real drunken pain in the backside, and he swayed in front of Mike and said in a slurred voice 'Hailwood you're a has-been'. Mike put his beer down and I thought he was going to wallop him, but he just said 'Well, mate, it's better than being a never-was'." Always there would be people invading his space, at traffic lights on the Champs Elysees, in hundreds at Monza, singly in bars. It was part of the price of a life, however unwelcome, and it had to be paid.

The centrepiece of the sportscar season remained Le Mans. "We went there with John Wyer and it was a very serious effort", Bell says. "We knew that one year we were going to win the bloody race. I did my stint, he got in and did his, I did the next and as I was handing the car over to him again I said 'Mike, I think there's something wrong with the gearbox. It won't last.' He said 'Don't you worry, I'll make sure we get to Paris for dinner tonight', and of course what happened? The car ran all the way to the end and finished fourth, which in one way was rather wonderful, but a bit of a pain in the ass in another. Mike was a bloody good driver, he was really very good, much better than anyone gave him credit for. He was a natural, a total natural, and there aren't many who are like that."

This is Mike talking at Le Mans in 1974. Question: Is it very difficult to drive at the speeds you do at night?

"Not really, it's fairly easy here because you have some long straights and the corners are relatively easy. The big problem is the differential in speed between the slower cars and ourselves, 70, 80 miles an hour in some cases. Some of the drivers are rather inexperienced, and don't seem to know what they are doing, they don't spend a lot of time looking in their mirrors. This is the biggest problem, but really it seems to be quite easy and rather boring. I've fallen asleep twice going down the Mulsanne Straight (chuckle). I don't think the race is dangerous from a fatigue point of view, but I think it's too long; 24-hour racing is a bore to the drivers, the managers, the mechanics, nobody enjoys it at all except the spectators, but they are the most important people. I prefer Grand Prix racing, but it's much harder." (I've covered Le Mans for a decade and a half and rarely heard such perceptive or honest words.)

In Holland he finished fourth. At this meeting he made a cryptic and instructive comment to Nigel Roebuck of *Autosport* about what he really thought of Grand Prix racing, too. "Have you ever seen", he said, scanning the paddock and the drivers all locked into themselves, "so many miserable buggers earning half a million quid a year?"

In France he was seventh, in Britain he spun off and, yes, it was hard. Ralph Bryans went to the race and "Mike invited us into the motorhome and we sat there. I noticed he was uptight. His finger nails were bitten down to the quicks. He looked to be a bundle of nerves, which was completely unlike Mike. Denny Hulme came in and they were having a discussion with the tyre people who were asking questions so I said 'It's best we go'. We shook hands and left it at that."

He qualified mid-grid at the Nurburgring despite going off heavily at the chicane at the end of the long straight when a front wishbone broke. "He wrote off the race car, chassis number one, in practice", Wybrott says, "so he raced chassis number seven, which was the spare car, and was having a very successful race." On lap 12 Mike was fifth behind Ickx and harrying him (you'd better believe it), Ronnie Peterson directly behind. Ickx and Peterson were in Lotuses and Mike was, as someone noted, "surrounded by them", or as Wybrott puts it, "sandwiched between them".

At the Pflanzgarten, a curve leading to a hard left with a rise, all three vaulted into the air as they would have to do, but the Yardley McLaren came down crooked. "It was", Wybrott says, "a particularly bumpy jump on the homeward leg and he landed wrong, he was unable to control the car and it went off. It spun over to the right and some 50 yards after it had landed went head-first into the armco." Mike stabbed the brakes hard enough when he landed to churn smoke from the rear wheels and lay rubber tracks. The front right of the car took the initial impact against the armco, and anyway hitting the armco "wasn't a bad thing of itself, but the car did it between two points and that allowed the armco to give way, so the car slid down it instead of glancing off. As it travelled down it hit the post and that actually stopped the car. That was the point of impact which drove the suspension through the car".

In fact it churned on for a little way, still going downhill. The front right wheel was torn away and cantered down that hill like a child's hoop. The nosecone had been savaged, shards of it flying away. The car pirouetted round the sharp right-hander at the base of the hill, but mercifully on the grassy verge which ran along before the armco. That was pure luck – and lucky. Peterson came upon it but had enough room to hug the far side of the track, missing the debris and Mike.

Mike stayed conscious throughout and busied himself directing the rescue operation. He was still in the car when Ickx and Peterson came past on their next lap, and laps were taking more than seven minutes. Mike had hurt both ankles and fractured his right calf and knee. He spent the night in hospital at Adenau near the circuit, was flown back to London and had the knee pinned at St Thomas' Hospital. "I broke a collar bone and an ankle when I was motorcycle racing", he said, "but never anything as bad as this". Brian Hart remembers talking to Hulme about the shunt "and Denny said Mike was pretty lucky..."

Mike confessed that while some people spoke of a car failure, something must have broken and so on, he felt it was his own lapse of concentration. No excuses. But he'd never made excuses, never would.

McLaren optimistically talked of Mike being fit to return for the Canadian Grand Prix two months away.

He never drove a Grand Prix car again.

"The 1974 season was the first time I'd met him", Edwards says, "and the very first sight of him I got was the receding rear of his Yardley McLaren as it lapped me in Argentina. I also had an accident at The Ring, but in a 5000 car, so the pair of us were in Farnham Park Rehabilitation Centre outside London. My arm was totally encased in plaster and his right leg was totally encased in plaster. They were working on us day in, day out and it was a great place, but the food wasn't so good and Mike said he couldn't take any more of it. But what could we do? He said 'Hang on a minute, you can press the accelerator and I'll steer the wheel'. We got to Farnham in his car and you can imagine what people thought when we got out of it. They couldn't believe two people like that were getting out of a car. We went to a little Italian place, absolutely wonderful, a lot of bottles of wine. Mike was somehow... majestic.

"He used to say to me he was thinking of retiring at the end of the season because for him bikes were – or rather had been – the thing. He was a real racer, he raced off the track as much as he did on the track. He wasn't the sort of man who was a technocrat, wasn't completely enveloped by it with all the testing and so on, he liked to get in and race like hell. He was just a lovely man."

Martyn Pass (who has given me so much invaluable help with background for this book) was a motor racing fan who had already compiled a scrapbook of cuttings on Mike and written to the Surtees team – the year before – for Mike's autograph, which he received; but that was a standard one across a photograph of the car. No doubt Mike had sat and done a signing session and the team fed them out as required. Now Pass wrote to Farnham wishing Mike a speedy and complete recovery. He received a hand-written note thanking him for his concern. It was and remains the action of a big man who was and remained a humble man.

While Mike was at St Thomas' a lady appeared quite unannounced at his bedside and said "You don't know who I am".

"Yes. You're my mother."

8

"The strangest thing he ever said to me, I think – or it seemed strange to me – was after the Nurburgring. We'd been together for God knows how long, we'd had two children (Michelle and David). We'd always said we'd go and live in South Africa when he finished racing, and the winter after the accident we'd gone back out there.

"We were sitting at dinner one night and we got round to talking about it and talking about he and I. He was really upset because he'd realized then that his racing was finished. It was one of the few times he showed what he was really feeling. Usually he was controlled and didn't show things that upset him too much, but he was upset that night, I'd never seen him so upset.

"We were talking about our personal relationship and he couldn't believe that I still wanted him just as him. 'How can you with a man with a gimpy leg?' – as he called it. I said 'But Mike, I love *you*, I love you the person'. He was in such a state.

"What I found so strange was we'd been together so long, had the children, and he still felt I might not care about *him*. We always had this thing, he and I.

I could never believe that he chose me, and apparently he could never believe that I'd chosen him. Someone had said to me once before 'You know he gets very jealous of you', and I'd thought 'What on earth? How can that be?'. He didn't think he was worthy, almost, which I found incredible.

"He'd always said from straight off that we would never get married. I didn't push him on why. I think he did have the danger in mind and then, after the accident, maybe he wanted to feel more sure of me. It wasn't going to hurt me any more or less if we were married and had a piece of paper, it was ludicrous really.

"You could have knocked me down with a feather when in South Africa he eventually said let's get married. Mike already had his South African residency and he said I'd better go down and get mine sorted out. My name was Hailwood because of the children. I'd changed my name by deed poll because I wanted the children to have their father's name. I went down to the office and they gave me quite a hard time, common law wife and all this business. At that time it wasn't so accepted, they were looking down their noses at me.

"I got back and he was in the bathroom. He said 'How did you get on?', and I said 'Stupid bloody lot down there trying to make me feel *this* big', and he said 'Oh well, we'd better get married then'. I thought *whaaat?*

"He said it in such a matter-of-fact way after all the years I'd been waiting. I told myself *no girl, you didn't hear that*. I walked out of the bathroom thinking *he didn't say that, did he? Did he?* I was too scared to go back in and ask. I didn't say a word for a couple of days. Then I said 'You know you were saying...I thought I heard something about...getting married'. 'Yeah, let's do that.' I was hot down the old registry office before he changed his mind again." Pauline Hailwood was poised to become officially Pauline Hailwood.

They didn't settle in South Africa, but chose New Zealand instead, to outsiders a mysterious choice. New Zealand, where the sheep outnumber the people, was so quiet and conservative he hadn't even liked it much when he'd driven the Tasman series there. So – why?

"It seemed a good idea at the time. Nothing else had come up anywhere else, he was offered a chance to go into business. I had never been to New Zealand, and when he put it to me that we should go there my only comment was 'I'll go anywhere you say. If you think you can be happy there that's OK by me'. Perhaps he thought it was a nice way of life for two kids, maybe it was a new life after racing. But New Zealand was too quiet for him."

Even moving through his mid-thirties it was always going to be that.

This year of 1974 a very determined Scotsman was riding Yamahas in the World 500cc Championship. While Mike settled into New Zealand's slumber this Scotsman began to find a plan marinating in his mind; and it would do so more and more strongly. He was only 23. He decided that the plan would take two years in the preparation, and he set himself a target: he would become ferociously fit. "I used to go out between six and eight every morning, no matter where I was – even if I was on a motorway I'd stop at a service area – and do my training session."

He was called Alex George, and as he pushed himself on dark winter mornings he saw clearly where each footstep was taking him. He intended to conquer the Isle of Man. So what? So nothing – yet.

9

Faces in the mirror, faces in the mirror – but spring 1992.

Jacky Ickx remains a neat and precise man, but matured now. He does Press Relations for a large construction company in Brussels and still rallies round Africa ("a superb and fascinating continent") when he's not acting as a consultant to Mazda. For a moment or two he gazes back:

"I am completely unable to say why Mike and I only had a relationship which was 'Hello', 'Good bye' and no more, full stop. I am unable to say why we didn't become friends. I met him through John Wyer in 1969; he was very close to David Hobbs and I never had much of a relationship with Hobbs. Maybe they thought I acted like a star, something like that, but at that age you don't pay attention to those things, you try and win and you try to be the best.

"Anyway, in racing, a person is always two different people. The one you see in the car is the total opposite of the one you see out of it.

"I had done a little bit of motorcycling, not much, but I gained the impression they thought the car people were in another world, which was more sophisticated. The bike people are more human – can I say that? – and very tied together. Maybe he felt like a stranger in car racing because he wasn't with his friends.

"I was always full of admiration for a man who had achieved what he had in bikes and then came to cars and did well there, too, and perhaps with not as much success as he deserved."

MIKE AND THE ISLAND

"It was a terrible risk. Here was a man who was pot-bellied, couldn't walk properly and was very conscious he might destroy his own legend or worse, much worse." – Ted Macauley

"He asked 'Can I have a lap round with you?'. It was like God asking you to explain a bit of The Bible to Him." – Mick Grant

"Motor Cycle News asked me to write the story. I remember the first paragraph. Mike Hailwood is returning to the TT full stop. He will win full stop. They wouldn't use it." – Charlie Rous

1

"That was a shocker when Mike said after the accident at the Nurburgring that he'd decided to go and live in New Zealand. He'd hated New Zealand in the Tasman Series and swore he would never go back there again. He went into a marine business, rebuilding boat engines and things", Rod Sawyer says. A shocker? These are commonly held sentiments.

Mike did, however, journey to The Island in 1975 as a spectator and covered a lap of honour with Geoff Duke – "It was a Honda road bike and I can't remember who asked me to do it. He sat on the back with his injured leg sticking out and he was so popular it was quite emotional." This is precisely the kind of ritualistic thing people succumb to when their racing careers are truly over, finished, done. Semi-crippled as Stan had been, married and with children, a businessman of sorts, a resident of New Zealand, he had become to some riders on The Island a figure of the generation before, or even of the generation before that.

Mick Grant first spoke to him, although "I'd be very quiet. I don't suppose I said much more than 'Hello'. However he paid me the greatest accolade you could ever be paid.

"I had broken his lap record at Oulton Park, which stood for a long, long time and in my own way that gave me an affinity with him. This was in the Seventies and he was still the guy to beat. At the TT I was on the Kawasaki in the 750cc race and on my second lap I nobbled his seven-year-old record, which was 107mph, whatever, he'd set on the Honda. I went round at 109mph and Ted Macauley said he and Mike were in the grandstand watching, and as the announcement came over that I'd just done it Mike turned and said to Ted 'The bastard!", which if you knew Mike was a wonderful compliment, it was an accolade."

Mike spectated at Silverstone, too, in August, where he covered another lap of honour. He had formally announced his retirement the week before, although that was little more than a formality, a way of giving an absolute and final end to it. You only had to look at him and the way he walked to know the great truth, anyway. "The reception I got was quite overwhelming", he would say so softly, not capable of masking the seam of sincerity. "It brought tears to my eyes, particularly when you think that three-quarters of the people never saw me ride. As I look around I see they are very, very young. It's quite amazing, really." Yes, the years had flown as quickly as that. "Fortunately, when I'm away from racing I don't miss it all that much, but when I come to a race like this and see all my old friends and hear the bikes and everything it's a bit nostalgic. I'd like to have a go, but it would be rather foolish. The last time I was on a road bike was a couple of weeks ago in the South of France. I borrowed a friend's 900 Kawasaki and I found the whole thing quite frightening, particularly in France, because they're all nuts anyway there."

2

And he went to New Zealand and the years drifted now, not flew; and something inevitable happened, born entirely of geography. He was bored.

"We went over to Australia a couple of times", Pauline says, "to do little vintage bike races at Bathurst, and that was OK for Mike because it wasn't high-profile or anything like that. The first of these races was also the first time he'd ridden a bike, and there were doubts about whether he could actually do it."

He could.

"I don't think the bike he was on was particularly competitive, but typically he made the best of it. I could pick him out among the field. It was the way he laid the bike over, his riding appeared so natural and easy. The style was there and I could see he still had *it*. I started to think then, *oh yes. I thought it's there, it hasn't gone away.*"

The years may or may not have drifted for Phil Read. "I stopped racing in the Isle of Man in 1972, and I said it shouldn't be a World Championship event. The last time I rode there it was a Grand Prix and a World Championship event and I got £25 expense money. It cost you to go over and the prize money was pathetic. I won one race in 1972 and got 250 quid.

"A very good friend of mine was killed there, and that was the last straw. He was leading the race, fell off on the Verandah and hit a concrete post which had replaced a wooden one. At that time we felt the organizers weren't doing as much as they could to minimize the risks.

"I had a lot of controversy and there were a lot of statements, the TT lost its World Championship status (in 1977), but I felt I'd like to go back. I'd still got lots more to do in the TT. I didn't feel satisfied that I'd done my thing over there. I contacted a few people, arranged three bikes, and I went over there in 1977 while Mike was living in New Zealand. The ACU offered me a lot of money to go back. I'd been paid £25, now it was £12,000.

"I had a Rolls-Royce Corniche and a van, and when I arrived I left them on the front. A policeman said 'I'd advise you, sir, to put them round the back, you're not particularly popular over here'. Some of the marshals were refusing to work if I raced. When I was driving the circuit with a friend in the Rolls we called in at a service station just past the Union Mills. I walked into the little shop and the bloke said 'Is that Phil Read's car?'. I said 'Yes'. He said 'I'm sorry, I'm not going to serve him.' My friend really let fly at this fellow, he said 'You are a pathetic little weasel, you don't know what Read's done for you'.

"I raced a works Honda, it was the first Formula One event to be held in the Isle of Man[1] and I won. They couldn't believe it. There was a downpour, they stopped it with one lap to go and so I'd won at over 100mph. I won the Senior on a Suzuki and then crashed my Yamaha the night before the last race. I think far away Mike said to himself 'Well, if a silly old git like Read can do it I can do it ...'"

Contrast this with New Zealand, where once upon a time the British Rugby League team were touring and passing through one lifeless town after another and began to call into the empty streets *bring out your dead!*

"Mike should never really have left Britain", Attwood says. "He was too British and missed a hell of a lot of the life and the fun that you only get in this country, particularly in London. In New Zealand there was absolutely nothing to do. He got bored completely out of his mind."

"I'd been at him for ages and ages to do something", Macauley muses. "He was getting restless, he was going to set up an air taxi business, but he was bored, terribly bored. He used to write me immensely funny letters and we were in contact all the time, even though he was round the other side of the world.

"He wrote to me. 'You're going to think I'm mad, and don't tell Pauline whatever you do, but I might – might – like to make a comeback at the TT. Either call me or write to me. If you think I'm mad, say so, if you think it's a great idea, say so, but I think the two of us could make a good few quid out of it as well'." The letter arrived at Macauley's home in Cheshire on July 11, 1977. Macauley began to test the viability of it as discreetly as he could, which wasn't easy. You still only had to mention the name Hailwood and light bulbs went on in people's minds.

"Then", Pauline says, "Mike started muttering about doing the TT. I was terrified about that, I really was."

"It's funny", Sawyer says. "I'd met Jennifer (my ex-wife) in July and started living with her immediately. When Mike called up from New Zealand and said he was coming over I had to tell Jenny that we'd got this friend who would be staying, and could he move in with us? I was living at Jennifer's house at the time. He arrived on August 10, which is Jennifer's birthday. I'd taken over one of the night clubs in London for the birthday party, 30 or 40 friends invited. It was in the King's Road and we had a discotheque downstairs. I said to Jennifer 'Look, you're going to be sharing your party because when Mike gets here there are a bunch of people he'd like to meet', and the party just got bigger and wilder.

"But Jennifer didn't understand who this person was! She knew absolutely nothing about motorcycle racing, very little about car racing beyond the times when she'd been to Grands Prix with me. And she had to share her birthday party

---

1. Mick Grant will be explaining this and its relationship to the other two big races, the 500 and the Classic, in just a moment.

with this total stranger and then share her house with him. He stayed with us for three or four weeks, and he and Jenny had the perfect chemistry together. They had so many laughs and jokes together, she was a very, very funny girl, a brilliant hostess and very good looking, which always attracted Mike, anyway.

"Mike was out and about doing little deals for the comeback. He'd have to borrow suits and shoes of mine because he didn't have any decent clothing of his own. You talk about lack of confidence. He hated to go and shop for things on his own. He'd look for somebody to verify whether he was buying the right things. I had friends who had men's boutiques and he'd go there and if he went in on his own he'd seek the guidance of the guy selling in the shop; if I was with him it was a matter of 'Is this alright?'. He always used to lie about how much he spent on clothes. If Pauline had ever found out how much he was spending on some of the nicer clothes to look the part in London ..."

(I'm not a betting man, but I'm willing to wager that Pauline was as perfectly aware of this as she was of so much else. Ordinary women, never mind worldly ones such as she, need only a glimpse of an expensive suit to know it's expensive; but never mind.)

Four days after Mike arrived, he and Macauley went to the British Grand Prix at Silverstone. Attwood was there and remembers Phil Read saying to Mike "It's a doddle if you make a comeback, no trouble at all'. I think that got Mike thinking about it."

Mike, as we have seen, was already thinking about it. At Silverstone he, Macauley and Vernon Cooper, chairman of the ACU and a leading official at the Isle of Man in particular, went quietly into a room and talked it over. Mike's presence and what that would mean to the TT hardly needed stating. A fee was agreed and the meeting concluded in about 10 minutes. But – should he, shouldn't he?

Mike consulted Surtees, who said "I'd prefer you didn't, but if you are, do it properly. I was very fearful because I questioned the motives. I was afraid that this was purely a money operation. I wasn't afraid that he would make a fool of himself because the man had ability, and that doesn't go away, but I didn't want him to hurt himself." Nor was Surtees alone in this. Geoff Duke: "To be quite honest I was worried about him. He was really and literally sticking his neck out. Knowing Mike, I was afraid because he would have so many fans expecting him to do well and I felt this would influence the amount of effort he put it. In other words, he'd put in more than was good for him. It really worried me. He could have hurt himself, oh yes."

"It was a terrible risk", Macauley says. "Here was a man who was pot-bellied, couldn't walk properly and was very conscious that he might destroy his own legend or worse, much worse. We had long heart-to-hearts. I said 'You have got to be well aware of the situation before we go any further', and he said 'I am very well aware of the situation. I can hurt myself very badly.' I said 'You haven't a thing to prove'. He said 'I've got something to prove to myself. I want to do it because I want to prove to myself that I can still do it. I can't race a car because of the foot, but I can race a motorbike'."

It's easy when you're simply reading words in a book like this to miss the passage of time. To have any clear memory of him a spectator would now have to be nearly 20 years old. He had not raced on The Island for a complete decade: June 16, 1967, when he'd won, Agostini had broken down and it had finished:

1	M. Hailwood	Honda	2h 8m 36.22s
2	P.J. Williams	Matchless	2h 16m 20.0s
3	S. Spencer	Norton	2h 17m 47.2s
4	J. Cooper	Norton	2h 18m 20.4s
5	F. Stevens	Paton	2h 19m 34.6s
6	J. Hartle	Matchless	2h 19m 50.0s

Mike was now 37. Williams had ridden his last World Championship 500cc race in *1973*, Spencer in *1970*, Cooper in *1968*, Stevens in *1967*, Hartle in *1968*. This was not the passing of a whole generation: this was another era.

Of the current riders, Read he would know, Mick Grant had ridden against him that once at Silverstone in 1971, and there were a few almost of the generation, almost of the era, like John Williams, who'd begun in the World Championship in 1969, and Tom Herron, who'd begun in 1971. Others were nearly young enough for him to have fathered them himself. Of them he would know nothing.

There was another generation of bikes, too. Could he actually ride them? He wasn't going to be nursing one of *his* era round Bathurst, wasn't going to nurse one gingerly down to the supermarket to do the shopping, he was going to fling one at and round The Island at a hundred and plenty, and if The Island was safer that was only relative to what it had been. Ragged-edged stone walls remain ragged-edged stone walls. Sawyer used to have bikes. "I'd play around on them and he'd say 'I don't want to ride because I don't think I can'. He was concerned about his physical ability, it was the foot that he was considering." Bathurst had taken him a step beyond that, but only a small step, virtually the smallest step. The Island was the biggest, rawest, most demanding, most daunting, dangerous, potentially deadly step a man could take. A moon shot would have been a safer option.

Macauley, a shrewd old professional, saw with perfect clarity that the thing could become an avalanche long before Mike proved he could physically cope with a modern racing bike. Macauley and Mike went to The Island in early September for the Manx Grand Prix, a race for amateurs.

Macauley had arranged for Mike to take part in the practice under the subterfuge of making a film. A camera was fixed to the bike. Macauley had arranged the loan of a 750cc Yamaha and Mike tried it at an airstrip in the north of The Island. He didn't enjoy the experience, thought it had the power and lift of an aeroplane, but was persuaded to do the practice on it. He felt his way in, did some real speed in bursts, but the power was so nakedly terrifying the "thing nearly threw me off the back".

He'd forgotten tracts of The Island in the sort of detail a racer needs and pondered the Yamaha. "Bloody fearsome." It was savagely true: 1967 was a long way away. He and Macauley had a quiet dinner and Mike said that at minimum, whatever he could do over the winter, he'd need to be on The Island at least three weeks before TT to relearn a whole career.

One damp day at a humble track in New Zealand late that autumn, he pulled his old red leathers from the boot of his car, slipped the helmet on, tightened the strap to his neck. A couple of people arranged themselves at the back of a 950cc Yamaha and, with Mike running alongside holding the handlebars, pushed it through puddles past a white van and out towards the circuit. He got on by instinct side-saddle, then neatly, easily, naturally flipped his body over into the tuck position, the engine beginning to grumble and growl. There were nine people watching.

As he moved onto the circuit the paunch of his stomach was visible straining against the constriction of the leathers. He went very prudently – damn near cautiously – in those first few moments as if he was examining himself as much as the bike. When he was ready, and only when, he made it go goddamned fast. The place was called Pukekohe. He was within a second and a half of the lap record.

Afterwards a New Zealand interviewer asked "What about your edge?" but – it must have been the accent, I suppose – it sounded like age.

"My what?" Mike said, craning that face, opening that smile.

"Your edge?"

"I thought you said my age."

"Well alright, I suppose edge is something to do with age if you like."

"Obviously I couldn't hope to go back and ride as well as I did in 1967. It would be facetious to think otherwise."

Mike now decided to transform himself into a racer again. His riding skill remained and so did his willpower. He gave up drinking, which he found particularly difficult, he stopped eating big meals, he bought the Canadian Air Force manual for fitness and followed that. "He went into this rigid training programme", Sawyer says, "and he worked very, very hard on that. It was a sit-ups, press-ups, running-up-stairs regime which he did with the manual.

"When he went back to New Zealand he phoned and said 'Are you coming down for Christmas?'. I said 'Yes, of course.' 'Why don't you bring Jennifer with you?' 'Oh, I don't know' – I covered the phone up with my hand and said – 'Jenny, Mike would like you and I to go down to New Zealand for Christmas.' Jenny said she'd love to. I told Mike to expect the two of us and he said 'Great, but you know you should marry that girl. You won't find a better.' I said I'd think about it. I covered the phone again with my hand and said 'Jenny, do you fancy the idea of getting married while we're down there?' She was dumbfounded for a couple of minutes and then she said 'Well, hell, why not?' I said to Mike that it was a great idea and would he be best man? He said 'Yes, and you can get married at my house'.

"That's what happened. We got married on Christmas Eve at his house. Mike organized it all, he even fiddled the paperwork because in New Zealand it's the same as in England, you have to have the bans read three times in advance. We arrived on the 23rd, we were taken immediately by Mike and Pauline from the airport to the Registry Office and we signed our names to the effect that we had arrived three weeks previously. Then off we went to the house. He had a Justice of the Peace come along, who performed the ceremony, Mike was best man and Michelle was Maid of Honour, and we had celebrations. Then we went on to Tahiti for our honeymoon."

Meanwhile, Macauley – based in Manchester, which is a lot of things but not Tahiti – had to stop thinking like a journalist and start thinking like a PR consultant, sponsorship finder and team manager. "We did it on the understanding that I organized everything. All he had to do was get himself fit. I went to sponsors, I was having dinners all over the place. The basis was 'Look, Mike's coming back, but let's face it, there are a lot of good runners about and if he gets on the leader board that will be a bonus. There is no way I am going to try and push him to win.' I'd got a private feeling about what he would do, and Mike was telling me white lies because he said he'd just go and ride round. I knew he couldn't do that."

What was he going to ride? Macauley found Martini as willing sponsors and Yamaha said just before Christmas – while Sawyer was preparing to fly off and get married – that yes they'd be delighted to supply Mike with a 500cc bike, the one Agostini had been using during the season (37 points, sixth in the Championship), but for the TT only. Steve Wynne of Sports Motor Cycles provided a 900cc Ducati.

The comeback was announced in January 1978 at Martini's penthouse guest suite in the West End of London. Mike wore clothes borrowed from Macauley. Attwood, who was present, knew no more about the Isle of Man than it was a place in the Irish Sea which bikes went round, but he said to Mike "I want to be there, I am going to be there".

A new generation were working at *Motor Cycle News*, too. "They understandably didn't really know about Hailwood", Charlie Rous says, "they couldn't remember him. They asked me to do the story and I did. I can recall the first paragraph even now. *Mike Hailwood is returning to the TT full stop. He will win full stop*. They wouldn't use it. One of them said 'Suppose he crashes?', and I said 'He won't crash, he won't come off, and I'll tell you something: he wouldn't race if he didn't think he could win. He never rode for the fun of it, he always rode to win.' But no, they wouldn't use the story."

Mike wanted Nobby Clark to be there. "At the time I was working for the Kenny Roberts team in Amsterdam", Clark says. "Mike asked if I would help him and I was really keen. He said he was to ride Yamahas in the 250 and 500 and 750 classes. The Roberts team all agreed I'd be able to go to The Island." Jerry Wood was working for Yamaha, too. "When I heard about the comeback I thought I've got to go and see that. I had a very understanding boss and I said to him I would take two weeks holiday. He said 'No, no, you can't go' – I didn't know it was a joke. He said I'd have to go and see the big boss and when I did the big boss said 'You must go and Yamaha will pay all your expenses'."

Whatever else The Comeback might be, it would be a gathering.

One person had to be missing, perhaps the person who would have savoured it most of all; perhaps the person who would have been least surprised at what happened. In February 1978 Stan had a heart attack while he was visiting Miami, was taken to Nassau, and died there a month later. He was 75. He also had known what it was like to be alive and it had been like *this*.

Mike flew with his family to England in April. He rode a couple of Ducatis in the rain at Oulton, the Yamaha at Snetterton. "They called me up and said 'Would you give a hand with his comeback?'" Iain Mackay says. "Mike was quite happy to ride the Yamaha as it was, but we kept working at it and working at it, and it got better, and we kept working at it. At the end of the session he ran 14 laps and 13 were on record pace. It was a very powerful bike and he could handle it straight away, no problems, and it was totally different from anything he'd ridden when he was competing – although he had been on one in New Zealand.

"When he'd last ridden regularly in competition you didn't have the possibilities to set up bikes. From the engine point of view they were very advanced, but the chassis had changed. The character of the Yamaha engine torque was that it didn't set off in one big rush, and that helped, but when he'd done the 14 laps it was simply ... amazing."

Mike was in demand. "I was racing for Ford with a Capri", Stuart Graham says, "and I was looking for someone to do the TT with me – the car TT at Silverstone. You had to have two drivers for a car. With an eye on publicity and everything else I thought it would be a good idea to get my old mate back to do it.

"The arrangement was straightforward. He'd be co-driver and we'd do one hour on, one hour off. Ford were keen. Whilst he wouldn't earn a fortune it was going to be worth his while. I contacted Mike and put the idea to him, and what was interesting was that the great Mike Hailwood was slightly unsure whether he could do it or not. He hadn't driven competitively since the crash at the Nurburgring, and he knew he'd be coming back to a fairly hot competitive scene. Saloon car racing was that.

"He wanted to test the car to be sure he wouldn't let anybody down, which was classic Hailwood. If he made a commitment to something like that he wouldn't just swan it, say 'Thank you very much', and take the money, he wanted to make sure everyone got their money's worth. I looked at sponsors and the financial side was getting complicated, but that could have been solved. What stopped it was that the testing of the Yamahas was taking up too much time."

This remains another tantalizing fragment of what might have been. Mike never did race any car again.

The gathering began and with it something of a mystery which leads to a question, and the question is how seriously Yamaha were taking it. Forgive them if they saw it as a middle-aged overweight cripple milking something from The Island and what he wanted was just bikes so he could circulate and out of politeness they were providing the means. A fine gesture, an acknowledgement, a touch of nostalgia. Yes. The way it goes.

"Before the season started", Clark says, "I sorted out all the spares and things we would be needing on The Island. There were fairings, tanks, mudguards to be painted, plus wheels. I got back to Amsterdam from a trip to check everything and all the parts were there, but the 500cc bike was on stands, no wheels. When I asked where they were I was told they had been stolen! Nothing had been done or was said as to where we could get replacements at this late hour. When we got to the Isle of Man I found that quite a lot of parts were missing, like different size tanks, the refueller and so on. The refueller was illegal, I was told – but the one we did use was banned everywhere else in the world because it worked on compressed air with no safety valves.

"I believe if you go racing it's always better to take too much rather than run out of parts. Before the truck left Amsterdam I was told that someone had gone through all the parts and said most were not necessary, and also there were items which had been stolen. We had to have tanks made bigger on The Island while the right sizes lay in the workshop in Amsterdam."

4

The composition of the TT had changed. The 350 and 500 races, called respectively the Junior and Senior, had been running since 1911, the 250 since 1922, the 125 since 1951, and throughout Mike's competitive career they had been the matrix, so to speak, of the meeting: one week of practice, one week of racing in the four classes. (I don't forget the sidecar men who were there, too, but aren't relevant to our story.) A race called the Classic had been added in 1975 and the TT Formula One in 1977. This was the race Read had won as well as the 500.

Let Mick Grant explain. "The people in the Isle of Man obviously want enough races to make it viable for the public to go over. It's always been the case that the bigger classes have the top names in them, and if you can get your Hailwoods and Alex Georges and Grants in three races spaced out – one at each end of the week and one in the middle – it's going to ensure that people stay for the full week." This means real money, all those hotels and boarding houses full, all those restaurants full, all those shops doing brisk business, and I don't forget the pubs.

"The Formula One race was part of a World Championship which was then Mickey Mouse, only two rounds – The Isle of Man and the Ulster Grand Prix – contested by production-based machines up to 1,000cc.

"The Classic at the end of the week was 500 and Formula One together, you could chuck in whatever machine you wanted."

Mike left Pauline and the children at her parents' home in Berkshire where, she says, they had a little house. "Mike didn't want me to go to the Isle of Man. It was this thing about not wanting me there if anything should happen, and he didn't want to have to worry about me. I knew why, I knew his reasons. I understood those reasons and you had to accept it, you couldn't argue about it."

Mike travelled to Manchester to stay with Macauley before they left for the TT. "He got so drunk at dinner in my house because he didn't realize he was drinking port, he thought it was wine on the table. He was ill. I had an E-Type and the next morning we went off to get some fresh air, get his head cleared. The brakes went on the car. He said 'That's alright, we'll be OK. You drive it and I'll work the handbrake, I'll stop it on the handbrake.' We went 30, 40 miles up the road like that. Nothing *fazed* him."

On The Island Mike and Macauley drove round the course. "I knew it then, I knew what his feeling was. Normally it would have been boring for him to ride round in a Rover 3-litre just looking at the track, remembering, but it was the amount of effort he put into that.

"Most of the time I found I was sitting on the racing line – I was on the left – in this Rover which he was throwing round with cavalier abandon. It got to such a stage that I said 'Stop it, I'll get out, this is getting a bit too serious for me'. I mean, there was traffic coming the other way. I went to the Highlander pub and said 'Come and pick me up when you've finished your particular bit of lunacy'.

"When it became evident he was taking it very, very seriously, from my standpoint it started to be a bit of a worry because I knew he could only do it to try and win. That's the way it had to be. He wasn't going to be sixth or tenth. Once he'd accepted that he was doing it he had a tremendous sense of responsibility. If you put something into him, money in particular, he had to give full value back. He couldn't do it any other way. He couldn't cheat."

Wood arrived. "I didn't want to work on the bikes because I had been out of it so long. I got drawn in more and more ..."

Carol and Lewis Young arrived – Carol, who had done the superb line-drawing of Mike all those years ago. Mike said to Carol "Why don't you get some prints done?".

"He gave me back the original", Carol says, "I took it to the printers and I had 1,000 black-and-white prints run off, then Mike sat for ages signing them just for me to be able to sell them. He said "Not everybody is taking this really seriously, they're all making a lot of money out of it, there's a lot of hangers-on. Why don't you make money out of it?'. No, I didn't sell a thousand because I've probably still got a hundred left. I could have sold a thousand but I'm not a very good sales lady selling my own things. I think I gave more away."

"Mike was in a shop buying postcards", Wood says, "and the place filled with people because he was there. My wife went in and he looked really uncomfortable. He said 'Help me to get out of here', and she made up some story about how he had to go to an appointment – otherwise he would have been there all day. Outside Mike said 'Thanks' and gave her £50. 'Try and win some money at the Casino.' You see, he never worried about money. In fact he didn't worry about very much at all."

The gathering broadened and deepened to embrace the general public, thousands upon thousands of them, and some at least would remember the great days, Hailwood-versus-McIntyre, Hailwood-versus-Hocking, Hailwood-versus-Agostini. These thousands were curious, but then they'd have to be curious. Mike was 38, the Island was still 37.75 miles long.

"I couldn't believe it", Grant says. "Mike asked if he could have a lap round with me. It was like God asking you to explain a bit of The Bible to Him. I said 'Yes, crikey, it's no bother at all'. He was on the 750 Yamaha, I was on the Kawasaki and we set off together.

"I let Mike go in front because it was far better me watching him to tell him what he needed to do to be on the pace. If he was following me that's all he'd be doing. I followed him right through to Ramsey and his racing lines were absolutely bang on, exactly. I reckon – it sounds big-headed, but never mind – that my lines round The Island were right. They suited me. Over the years people have said 'You don't look to be going so quick', but if you're doing it right it does look like that. I was very economical on using the road and, again, I was of the old school. I spent a lot of time working at it, hours and hours, because it was a big part of your annual income. You needed to do your homework.

"You don't forget, but what you do is brush up on your weak points all the time. I would rather go round lap after lap in a van, look at places where I'd felt uncomfortable in practice, and that's OK for two or three years, then you have to go round in the van again."

Apart from a minor excursion the year before Mike hadn't been round since 1967.

"Mike was slightly wrong at Greeba Castle coming out. He was about three foot off where he should have been, which doesn't sound much but it's quite a lot really. There used to be some tarmac on the left as you come over the hill and you're turning right. You clip the kerb on the right then you tip left, but he went extreme left along the wall in order to turn right. It was so bumpy there that it upset the bike. Where he went was the natural racing line, I can understand why he went there, but in actual fact you stayed off it.

"On The Island you don't always take a Grand Prix or a classic line, you use the cambers, you use where the grip is, and if it's raining you may not use the same line. It's all knowledge. If you had a plan and drew on it where the correct line should be he was on it, but The Island isn't always like that.

"He was off-line somewhere else – I can't remember where – but other than that he was absolutely bang on to the inch and I was quite amazed. But he was hopeless on the brakes! I couldn't believe it. He wasn't using the brakes at all. He was very fast on the fast corners, he was comfortable through them – which was the whole idea of the exercise – but logically he was using the brakes as they would have been in 1967 and they never really had brakes (in the ferocious modern sense) in those days.

"We came towards Ramsey hairpin and he slowed down and waved me by. That was for me a sad thing. You can put the course into three sections, the flat bit from Bray to Ramsey, the uphill bit and the downhill bit. I don't know why, but looking back at the times when I gained on people and lost on people I was average on the flat, at that time I was useless going up The Mountain and I was brilliant coming down it. I could make up anything on anybody coming down. My weakness was going up.

"I'd have been quite happy for him to follow me anywhere except there. I hadn't a clue where I was going, I just hadn't. When he waved me by I was horror-stricken, I almost wet my pants. This was supposed to be me showing God round, he's asked me to do that, he obviously thinks I'm the ideal man to do that. I'd rather have given him a *piggy-back* up the mountain, but you can't stop and say 'Hang on a minute, Mike, I want to follow *you* to see where *my* problem is'. Everything compounded at the wrong time.

"I kept out in front and I did an unforgivable thing which was so stupid. I took lines going up The Mountain like the ones I thought *he* would take. I should have done my own thing. We went up, we came down and we reached the start-finish. He said 'What do you think?'. I said 'Your lines are absolutely bang-on except for a couple of places, but you were hopeless on the brakes – but there again you've never had real brakes before'. He knew. It had sunk in. I said 'You're losing 50 yards everywhere on the brakes', and he said 'OK, I am, but what the (expletive) were you doing up The Mountain, you were all over the shop?'. I never told him, I never told him. I mean, Hailwood was the classic on classic racing lines, you'd watch him at Donington, he goes *past* the corner and *then* turns in.

"I was almost trying to do a pleasing job and the one thing you can't do up The Mountain is go in late. You go in early everywhere. He didn't clamber all over the bike, but neither did I. We were very similar from that point of view.

"I never shifted my backside off the seat. Maybe I stuck my knees out, but I never actually moved off the bike. I've got theories on that and I still think it's the way to do it. The style of people leaning off was in full swing – that's the modern style and it suits circuit racing, but it doesn't suit road racing because when you have races like the North West, the Ulster Grand Prix, the Island, if you start moving about on the bike you're making it wobble and in 140, 150mph corners you want the bike as *quiet* as it's going to be. If you are jumping all over the bike you're upsetting it. As the road race circuits have gone into demise we've seen less and less of that" – riders with bums on seats. This question of style is interesting because there was a purity about the way Mike and a bike moulded until they welded into one. He wasn't *riding* the bike, he *became* the bike and the bike *became* him. This did look amusingly old-fashioned and there were plenty of people on the Island, riders among them, who smiled and shook their heads and spoke no doubt of dinousaurs and how extinct they had been for so long.

Rob Walker once asked Mike in more recent years why other riders lifted their legs up and pushed their knees out when they were going round corners, "You never did that, even at the end', and he said 'It's to show the sponsor's name on the petrol tank'!"

"Mike could never do a wheelie", Macauley says, "and in fact a false photograph was put out. It was taken from underneath a bike, a very daring picture, the bike on its back wheel, the front up in the air. The caption said 'Mike

Hailwood practising for the TT', but it wasn't, it was somebody else, and this was a constant source of embarrassment to him. The picture was used worldwide.

"Mike could not get the front wheel to lift deliberately, it would only do that under normal speed and acceleration. His feeling was that you can't race if the wheel is up in the air. He could no more do a wheelie than stick his leg out – and he couldn't put his leg out of the fairing, either. There are wonderful pictures of Mike coming round Quarter Bridge where they all put their legs out and Mike is totally tucked in; but his bike is at just as big an angle as anybody else's. He said he'd love to do a wheelie 'but I just can't get the front wheel up'. I said 'Have you tried?', and he said 'Of course I've tried, and I can't'."

Mike practised on the Ducati and for reasons of clarity let's look at the racing week he faced: The Formula One on this Ducati, the 500, 250 and Classic on Yamahas.

"Mike went off on the Ducati and did a couple of laps and came back, and we said 'How did it feel?', and he said 'OK'. The suspension man had been down at the bottom of Bray Hill[2] watching, and when he got back Mike was in the paddock", Macauley says. "The suspension man was nearly shaking. He said 'God only knows how Mike is handling the bike down there. The suspension is awful'. This guy fiddled about and it was just a question of fiddle-fiddle-fiddle and it was done and Mike went off again, came back and said 'Bloody marvellous'. The bike had been shaking and banging and clanging away down the hill and Mike had thought the bike was just like that."

Rod Sawyer went to the Island for the practice. "It was all very new to me. Denny Hulme was over there as well and Denny and I went out onto a wet and windy circuit. I was in total awe of the distance of The Island. I'd had no idea what it was like. It was the Nurburgring all over again, but in streets, no protection whichever way you looked at it, a frightening thing. It's the easiest place in the world to hurt yourself. But Mike had an incredible amount of ease being there, he was at home, he was relaxed in the evening. He did spend time going up to the garage and checking out with the mechanics. He'd say *Jesus, did I ever scare myself at such-and-such a place*. You don't realize until you've driven round the circuit how scary it can be, how sincere he was when he said that."

Yes.

"It didn't matter what time of the night it was", Wood says. "He would always come and see how the mechanics were doing and bring them tea and coffee." This is how very big men behave, and if you're working through the night and a Living Legend, truly, is humbly there with a cup of tea for you, you won't just work a night for him, you'll work forever for him.

Sawyer couldn't stay for the Formula One race. He had a business transporting people to and from car races and that's where he'd have to go.

Dickie Attwood: "I was on holiday in Anglesey with my family and I'd said all along to my wife that I was going to the TT. She said 'What do you want to bother to go there for?'. 'Well, Mike's going to be there.' 'Bloody Mike Hailwood.' Veronica and Mike didn't really get on very well because whenever I went out with him I came back in a terrible state".

"The weather was fantastic, we were having a great time, and I really felt a

---

2. The sharp descent and right-hand corner shortly after the starting line and, for spectators at least, a superb vantage point.

right bastard for leaving my family. We had a small caravan overlooking a bay and it was really beautiful. It was a hell of a wrench to go. I thought God, it would be much easier to stay here, but I'd said I'd go and I wanted to.

"I had to drive round to Liverpool. I'd never been to the Isle of Man and that's another reason I wanted to go. It was one of those things I didn't know anything about really. I got on the ferry and I was absolutely staggered. It was full of bikes and people, and I didn't know one person. I felt an alien. I got to the other end and it was evening. I didn't know where I was going. I asked for the such-and-such hotel and somebody said it was over there on the other side of the bay, so I started to walk with my bag. If I'd known the Isle of Man at all I'd have nipped on one of those horse-drawn things that go round.

"I reached the hotel and it was funny because you went through the ground floor and the reception was upstairs. They had a room for me, which was fortunate because I wasn't really sure. Mike had booked it. I was just about to get into the lift and by sheer chance Mike breezed through. I was so relieved. For four hours I hadn't seen anybody I knew. He said 'You old sod, what have you come for?', and I thought what have I bloody come for? But meeting him like that started it on the right foot and we had dinner. It was extraordinary how relaxed and at ease you were with someone like that. He was such an enormous person to me, how proud you were to be with him – it's daft but absolutely true. I got involved, oh yes, although I didn't know what I was doing ...

"Mike had made a big commitment and he got fit and he was really in shape. I'd heard stories that he'd been boozing a lot in New Zealand and had a lot of weight on, which I found difficult to understand, but I'm sure it was true. When he came back you could tell he'd done a good job on himself and the Ducati people were doing what I would call a really professional job.

"There was early morning practice when you got up at five in the morning and it was still dark. I said to Mike 'Look, when you get up, just bang on my door because I want to come with you.' 'Nah you don't, you don't want to bother with that, it's cold.' He didn't bang on my door, but fortunately he was in the room next to mine. He didn't slam his door, but I heard it shut. Subconsciously I was probably waiting to be woken up anyway, and I was somehow ready for that although we had had quite a late night the night before. I realized what it was, got up, rushed out and Mike was walking down the passageway.

"I shouted 'Hey, wait for me, wait for me!' 'Nah go back to bed.' I said 'Wait, I'll only be two seconds.' He said 'I'm going with Ted', and disappeared round the corner. I threw everything on and rushed downstairs – Mike was in his leathers – and of course, daft bugger that he was, he was waiting in the car, wasn't he? He'd waited a bit longer than he'd wanted to, he was getting a bit irate sitting there. You could tell he was. He said 'Come on, you prat, you're making me late'.

"It was dark and we went up to the circuit and the atmosphere up there – I wouldn't have missed that for the world. It was an atmosphere I have never experienced in any other way. As it got a bit lighter bikes were starting up, there was the smell and the noise and so many people. I thought what are all these people doing here? Obviously they had found the same thing as I had: this atmosphere. Mind you, you had to be wary of where you were standing because bikes were being push-started and they don't make any noise until the engine fires and they're moving..."

This was the morning of the Formula One race, although Mike went off on the 250 Yamaha – practice was a rolling thing, you'd already practised for the Formula

One, the bike was set up poised and ready for it; now you'd do the 250 and perhaps on the morning of the 250 race you'd practise on the 500 and so forth.

Mike nursed the 250 round because it had a new front tyre and they're slippy until they've had the sheen burnt off. He lost control at Braddan Bridge, the front wheel skidded and he was flung off. The bike ricocheted against a wall, tearing the fuel tank loose. Mike was badly shaken and said he was. He even *looked* shaken.

"We went back to have breakfast", Attwood says. "Ted was worried, he really was. I said 'Don't worry, it'll be fine'. Ted was at a total loss what to do with Mike just before the big race, and he said 'Oh, well, you'd better go and see him'. I said 'He probably doesn't want to see anybody, but I'll go and I'll be around if he needs anything'. There's nothing you can do, small talk is really not necessary to a rider or a driver at that point."

Attwood also told Macauley that the crash was probably one of the best things which could have happened, you know. "That'll really make him sharp – because it's not a piece of cake. Not that Mike would ever have thought it was, but it sharpened him up rather than destroyed his confidence. I thought to myself: he'll he *more* determined. There had been absolutely no indication in practice that he was going to do well. Right towards the end of practising he started to get towards the pace he'd need, then he fell off the 250..."

He'd hurt his hands badly, but about that he said not one word.

"When he was on a grid anywhere", Macauley says, "people were looking at him and it was a psyching-out situation. He had this wonderfully calm exterior, although he would admit that inside he was fluttering like everyone else. The only time that I ever knew him put any time into wondering about the opposition was in 1978 in that first race. He'd been away so long and hadn't necessarily followed motorbike racing. He knew a few names, but he didn't know too many.

"I had to sit one breakfast with him and give him a run-down of maybe the top 10 or 12, what their potential was, what their capacity was, what their danger-levels to him were on a 0 to 10 basis. Maybe he hadn't needed to do that when he was competing all the time, but now it was an indication of his professionalism, a new professionalism that he was in the TT and he wanted to know where the main dangers were. We went into it very, very thoroughly all the way down to personalities. Obviously Mike was thinking without revealing it whether a fellow could be psyched out or not."

Now, on the morning of June 3, 1978, while Attwood waited to be of service, Mike napped in his hotel room and Macauley sat on the bed in his room gazing out over the Irish Sea wondering if he'd made the biggest mistake of his life and the most public big mistake, too.

On the main road between Madrid and Burgos there was another gathering. It was the second day of qualifying for the Spanish Grand Prix, Jarama, and by a paradox Mike's generation were here. Peterson, Lauda and Reutemann had all been fast on the Friday, but not fast enough to catch Andretti, who sat on provisional pole in a JPS Lotus-Ford. Hunt was in there and Watson, Emerson Fittipaldi, Scheckter, Depailler, Jabouille, Mass, the whole bunch from the Formula Two Championship of 1972. Oh, and Clay Regazzoni...

But in the six years between the Nurburgring of 1974 and now a new generation had arisen here, too, Gilles Villeneuve, Riccardo Patrese, Didier Pironi, Patrick Tambay, Alan Jones.

It was hot in Spain, very hot as the minutes ticked away to the second and final session for the grid.

Sawyer had arrived, his thoughts no doubt resting elsewhere. At moments Brian Hart's certainly did. "We were waiting for the newspapers to arrive so we'd know how he'd done in practice and I was hovering over the radio trying to get the BBC World Service to see what was happening. We all wanted to listen. That's the sort of effect he had on people he'd become friendly with and spent good times with. You didn't forget the bloke."

As the sun burnished and parched the circuit of Jarama, Andretti – who Mike had raced against so many times – eyed pole position. On The Island Phil Read eyed Mike. "On the last day of practice Mike lapped about 10 seconds quicker than me", Read says. "There was no acrimony between us. I was delighted he came back because it added a lot of prestige to the race, so it was between Mike and myself..."

5

It was warm on The Island and Mike, stripped to the waist, hung around the bike without paying particular attention to it.

"His trust in people was infinite", Macauley says, "and that included the mechanics. They'd wheel bikes out and the riders, subjected to extreme stresses and strains, would look at their bikes, touch things, feel things. I can't remember Mike ever looking round his bike. He looked at riders. I have a picture in my mind of the bike coming up in the truck and being wheeled out, brought into the *parc ferme*.[3] I'd driven up with Mike. He didn't gaze at it to see if anything was hanging loose, didn't even walk round it. He'd get on it because the mechanics had done their job, yes, that was it, he'd get on it and ride it. I repeat: he had enormous trust in people."

Macauley had arranged for Mike to go number 12 (a nice touch, reflecting the number of his TT victories, but also more practically because the fast men would all be in front and he'd know what he'd have to do). Read was number one on his Honda. But the prelude to the start was taut, tight and acrimonious.

Suzuki were not happy. Their mechanic Martin Ogborne says that "We had trouble with Honda. They refused to allow Graeme Crosby[4] to change his number. I forget who was next to him, but it was a Honda rider. Crosby said 'I'm capable of winning, but not if I've got a Honda rider next to me'. (This was a deep and perhaps psychological matter with a lot of permutations.) Graeme was number 18, I'm pretty sure Roger Marshall was number 19. So we wanted a change. At first the organizers agreed, then they dreamed up some rule that Honda had objected and wouldn't allow it. We had a great argument, but the organizers insisted.

"We got to the line and we were told Crosby had to go at 18. Crosby was fuming, steam was coming out of his ears. This is what Honda wanted. It was

---

3. Parc ferme, a French expression (closed park) for the official area where bikes and cars are put for examination – and so nobody can get at them. In rallying this is where cars are kept overnight.
4. A New Zealander who competed in the World 500cc Championship between 1980 and 1982 on Suzukis and Yamahas. He finished second in the 1982 table behind Franco Uncini (Italy), but in front of Freddie Spencer, Kenny Roberts, Barry Sheene and Randy Mamola.

what we call head-banging: get a better bike, then unnerve the opposition. It almost worked – but it didn't. Mike Hailwood came over and said to me 'Tell him to calm down, calm down. You don't start a race in an agitated mood like this'." These were the very first words Mike and Ogborne had ever exchanged, itself a testament to the passage of time. Ogborne was Barry Sheene's mechanic – and Sheene had ridden his first World Championship 500cc race in 1974, seven years after Mike rode his last. "Then Hailwood threw his voice behind us. He told the ACU that it was "wrong because I did exactly this when I was up against it on Honda against MV, I changed my number', and he quoted that instance."

The bikes are ready to be fired up, the crowd waits, Mike faces the greatest personal risk and the most profound personal examination of even his life, and amidst it his thoughts are for fair-play and just as pertinently the well-being of Crosby who he can scarcely ever have met. "You don't start a race in an agitated mood like this."

Read moved away fast, Mike moved off 50 seconds later and now an irony: Read wasn't going as fast as he had in practice, and an Ulsterman, Tom Herron, on a privately owned Honda, was suddenly emerging as the Man Most Likely.

They flooded across the line to complete lap one and Mike led Herron by nine seconds, led Read by 20.

Macauley rushed up to Attwood and shouted wildly "He doesn't have to do any more! It doesn't matter what happens now! He's done enough!". Attwood remembers Macauley as "gone, gone".

Read: "He caught me on the second lap going into Ballacraine. He passed me in that corner. The crowd were leaping up and down and for two and a half laps we diced together. I thought: I've got to stay with him for the sake of the crowd." Herron had broken down and now it was one old man against another old man and "it was great ... fantastic ... just like the old days. There was no way I could beat him unless he had trouble or he was delayed in the pits. I'd have to get the 50 seconds back to regain the lead.

"We swopped places, I'd outbrake him into a corner because the brakes on my bike were better, and he'd come by and we'd go thumbs-up and we'd whistle through the corners – but in the fast ones the Ducati was superior. The Honda was better on acceleration up to about a hundred so I'd pull him back on that. I'd drop back a bit and catch him up and get alongside him and we were really enjoying it. He knew the deal, he wasn't about to move over on me, he trusted my ability and he knew I wasn't about to move over on him.

"Following him down to the Cronk-y-Voddy straight on the last lap I was really having to rev the Honda to stay with him. The oil tank and cooler blew up and covered me in about a gallon of oil. I stopped there and watched the other riders come through. I was talking to spectators and they said 'How is it that you two old guys can do this – about 10 miles an hour quicker than anyone else – and you look so much neater? I said 'I dunno' and I got a lift back."

Mike was alone.

Surtees: "At least he was on a Ducati, which related to his past. He related to it, he switched on to the automatic pilot which top riders and drivers have and it was a superb combination."

Duke: "It was the right machine for him to make a comeback on. It was a good job he wasn't on the 1967 Honda. The Ducati handled well, and as I watched I saw the old Hailwood, the old touches. I thought: because he's ridden so many different bikes in his career, and although that might have been difficult at times, it was of long-term benefit."

Yes, all the way to here.

Pauline: "I was being kept in touch by telephone, somebody ringing me from the circuit. That was pretty nerve-wracking."

That last lap expanded itself until something much bigger happened and it was a peculiarly British profundity. No other description will do. Mike became the bike, the bike became Mike, and the thousands upon thousands were joined to them and became one with them as Mike and the bike were at one with each other. As Mike passed – it didn't matter where, town and country – the thousands were drawn instinctively to their feet in precisely the way people are in the presence of something momentous. Kids born after he'd retired waved their programmes, waved their arms. The cheering grew to such a swell at Ramsey that he could hear it above engine noise, something he had never experienced – or imagined – before.

There was no riot, no hysteria, no tears. It ran deeper than that, didn't need that to be expressed, couldn't be expressed by that. It was the British doing what they do, surrendering to another Briton by ordinary gesture and a great communal groundswell of polite noise which flowed to him as he flowed back to them; and the gesturing, the groundswell meant more than any riot, any hysteria, any tears. It came from a deep clean-water well, it was what the British do best, just as there in front of them the Briton was doing what he did best, and doing it better than anyone who had ever lived could do it. He was as ordinary in his own eyes as they, as polite as they.

And that was the consummation.

There was no pressure now. John Williams on another Honda was two minutes distant and would finish thus, Williams, who was riding as if in another time-zone, another dimension, another life, a time-warp. Two minutes. Mike came down The Mountain stately in splendour, stately in splendour and still alone, moved through the places of the descent still alone, crossed the line absolutely alone. Then there were tears.

Macauley: "I'm a hard case, and if I've cried twice in my life that's about it, but the tension because I'd organized it and I'd known I could be responsible for Mike Hailwood getting killed ... when he was coming across the line and he'd won I burst into tears."

Duke: "I spoke to Mike briefly and he was emotional. This was the greatest performance of all time on The Island."

Just for a moment the handsome face looked craggy and creased and worn. Just for a moment his left hand went up and brushed a tear away. A couple of moments later he was smiling that smile.

Read: "I went into the hotel, the Palace, in my leathers. I'd wiped a bit of the oil away. I tapped on the door of his room and he was just getting stripped off. I said 'Mike, I'm really delighted, well done, come down for a drink.' We went down to the bar, me in my greasy leathers and him in his tee shirt and jeans, and I bought him a drink."

M. Hailwood	864 Ducati	2h 5m 10.2s (108.51mph)
J. Williams	890 Honda	2h 7m 9.6s
I. Richards	984 Kawasaki	2h 8m 7.4s
H. Dahne	860 Honda	2h 8m 26.8s
A. George	855 Triumph	2h 8m 28.2s
C. Mortimer	1000 Suzuki	2h 10m 50.4s

At Jarama, Andretti did get pole. Word reached Sawyer from The Island and "I was able to take the news down the pit lane, and that was a marvellous moment because a lot of motor racing people were wildly keen on Mike as a personality. Peter Warr[5] really surprised me. He whooped and jumped around and rushed off to tell a bunch of other people. Everybody was talking about it."

Yes.

Attwood: "That night we had an enormous party and he'd actually gained another World Championship" – only this and the Ulster counted towards the Formula One title, remember. "That day and night all slotted into place as if somehow it had been meant to slot into place."

6

"The one balls-up at the TT was made by Mike. He wanted to change the steering damper on the Yamaha 500, a bike which was going to win the race, no question, the mood he was in. For some reason – and I don't know to this day why – he was unhappy with the damper. Maybe somebody had said something to him. He asked for it to be changed and they put on a Kawasaki damper." Ted Macauley is still musing and wondering about that and will always do so, will always have to do so.

Nobby Clark: "Mike would never tell the mechanics to do this or that, he always asked them and many times he'd say 'if you have any time over could you have a look at this for me?'. He never expected the bikes to be perfect, although of course we always worked with that goal in mind. I think he was a born genius, he made riding a racing bike look easy. He knew what he wanted from a machine and he was quite technical, but he didn't know how to get there. This was where we had to decipher what he told us. If there was something wrong he said that. He was an extremely honest person."

This makes The Affair of the Damper even more mysterious, impenetrable, almost a violation of character and creed, a side-stepping of the ground rules which had governed a life and served it well. "He'd broken rule one", Macauley says. "Leave it to the lads, don't go messing around."

Attwood had been pressed into active service for the 500cc race. "They said it would help if we could get some information to him on the other side of The Island so that he doesn't get it a lap late" – when he crossed the start-finish. "We would be in radio communication, me to the pits, I can't remember how. I had a board I could write on and stick out to tell him who was still in the race, who was out of the race or how far behind he was, how much in front he was. It was a proper pit board, but I had to write everything on it, there weren't numbers and things. I was going to be positioned at Ramsey. I borrowed a motorbike to ride there. I was late leaving, I had to go the wrong way round the course" – into the direction the racers would be coming from because this cut the journey from the pits to Ramsey by a third.

Thus it was that Attwood's Epic Ride joined John Cooper's Epic Ride from all those years ago and, a complete stranger to a motorbike, Attwood's was more dangerous.

---

5. Peter Warr, long-time senior member of the Lotus team, who managed it in 1982 after Colin Chapman had died and is now Secretary of the British Racing Drivers' Club.

Mike enjoying a cuppa with Tommy Robb during the Dutch GP meeting at Assen in 1967. (*Picture courtesy Tommy Robb.*)

Mike on the top step of the podium, flanked by Giacomo Agostini and John Cooper, for the prizegiving at Brno, Czechoslovakia, in 1967. (*Picture courtesy John Cooper.*)

The 1967 Belgian GP, when Mike finished second to Bill Ivy in the 250 race on his Honda. (*Picture courtesy Mick Woollett.*)

Crucial pitstop during the 1967 Senior TT. Mike about to restart the four-cylinder Honda while Giacomo Agostini's MV is still being refuelled. (*Picture courtesy Mick Woollett.*)

Mike, seen here with Nobby Clark at Brands Hatch in 1967, was not mechanically minded, though on this occasion he tackled a plug change on the Honda. (*Picture courtesy Mick Woollett.*)

A picture that says it all. Mike pulls a face as he passes Mick Woollett during his vain pursuit of Agostini's MV Agusta during the 500cc race of the 1967 Belgian GP. (*Picture courtesy Mick Woollett.*)

Mike, an avid reader of almost anything, catches up on the latest racing gossip with Ago in 1967. (*Picture courtesy Mick Woollett.*)

Mike with Honda's Aika-san and mechanics at Hockenheim for the 1967 German GP. (*Picture courtesy Mick Woollett.*)

John Hartle receiving the Fred G Craner Trophy from Mike, who seems to be disappointed by the lack of 'bubbly' inside. (*Picture courtesy Nick Nicholls.*)

Bill Ivy and Mike, the master pranksters, indulging in a demonstration of hippy-style flower power in the paddock at Snetterton. (*Picture courtesy Jim Greening.*)

Mike didn't enjoy his first foray into motor racing in the early Sixties, but became one of the stars of Formula 5000 on his return to four wheels in 1969. Here he prepares for the Guards Championship race at Brands Hatch in Jackie Epstein's Lola-Chevy. (*Picture courtesy Fred Taylor.*)

Mike the Bike left it to Jackie Oliver to demonstrate the Gulf team's Le Mans mascot in 1969. They used Ford GT40s for the race, which Mike and his partner David Hobbs would have won comfortably but for a fractured brake pipe. Instead, Jacky Ickx, sharing with Oliver, beat a Porsche to the line in the closest finish in the race's history. (*Picture MRP archive.*)

Mike, who drove a Surtees-Ford TS10 to the European Formula Two Championship in 1972, leading a bunch of cars away from the Mallory Park hairpin. (*Picture courtesy Gerry Stream.*)

Formula Two produced close-fought racing between drivers on the way up and established Formula One stars having a change from Grands Prix. Here Mike's Surtees is running a close second to Jody Scheckter's McLaren at Crystal Palace in 1972. (*Photograph courtesy C W Mark.*)

Mike leaves the Silverstone pits in his Surtees-Ford for the start of the 1973 British GP, but he would soon be back. All three Surtees in the race were amongst the eight cars eliminated when Jody Scheckter lost control of his McLaren and caused a multiple pile-up at the end of the first lap. (*Picture courtesy Martyn Pass.*)

Mike enjoying himself through a tight left-hander at the wheel of the Ford-powered Yardley McLaren M23 during 1974. (*Picture courtesy Martyn Pass.*)

Thanks to his motorcycle background, Mike was a highly competitive racing driver in the wet. Here he is heading for a close fourth place in the 1974 *Daily Mail* Race of Champions at Brands Hatch, when he finished on the tail of McLaren team leader Emerson Fittipaldi. (*Picture courtesy Chris Buckler.*)

The smile that suggested calm confidence. After three rounds Mike was lying joint second in the 1974 World Championship, but then things started to go downhill until his final season of motor racing ended abruptly. (*Picture MRP archive.*)

This much-handled print remains Pauline Hailwood's favourite portrait of Mike. (*Picture courtesy Pauline Hailwood.*)

The family man. Mike with Pauline and their baby son David in 1974. (*Picture courtesy Pauline Hailwood.*)

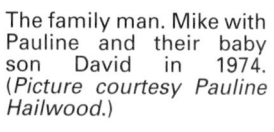

Back to his racing roots. In 1975 Mike did a lap of the TT course on a 350 Yamaha, although there was no intention of a racing comeback at that time. (*Picture courtesy Mick Woollett.*)

Geoff Duke and Mike meet again on The Island in 1975. No sooner had he arrived than the autographs began to flow again, many of them for youngsters who were seeing him for the first time, but knew all about the legend. (*Picture courtesy Mick Woollett.*)

Ian Richards, who would finish third on his Kawasaki, holds a momentary lead over Mike's winning Ducati at the start of the 1978 Formula One TT. (*Picture courtesy Mick Woollett.*)

A master never loses his touch. Mike's immaculate style is captured as he accelerates away from Quarter Bridge during his winning Formula One ride. (*Picture courtesy Mick Woollett.*)

Rounding Governor's Bridge ahead of the Honda of the previous year's Formula One race winner Phil Read. (*Picture courtesy Mick Woollett.*)

Mission accomplished. Mike accepts the congratulations of second place man John Williams after his successful comeback ride; his winning margin was almost two minutes. (*Picture courtesy Mick Woollett.*)

A week after his TT success Mike was at Mallory Park, where Barry Sheene couldn't resist climbing on to the Ducati. (*Picture courtesy Nick Nicholls.*)

Mike was less lucky in his other three 1978 TT races, in each of which he rode a Yamaha. Here he is accelerating out of Quarter Bridge shortly before retiring from one of them. (*Picture courtesy Mick Woollett.*)

In action again at Mallory Park. Here he is taking the hairpin on the Ducati with Phil Read's Honda in the background. (*Picture courtesy Nick Nicholls.*)

Mike raises a cheer from the crowd in Parliament Square as he sweeps through on his Suzuki in the 1979 Schweppes Classic TT. Mike's battle with Alex George and his Honda made it an epic race with the result in the balance to the end. At the finishing line the margin was just 3.4 seconds, and this time Mike had to settle for second place. (*Picture courtesy Nick Nicholls.*)

One of the last pictures taken of Mike was this shot of him with Charlie Rous, a friend over many years, who in 1964 had been part of Mike's support team for his successful attempt at the one-hour speed record at Daytona. (*Picture courtesy Charlie Rous.*)

"They were shutting the circuit all the time and I thought *Christ the team is relying on me with this signal board and at this rate I'm not going to bloody get there.* I was stopped so many times and as soon as I mentioned Mike Hailwood there was no problem, though that didn't work a couple of times. *'You're with Mike Hailwood? Everybody says that.'* I was a jibbering wreck when I reached Ramsey.

"I was standing coming out of Ramsey at a garage – I was standing on the side of the road really. There were two or three other people near me, that's all. I was in an area that other people weren't and I probably wasn't meant to be there, either, but Mike knew where I was. The race started and I was giving him information that Ted was giving me from the pit area.

"On the second lap I saw Mike coming towards me and he was stopping. He was in quite a state as I realized later. He had to switch the bike off or we'd not have heard a thing we were saying to each other. He explained that the steering damper had broken and if you haven't got a damper the steering can do anything. He'd got into the most horrendous speed wobble and the bike had nearly thrown him off. He could have been killed and nobody would probably have known why. 'For Christ's sake tell the pits to get another damper ready.'

"With that he started to push to bike off. Seeing him do that – and he had the bad leg anyway – I started pushing the bike as well, which of course you're not meant to do. Outside assistance. I was pushing as hard as I could and he, not seeing me, must have thought pushing the bike was a good bit easier than he'd reckoned it would be!

"It fired up and off he went. A policeman came over and went mad. *You shouldn't be on the bloody circuit, what are you doing on the circuit?* I suppose he thought I was in a dangerous place. I couldn't have cared less. I was helping my mate, that was all. It got heavy, I nearly got locked up. The policeman said *you can't stand there*, it was dramatic and noisy, but he didn't stop me doing what I was doing."

(Later Attwood would learn about life without a damper; "once you get up to any sort of speed the whole bike starts to go out of control. If you get into a speed roll you are a passenger and how you prevent a speed roll happening I don't know".)

Mike finished 22nd.

"The steering had been all over the place and Mike asked for another damper", Wood says. "At the end of it Mike didn't blame anybody, he just said 'Thanks guys for all your help'. That's the sort of person Mike was" – to which Macauley adds: "He wanted it changed so it's changed and it cocked up. Even Mike couldn't handle that, he couldn't steer the thing. He said 'I dropped a clanger, it was my mistake', and he was most gracious."

An American, Pat Hennen, crashed on the last lap (and would be in a coma for three months). Mike went over to the Suzuki team and asked Ogborne how Hennen was. "Very serious", Ogborne said. "Hailwood asked about a visit to the hospital, but there was no point. Pat was simply too ill." Martin Ogborne remembers that, the coming and the asking.

In the 250 he was 12th – he hadn't expected to do particularly well and was gazing ahead to the climax, the Classic, anyway. The Classic was a misnomer.

"We were absolutely level on time", Grant says. "I used to have a signal point just coming out of Laurel Bank. A friend would go with a board. They had a commentary point at Ballacraine and, believe it or not, he just had time to put my position on the first lap on the board. This was an enormous help because riding round the TT circuit is the loneliest place in the world. Unless someone comes past you you haven't a clue what's going on so to have signals is very important.

"I had three or four signal points around the circuit, sometimes a lot more than that, but the first one gave you an indication as to where you were. Mike and I were level at my first signal. I got *P1 plus zero* (first place but no lead in seconds, i.e. first equal). I thought: Bloody hell, this is going to be a tough one, this is. Then the next signal I got Mike was out. His bike had stopped." The crankshaft had broken.

"It was an anti-climax, I'm sure, to everyone on the Isle of Man, everybody moaned and groaned, but to me it was a great relief. I cruised on and won it, but looking back now I'd have liked Mike not to have dropped out of it ..."

Quiet, almost private of postscripts. After all the traumas with the Yamahas "no wonder at the end of the week Mike said there were only two losers, him and I. All the hangers-on were gone. Mike really felt he had let the fans down badly" – Nobby Clark.

Martin Ogborne: "We watched the Yamaha fiasco. They'd arrived with a 250 straight out of the box,[6] a 500 old ex-works thing and a 750 straight out of the box. In those days there were certain things which were wrong on Yamahas. We knew that, but of course we didn't say anything. The 750 kept seizing. Hailwood never did a lap: he'd set off, it would seize. I think Nobby Clark and the other mechanics were dropped in at the deep-end. They had so much work to do on three bikes. The mistake was in sending new bikes. You never take new bikes to the Isle of Man. It's a stupid idea. You take what you know works unless you've got lots of practice time or lots of money, and even then you're gambling."

Jerry Wood: "On the last night Mike came up to me and said 'Here's a letter for you, but don't open it'. I thought that was odd. When I did open it I was flabbergasted. There was £200 and a note, *'Thanks for all you've done'*. I was driving one of the trucks home and we weren't leaving until the following evening. I went to the hotel and said I would need the use of the room during the day after I would normally have checked out. I was prepared to pay the amount of an extra night's stay. They said 'But the room has already been paid for by Mr Hailwood'."

Mario Andretti won the Spanish Grand Prix at Jarama, June 4, 1978, from Peterson, Jacques Laffite, Scheckter, Watson and Hunt. Regazzoni was classified 15th, but not running at the end. A broken fuel line. It did not catch fire.

"I didn't know that he'd won the Segrave Trophy, and I didn't know he'd recommended me for the Segrave medal as the man responsible for the TT comeback.[7] He kept it very, very secret and it came out on PA.[8] The office rang me and said 'You've been recommended', and I didn't even know. I told Mike and he just grinned", Macauley says.

---

6. A motor racing expression which means what it implies: a bike or car freshly made, untried and untested, straight from the factory.
7. For services rendered to the sport.
8. The Press Association, Britain's national news-gathering service, which feeds virtually every newspaper, TV and radio station and is also widely used for official announcements because all subscribers get them and simultaneously.

"Anyway, we went for the awards and he was introduced to Cats' Eyes Cunningham – I forget his first name – but he had been a pathfinder pilot who led Lancaster bombers in raids during the Second World War. Mike had heard of him and was in awe of him. It was the only time I heard Mike say 'I've got to get his autograph, please go and get his autograph for me. I can't go and ask him.' I said 'I don't believe you'. Mike said 'He's a hero of mine, he's an absolute hero of mine.' I went over and Cat's Eyes Cunningham said 'I'll do it on one condition – that Mike gives me his', and it was a lovely situation." It was another consummation of the British finding something in the British and holding hard to that, expressing it so awkwardly, diffidently, gently.

"In general, Mike had a healthy appreciation that people wanted to be near him or talk to him, but he still couldn't understand it. He just couldn't understand it. After the autographing I said 'Now, Mike, you can go some way to understanding why people want some attachment to you'. How could he possibly not have realized that? Well, he didn't. Take his attachment to trophies, for instance. After he won the Formula One race we went to the prizegiving and he gave me the trophy, the winged Mercury, and I've still got it.

"Mike went through his trophies and made sure they were all silver (and contemplated having them melted down to make a table, though he never did) and he made sure his gold medals were gold." It still left a lot of trophies and more were coming, more were coming. "I opened a cupboard one day and they all fell out and I claimed one, I said I'd like one of those. He said 'Find the biggest (expletive) one you can and get it out of here'. It was for winning a car racing championship in Brazil. I carried it home on the train. I've still got it, too."

This is (inevitably) something of a digression as the last of the ferries churned their way from the Isle of Man and an emptiness returned to The Island, but it's also another face in the mirror.

Anyway, "I think we earned something just short of 70,000 quid for one week's work, which was unbelievable, and more came in a little bit later" – Ted Macauley.

The real postscript is forged by Dickie Attwood and belongs to him. Naturally enough, it takes as its centrepiece the Formula One win, although all unknowing it broadens and widens to embrace the whole of The Island those June days. It is only a sentence, only nine words, and better for that because for once it's not a singular example of British understatement.

"1978 was a dream, no, it was a miracle."

THE MOUNTAIN

"He said 'How am I doing?' and I said 'Fine'. That was the sum total of it. We had to shout because the crowd were going berserk." – Martin Ogborne

"I never want to go that fast again." – Mike Hailwood

"On The Island it's very much you against the circuit." – Mick Grant

1

"He decided to come back again, which I was against, a personal opinion. I'd been against it in 1978, although not in the least because he was competition – from that point of view it was a plus. No, I thought he'd an awful lot to lose if it went wrong." These sentiments are cast into great irony. The speaker, Mick Grant, was to be a central player in 1979 and it went wrong for *him*.

There was never much doubt that Mike would come back to The Comeback again. "The 500 was the one Mike had really wanted to win", Attwood says. "It's like winning a Formula One car race instead of a Formula 5000 race."

Macauley, who'd vowed to himself that he'd never go through it a second time, drew a lot of deep breaths and started organizing bikes. He stayed with Ducati for the Formula One and contacted Suzuki, who saw everything all in one moment, said "Yes please", and provided a 500cc machine. Suzuki also offered a 750 superbike, but even Mike baulked at that.

The Ducati was the problem. Macauley estimated that it had gone backwards from the year before, the handling wasn't good and they'd moved the gearchange to the other side. That was of enormous significance and potential danger to a racer who reacted instinctively and whose reactions were governed by the habits of a lifetime. Mike flew to Misano, in Italy, to test it, the back wheel seized and he was thrown off. He landed heavily and broke his ribs. "I retained no control of myself whatsoever, which was incredibly frightening. I just went tumbling down the road like a rag doll, arms and legs everywhere." He flew immediately to Heathrow and was in such agony that he booked into an airport hotel for the night. He was unable to move further.

He recovered enough to be able to test at Donington and Oulton. "Ducati went serious testing and did quite a lot with Mike before the TT", Attwood says. "He'd had that big accident in Italy because he went for the wrong thing while he was changing gear. He was off in no time and he really hurt himself. I remember going testing at Oulton, and he was trying the Ducati. He had difficulty getting in tune with the gears and the brakes."

On March 18 Barry Sheene won the Venezuelan Grand Prix on his Suzuki, Tom Herron third on another. Ogborne and fellow mechanic David Cullen, an Aussie known universally as Radar, returned to the Suzuki headquarters in Britain. "Maurice Knight[1] called us upstairs and said Suzuki were going to enter the Isle of Man. We knew Crosby was going to do it, we knew obviously Barry wouldn't[2] and we knew you always had a spot rider.[3] We had no idea who it was going to be. Maurice said it was Hailwood. I thought *Gordon Bennett*.[4] We were asked to keep it secret. I said to Radar 'We're going to be 100 per cent on the bike because if anything goes wrong Suzuki will go down the plug hole so fast it won't be funny'." Ogborne, incidentally, always refers to Mike as Hailwood. This I suspect is both a mark of respect and recognition that he didn't actually know him.

"We hadn't a bike so we assembled one in the workshop. We had enough time. It was a 1978 machine, and we made it Isle of Man-survivable. Come the month of May, we'd been out to more Grands Prix" – Austria, Hockenheim, Imola and Jarama – "and we were told Hailwood was arriving to measure himself up for the bike.

"The workshop was cleared and everybody went home. About eight o'clock in the evening Radar and I were waiting, Ted brought Hailwood in. We were introduced and he remembered me from 1978. We sat him on the bike, adjusted the handlebars and the footrest, things like that, so he could get to the controls.

"Radar and I had decided it would be a good idea to go to Donington to test because he hadn't ridden a Suzuki. A couple of weeks later we did go to Donington. Some wealthy pop star – I can't remember who – was having driving lessons in a Merc, he cleared off and Donington said: 'Right, off you go'. We didn't exactly set the bike up for a beginner, but we didn't set it up the way we would have done for Sheene and Herron, either. Hailwood went round and round getting used to it, the power, the brakes, what it did, what it didn't do. He came into the pits and I said 'Anything to report?'."

Mike: "No."

Ogborne: "What's the bike like?"

Mike: "Perfect."

Ogborne: "It might feel like perfect to you, but it's obviously not."

Mike: "No, no, perfect."

Ogborne: "*No, no, no*! They aren't perfect. Let's start again. Let's start at the front end. Is there anything you don't like there? Is anything giving you problems there?"

Mike: "No."

Ogborne: "Are you sure?"

Mike: "Yes."

Ogborne: "Alright, let's talk about the brakes."

---

1. Head of Suzuki-GB.
2. Sheene rode on The Island once, crashed, vowed never to ride there again and never did.
3. Guest rider.
4. A slang expression meaning strewth!

Mike: "Well, I could do with this..."

Ogborne: "Right, now we're getting somewhere."

And that is how it happened. "It took him ages to open up to us. I know what he was comparing it to, the Honda he'd ridden all those years ago and the Yamaha in 1978, which was past its sell-by date. This Suzuki was better, a lot better, and he took that as being perfect. He was unassuming, he didn't want to put anybody to any trouble, he didn't want to go further in setting the bike up, but I said 'You *can* go further. Cut the bullshit. What is it really like?' Slowly we got more sense out of him. He made a few adjustments, but still nowhere near enough, and we could tell that. You can't arrive, ride a bike and say it's perfect, you *cannot*.

"We made changes, he went out and came back in and I said 'Right, how are you feeling now?'. I said 'Now you understand. OK, we'll change the engine setting for a short-circuit specification, which is like a Grand Prix. You'll feel the difference.' We changed the ignition timing, sorted the carbs out and said 'Try that, but watch it, this thing's quick now'. He came back and said 'Bloody hell, you weren't kidding'. Of course we'd set it up for 15 super-quick laps, we weren't going to run it round the Isle of Man like that.

"In Hailwood's day, if a bike was wobbling they'd say hang on to it, or turn the steering damper up one more notch. On the Hondas which he'd ridden you'd look at the rear units and there was just nothing. If it was bottoming out you went the one notch up and they said *that's it, forget it*. We could go anywhere because we had a side-loading gearbox. I explained that to him. I said 'You can have any ratio you want. We can change this in eight minutes. You tell me what gear is too high, we can change it to suit you.' He was afraid that when he got to Waterworks and Governor's Bridge he'd burn the clutch out. I said it wouldn't happen, it would handle anything he wanted, 'but if you're saying you're afraid of that we'll put a low first gear in it and bring second gear close so when you go from second to first it won't stand the thing on end'. We played about with the gearbox and on The Island he used it like that.

"His right ankle was unusable. He said 'I cannot use it at all' and he couldn't. He had no movement in it, the movement came from the knee. His ankle was sort of locked."

The pressure began to mount, different and sharper than in 1978. "Everybody", Sawyer says, "was expecting much bigger things now he was on the Suzuki, it was a Grand Prix contender and so, yes, the pressure was much greater the second time around."

It increased in the hardest way. Two weeks before the TT Mike was invited to watch the North West 200 in Ulster. During it Tom Herron crashed and was killed, Mick Grant crashed and was badly hurt. "I had a mechanical problem and a rear wheel adjuster snapped as I went into the hairpin", Grant says. "I hit a lamppost, broke my pelvis, two or three ribs. It was the only time I was detained in hospital overnight because of an accident. It was in Coleraine. I signed myself out, they took me to the airport in a wheelchair, I flew to The Island and there was a wheelchair to meet me.

"I went to The Island because it was my job. People expect to see you, I was one of the top names at the TT – apart from Mike. People had booked their holidays, it was a good pay packet and, as I say, it was my job. The difference between a professional sportsman and someone else is that if you break an arm, see a doctor and he says 'It'll have to be in plaster for six weeks', the sportsman replies 'Hang on a minute, I want it off as fast as possible, I want it off in two weeks, can you mould the plaster so I can use a throttle?'.

"I went to see a friend, a lady who was chief physiotherapist at the hospital, and she said the chances of me being fit were remote. My pelvis hadn't actually come apart, but it was quite a bad fracture and I'd got the ribs. The biggest problem was that my leg hadn't been drained and there was an awful lot of blood in it which shouldn't have been there. I went swimming three times a day, she was physio-ing me three times a day, and after a couple of days I could just about get around on crutches."

By now the pace on The Island was quickening. Every boat disgorged more and more people. The very atmosphere was spiced as it had been in the Sixties by a single man and what he would do, what he could do. There was a vivid sense of history as well as curiosity threaded through it. The past and the present would be reunited – another consummation.

What Mike needed was some measure of escape. "Macauley rented a house quite a way from everywhere and I went there for a couple of nights", Attwood says. "Mike handled the pressure very well, there was never any problem in that." Everyone wanted Mike, and as Attwood puts it, "he had to attend all the pre-race events, the wet tee-shirt contests, all those sorts of things. The places were absolutely packed because he was there."

"They had a competition in the Palace Hotel", Carol Young says. "In those days people were doing silly dances on their own and the competition was for motorcyclists who wanted to dance. They asked Mike to be the judge. He said to us 'I don't really want to do it, but I will'. We were sitting there with him watching these dancers and he didn't know which one to choose. They were all pretty good in their way, blokes and girls, but funnily enough the blokes wore leather jackets and chains. Because they knew Mike was judging they were doing their best. Mike awarded the prize, he had his photograph taken with the winner and they were all thrilled to bits.

"There was a little go-kart circuit up at Onchan Head[5] and the next day Mike said 'Come on, let's go up there and have a thrash'. We went, we were on the karts and a gang of bikers turned up. They were the group who had been dancing. They had the photograph from the night before and they approached Mike to sign it. If you'd see these guys on the street you'd have crossed over and walked on the other side, but he stood there for about half an hour laughing and joking with them."

Grant was doing no laughing and joking. "I went to see the official doctor and he showed me things I'd got to be able to do, some press-ups, stand on one leg, and so on. He said unless I could do them he wouldn't sign anything to clear me for the races. That was the challenge."

Mike had a brief moment to gaze back. "The whole Honda 1966 team was reunited and we had a super party", Stuart Graham says. "There weren't so many of the mechanics, but the guy who was running the works-backed Honda team – HRC as they called it – was Aika-*san*, he'd been team manager in 1966 and he was still going strong. We were all astounded and proud that Mike was back again after all these years with a gammy foot to show another generation how it was done."

The Formula One race began to loom. Grant went back to the doctor who,

---

5. On the opposite side of Douglas Bay to the town centre.

during practice, "was going in the helicopter up to the top of The Mountain. The doctor said 'Right, you can have one lap, but you must stop at The Bungalow. I want to check you.' I daren't put my left foot down, I couldn't put weight on it. To stop I could only use my right foot and when people were shoving me off I'd say 'For God's sake make sure it goes to the right.' They pushed me on this big Honda and I had a steady run round and stopped where the doctor was. There's not much lock on a racing bike, it was a heavy old bike and I'd got to turn it round in the road on just the one foot. I daren't take the other off the footrest. He said 'How did you come on?' and I said 'No bother at all, perfect' and he said 'Well, you'd better finish the lap.' Some guys up there gave me a shove and ... I'd got away with it.

"The following day I had to go round to his office. I hadn't been taking pain-killers. I did the press-ups, I did the standing on one leg and he said I could ride. I missed the Formula One race. I thought I'd do the 500 and the Classic at the end of the week because every day I was getting better, measurably better. Swimming is the best thing in the world. Everything was still broken, but the muscles around were coming on a treat, and if you're fit anyway that makes a difference. In those days I'd usually run seven or eight miles every day because if you're fit you can take a knock and come back a lot quicker."

The Formula One race itself? The Ducati was far off the pace and the battery box came loose. Then Mike lost top gear, too. He was fifth.

A. George	(997 Honda)	2h 2m 50.6s	(110.27mph)
C. Williams	(900 Honda)	2h 3m 46.2s	(109.74mph)
R. Haslam	(997 Honda)	2h 5m 00.0s	(108.66mph)
G. Crosby	(994 Kawasaki)	2h 6m 28.2s	(107.39mph)
M. Hailwood	(864 Ducati)	2h 8m 03.6s	(106.06mph)

Alex George was now in the second year of his two-year plan. The first year, 1978, had been perhaps preparation, a rehearsal – fifth in the Formula One, fifth in the 500, third in the Classic. Now, riding Grant's bike, he had conquered. He fully intended to conquer the 500 and then the Classic and by now he judged himself "super-fit".

Mike had altogether different considerations to ponder.

"That Ducati was as much a physical and mental effort for him to ride as the big Honda had been", Sawyer says. "It was a pig. He was having to hold the battery in with his calf muscle, it kept on misfiring and spluttering and he was still hanging on in there riding this thing round." (Sawyer expands on that with a more general but no less pertinent observation. "What you forget is that the circuit would be closed because there was mist on The Mountain, and then somebody would go and do an exploratory lap and they'd start. Where there is mist there is wet. Mike would say 'You go barrelling along quite merrily and all of a sudden you look for a colour change and sure enough just where the fog's been that's where you start seeing the damp line and it's a frightener. And along the long straight to find the front wheel coming off the ground at 180mph is ... an experience.' I don't think people ever realized quite what The Island really was." And Mike had been riding it holding the battery in.)

"He was very, very uptight when he came off the bike", Sawyer says, "he was really screwed off because he had not succeeded and he'd had problems trying to get the Suzuki to perform in practice. He was despondent when bikes let him down because he was as determined as ever. He suffered these enormous mental and physical strains. However, on The Island he had Barry Sheene's mechanic, a wonderfully conscientious lad."

Martin Ogborne, in fact. "We practised on the Friday", Ogborne says, "and enginewise we didn't touch it until Sunday morning" – the day before the 500cc race. "As soon as we started it we knew something was dreadfully wrong. We started it two or three times to try and convince ourselves that there was nothing wrong. I said to Radar 'We've got to take the engine out', and we knew what a big step that was. We lifted it out mid-morning.

"It was a crankshaft oil seal. We had to have the crank pulled apart, then we had to go round to an engineer, and as soon as he pressed the bearing off we saw what had happened. On an oil seal there is a spring ring which always grips. That had jumped off because of the way it had been put together and you couldn't check it – you received it as a sealed unit from Japan. Only when you run it do you find if there's something wrong with it. At least we had found out what it was. If we hadn't we'd have had to cross ourselves...

"The Isle of Man is not like a Grand Prix with a 10-minute warm-up. We'd have had to start the bike, we'd have seen smoke. Off Mike would have gone and as the engine tried to run it would have drawn transmission oil into the engine. It's not running on one cylinder so effectively it becomes a three-cylinder four-cylinder. He would have gone down Bray Hill and probably stopped at Quarter Bridge with no throttle response, nothing.

"We got another oil seal and tapped it in. At five o'clock Hailwood came round because he wanted to check the bike over. I'll never forget his face. He expected the bike to be ready to go. Normally riders like to come along and just sit on the bike for their peace of mind. Of course the whole engine was in bits. I said 'Don't worry, we'll have it fixed by tomorrow morning. We've found out what it is, it's only minor.' I even pointed out what it was. I said 'Toddle off back to your hotel' – I had to tell him *something* – 'we'll see you first thing in the morning. We're sorting it out now.' He knew it was more than minor. He wasn't stupid, and anyway a rider can get detuned so quickly if he watches the people around him and they show any attitude of cruising.

"We worked meticulously all that evening to get it back together. Our workshop was underneath the staff quarters at the Majestic Hotel. The waiters came down to watch us work and stayed most of the night. There were so many of them standing around that we had to ask them to leave. We finished around four in the morning. We fired the bike up and the staff didn't mind because if they hadn't been watching they'd heard us working and in any case the workshop was well away from the hotel.

"We started it up and we knew the bike was alright. It was dark, we had a torch and shone it across the back of all four exhaust pipes, which is probably the best way of doing it. This is a bit like watching for fog. We didn't see any and that's how a two-stroke runs. Straight away it felt proper. We went and had breakfast at a little place down the road which was open all night, and by then it was time to practise our quick-fill drill because at 10 o'clock you had to put the bike in the scrutineering bay.

"We loaded the bike, went up to the pit lane at six o'clock. We had a 100-gallon tank and we erected it, put the quick-filler on. We had it 15 feet in the air and with the 100 gallons it put in five gallons in two seconds. They were aircraft fillers, one at the side, one at the top, it was gravity feed,[6] you plugged them in and *wham*.

---

6. Using the weight of the 100 gallons to force-feed petrol into a bike.

We got a guy to sit on the bike and Radar and I practised our drill three times."

Grant woke to this dawn still in pain. He would race, of course, "and on The Island it's very much you against the circuit. The first lap is the dangerous one because if you're in the leading dozen it's the guys with low numbers you're going to have to pass: they're going quick and it can be difficult. Once you've got that first lap out of the way the race is established. You're lapping the ones who are maybe a few miles an hour slower, you wait a couple of corners if necessary and then pass them and that's not a problem."

Grant's problem was, of course, his injuries. Their effect remained completely unknown. How much pain would they give him? How long could he tolerate it – two miles or two hundred? And he had Alex George to contend with as well as Mike...Alex George, a tough and talented Scotsman who had won the Formula One race and in this year 1979 was flying round The Island.

Interviewed, Mike said "We've had our problems with the bike and we'll have to see, but I'm definitely going for a finish." More privately he confided to Ogborne that he had a plan "and he told me what it was. 'The first couple of laps I won't go that quick.' At the start of the race he wouldn't be cruising, but consolidating his position, working out where he was going to make his move."

With the noise of engines rising like a chorus in the background Grant levered himself awkwardly and very gently onto his bike and felt tentatively down with that left foot. He settled in the saddle. "Talk about 'Let us pray'," he said.

Mike went number eight, a muscular shove, a springy few steps and he was away. George and Grant were on the next row and 10 seconds later they moved off, Grant needing a pusher, who peeled away as the bike fired, George already travelling fast. At Ramsey – and moving almost in tandem – Grant and George had clawed four seconds back on Mike.

"If I'd been a rider who moved around on the bike", Grant says, "I wouldn't have got as far as Quarter Bridge. I locked my elbows into the tank and crouched. My pelvis wasn't the problem because in a race your pelvis doesn't actually do anything. It was the ribs which were giving me the pain."

At Governor's Bridge Grant was in the lead on overall time and actually catching Mike physically. As Mike cranked the Suzuki over for the slow, slow hairpin, straightened it and accelerated down the hill Grant was already turning in a mere 70, 80 yards behind. As Grant accelerated down the hill George was already turning into it a mere 70, 80 yards behind ...

Lap One:

Grant	111.59mph
George	111.17mph
Mike	110.93mph

This was the peak of Grant's effort and he began to drift back. In his dogged Yorkshire accent he says "It was quite painful". On lap two Mike squeezed his speed up to 112.17mph.

On lap three Mike destroyed Grant, George and everybody else. On lap three he destroyed the 500 lap record. On lap three he bent The Mountain to his will. 114.02mph.

Grant was moving slower and slower. "Going down towards Hillberry the crank went. By that time I was all in, I'd had enough anyway. When I stopped I had to be lifted off the bike by a spectator. It's one of the few times in my life I had bother with a leg over ..."

The pitstop was crucial, Mike leading by three seconds. Ogborne and Radar waited. "Radar was on one side and I was on the vent.[7] I vented the tank to let the air out because if you didn't you'd blow the fuel-lines out of it – so much fuel was going in so fast. I used a cloth to help, Hailwood picked it up and wiped his visor. He said 'How am I doing?' and I said 'Fine'. That was it, that was the sum total of it. We had to shout because the crowd were going berserk.

"At the same time as we were shouting I was looking at the vent tube, I was looking for neat fuel coming out because the moment you see neat fuel the tank is full – not froth, it's not full then. The crowd were looking for that as well, the crowd were roaring '*off, off, off*' wanting me to tell Radar to back away and let Hailwood go.

"I watched, I shouted to Radar '*off*'. He had to do that first. If I had, the tank would have split – all that weight of fuel going in and no vent for it to come out. We'd worked out a system. The vent tube was strapped to my back so I didn't have to put it down. Radar stood back with the hose. It's heavy, it's four inches in diameter, 12 feet long and it alone holds six gallons of fuel. Radar held that up, I went round to the rear of the bike and pushed it and Hailwood went.

"When a rider comes in he loses his rhythm, his momentum, and it takes him a lap to get back into it. The bike feels different because it's just been almost empty and now it's full. We were running larger than usual fuel tanks, 36 litres instead of 32. He began to pick up his pace ..."

Not for long. "The steering damper runs from the cylinder head right up to the radiator. Because the engine is running such a long time the damper became so hot it got very stiff, almost jammed," Ogborne says. "At Governor's Bridge round the hairpin he turned, it hit a tight spot and then slackened off. He had to put his foot on the ground. He didn't know what it was. He thought 'Oh God, what is this?'. Later we worked out that the heat had made the oil very hot, almost boiled and that pressurized the steering damper and momentarily it locked ..."

Mike would tell Macauley, "The bloody handlebars wouldn't let me turn acute right-hand bends. It was OK on the fast bends, but I had to heel it over and put my feet down to *tap-dance* my way round on the acute corners."

George dropped out, ignition, his hat-trick now no more than a wistful wish. It left Mike quite suddenly in splendid isolation. A rider called Tony Rutter was second, but far, far behind. On lap four Mike did 112.06mph, on lap five 112.15. "He was two and a half minutes in front of Rutter", Ogborne says. "It was almost like a demonstration run. He'd done the practice, he knew everything about the bike, he was confident. At the beginning of lap six we'd already started to take the quick-filler down and pull it apart. We looked at the signboard and saw his light come on[8] and we knew that he was going to win. Then we went down to the finish area and waited for him to complete the lap."

---

7. Without labouring the point which Ogborne explains so well, as fuel empties from a tank air rushes in to replace it. When you come to refill the tank with petrol you need a vent to allow the air to escape.
8. The system worked like this: on a big scoreboard by the grandstand a Boy Scout moved an arrow on a clockface over each rider's number as the rider reached specific places (Ballacraine, Kirkmichael, Ramsey, and so forth). When the rider reached Signpost Corner an electric light went on and people in the grandstand knew he was only a couple of miles away.

Mike covered that sixth and final lap at 111.62mph. That's when he heard the ripple of cheering at Ramsey, that's when he cranked the Suzuki over, dipped down another gear so that for an instant the engine shrieked in pain, cranked it over the other way to curve round the left-hand corner just across the little town square; that's when the bike wailed up The Mountain, wailed down The Mountain and ran for home, each place a familiar marker, each place a memory: the left at Keppel Gate, the hard right at Creg-ny-Baa, the descent to Brandish Corner, to Hillberry, the hard-right at Signpost Corner, the hairpin at Governor's, the hammer-hammer-hammer to the line; that's when he raised his left hand to acknowlege the crowd in the grandstand, every one of them on their feet, that's when he made the small, polite, modest movement, nothing more. It remained utterly typical.

M. Hailwood	(500 Suzuki)	2h 1m 32.4s	(111.756mph)
T. Rutter	(500 Suzuki)	2h 3m 39.4s	(109.843mph)
D. Ireland	(500 Suzuki)	2h 4m 7.2s	(109.433mph)

"When we met him he was ecstatic", Ogborne says. "Ted was there, the crowd surrounded him. We caught the bike and he said 'Thanks a lot, brilliant, I couldn't have done it without you'."

Someone said: "You know you've done the lap record?".

"Really?"

Leslie Nichol: "A hundred and fourteen."

"Nooooo. You're joking."

"No, you did it."

"Bloody hell, I wasn't even trying very hard."

Mike moved to the high winner's platform and he was still isolated in this splendour. As Ogborne puts it cryptically 'Nobody else had come through. Two and a half minutes is a long time." Up there a few minutes later when Rutter had finally arrived Mike paid the compliment Ogborne still remembers and will always remember. "With modern riders you've good and bad", Ogborne says. "You've people who snap at you, people who forget you. Hailwood seemed almost too good to be true – but that was his nature, it wasn't anything else."

Up there, the hewn face slightly stooped towards a microphone, a garland round his neck, he said "The whole thing went a lot better than it did on Saturday, and I'd like to thank Martin and Radar who've been working on the machine, because I know they worked all last night. They found a seal had gone in the crankshaft or something technical (dismissive wave of hand indicating his continuing bafflement with the mechanical world) and they spent all night ripping it apart and putting it back together. I'd like to thank them for all their hard work and of course all our sponsors and congratulations to Tony (Rutter) and Dennis (Ireland)." He did not mention himself and that remained utterly typical, too.

"After the 500 I was out of my brains", Ogborne says. "I was tired, I had some champagne and I don't know how we got the bike back to the garage. We managed. By then three or four hundred people had gathered because they'd heard that's where we'd been working. We'd tried to keep it a little bit secret because you don't want too many people in, but they had heard. We lifted the bike out of the van and there was a great cheer. We put the laurel on the front of it and we went down to the hotel. There was another great cheer when we went in because I think all the staff had realized how hard we'd worked. There were about 15 drinks lined up for us, everyone had gone mad.

"I remember a poster and it showed Hailwood flicking through one of the bends – a normal three-foot-by-two poster, they were all over The Island – and the caption to it said *Hailwood chooses Castrol*. There was one in the hotel foyer, and by the time we got back there someone had crossed it out and written: *God chooses Castrol*. I wish I'd got it and kept it..."

That was the emotion of it. The lap of 114.02 can be better evaluated by scanning forward and back. The first 500cc race had been run in 1911 and a rider called Frank Phillips (on a Scott) set fastest lap, 50.11mph. The progress of technology (and no doubt riding skill) was as evident then as now, and although the speed dipped to 49.44mph the next year, it rose steadily, almost remorselessly, reaching 90.27 in 1937 and teetered on the very edge of 100 by 1955 – Geoff Duke, 99.97.

McIntyre went through the barrier on a Gilera in 1957, 101.12, but across the mid-Sixties that rose and fell before Mike himself did 108.77 on the Honda bronco in 1967. Thereafter...

1968	G. Agostini	MV	104.91
1969	G. Agostini	MV	106.25
1970	G. Agostini	MV	105.29
1971	G. Agostini	MV	104.86
1972	G. Agostini	MV	105.39
1973	M. Grant	Yamaha	104.41
1974	C. Williams	Yamaha	101.92
1975	M. Grant	Kawasaki	102.93
1976	J. Williams	Suzuki	112.27
1977	P. Read	Suzuki	110.01
1978	P. Hennen	Suzuki	113.83
1979	M. Hailwood	Suzuki	114.02
1980	S. Woods	Suzuki	111.37
1981	M. Grant	Suzuki	112.68
1982	C. Williams	Yamaha	115.08

Twice Mike reversed the flow of techology or, putting it another way, defeated the flow of technology. His 1967 lap record lasted well into the next decade, and his 1979 lap stood for three years.

The 1967 lap was the fastest any man had been round The Island, and it stood until 1975 when Mick Grant took a Kawasaki to 109.82 in the Classic for *1,000*cc machines. The 1979 lap was not an outright record because by now the Classic, with its possibility of so much more power, was into its stride. In 1978 Grant did 114.33, in 1979 Alex George did 114.18. It remains deeply astonishing that Mike was within decimal fractions of these times on a 500.

You know the hoary old saying about lies, damned lies and statistics. This time they contained a very great contradiction to that. This time they told the truth.

2

"We'd worked on the bike all Sunday night, the Monday night we went out to a party, we ended up at The Casino with Hailwood", Ogborne says. "Tuesday was our day off. We hadn't slept at all. I think someone from Suzuki had asked Hailwood to take him round, he borrowed a few road bikes and said he'd take us round, too. We all had bikes, we followed, and although he had his Mike Hailwood helmet on I don't think he was recognized because a lot of people were running that type of colour scheme. God, we couldn't keep up with him! He'd have to stop and wait for us. We'd say 'Hang on a minute, we're not a quick as you are', and then he'd set off again.

"I remember a Suzuki director saying to me 'How can you do it – work Sunday night, Monday night no sleep, Tuesday morning and you're still OK?'. I said 'If you want to win you can do it. If you want it badly enough you can do anything'."

Ogborne might have been speaking of Stanley Michael Bailey Hailwood and what he had done in the 500cc race on the Isle of Man, June 1979. It was Mike's 14th TT victory. To Attwood again belongs the postscript.

"1979 was probably more *complete* for Mike because it was the one he wanted to win again, the 500."

"After all the ballyhoo, we were going back to the Majestic and Hailwood said 'I'm using that bike for the Classic'. He'd had so much trouble with the Ducati in the Formula One. We said 'Still bring the Ducati up in case we've got problems. You'll have a choice of bikes.' The Ducati people came up for scrutineering, but Mike didn't even want to look at it," Ogborne says.

"We changed the steering damper for the Classic and it was the only change we made. Everything else was the same, even the chain (chuckle). The Reynolds idea[9] is to take them off and throw them away, but I knew a chain can do 12 racing laps. The Reynolds people said 'No, no, we don't want to take that chance, not with Hailwood' and they gave me a new chain, but I didn't put it on. I didn't tell them, either. If you fit a new one on you have to guess how much slack to put into it because during the race it really does slacken off, but one which has done six laps is already prestretched. I took it off, cleaned it, put it back on and told Reynolds I'd put the new one on."

That morning Alex George lay on his hotel bed carefully stretching all the tendons in his legs. He knew it was a long time to be on a motorbike: two full hours. His last proper training session had been the day before; he would not risk another now, would risk only some more stretching on the grid itself before he actually mounted the bike.

The Classic, as it unfolded, was aptly named this year, 1979, not the misnomer of '78. The Classic was a distillation of simplicity and complexity, but built around one man against another man, Mike against George, one machine against another machine, 500 Suzuki against 1,000cc Honda, but that was deceptive. The Suzuki was quicker.

"We'd spent a lot of time together", George says, "and we had a very good relationship. In the Formula One I'd used Grant's bike, now I used Ron Haslam's, although they were virtually the same. I'd done a bit of testing on it. I felt good enough, I'd won the Formula One and it didn't matter who was out there, I was going to have a go. No, I wasn't intimidated by Mike at all, I had great respect and admiration for the guy and I used to say that if I ever became partly as good as him I'd die a happy man...

"Mike was on the Suzuki and there were the Suzuki followers, I was on the

---

9. Reynolds, the company Ken Sprayson worked for, were famous chain makers.

Honda and there were the Honda followers, and they built it into an all-star wrestling match." George could distance himself from this rising emotion. He had an uncomfortable fact to contemplate. Through the speed trap in practice Mike had done 162mph while "Me, flat on the tank, coaxing every effort out of the Honda, got 154". Honda wondered if their bike really could get round The Island quickly enough, and that was something George was entitled to wonder, too. "The Honda had a lot of torque and could drive through the corners quite fast, but it was down on top speed by nearly 10 miles an hour. The Suzuki was light and more nimble, and definitely handled better, braked better." That was another aspect of the distillation, the strengths and weaknesses of one bike pitted directly against the strengths and weaknesses of another.

George felt the responsibility keenly enough. "A lot of people were depending on me when I was on that bike. The team had been working towards it for weeks and weeks in the UK, and probably months if not years before that in Japan. It's a lot to carry on your shoulders."

Macauley drove Mike to the circuit. On that journey Mike said – nothing.

When they reached it Macauley glanced at George's face. On it he could read – nothing.

And they came to the race. "We had a laugh and a joke before it. I said 'Watch what you're doing, be careful', and he said the same to me. He was generous and I hope I was. It was obvious in his eyes that I was the main threat, and equally obvious through my eyes that he was going to be the main threat." Yes.

They waited. George did the last of his exercises, a slackening and elongating of the body in controlled, easy movements, just loosening, loosening, loosening. Don't pull a muscle now. Then he prepared himself mentally, as he did each time on The Island. "When the flag drops you've got to go from that instant. You can't get to Quarter Bridge and then say to yourself '*Here we go, here we go*', because you will already have lost 10 or 15 seconds..." Please remember that statement.

Mike went first, the strength of the shove as it had always been, power from the arms and shoulder-blades. George went two rows behind Mike – 20 seconds. George went hard and immediately.

Lap	George	Mike	
1	112.10mph	111.26mph	(George leading by 9.2 seconds)
2	112.74mph	112.56mph	(George leading by 4.0 seconds)
3	113.20mph	113.08mph	(George leading, just...)

Half the race had gone in less than 60 minutes, something totally unknown on The Island. "The pitstops were important", George says. "We got in and out pretty quickly, and so did Mike. Everybody gave their absolute best in both camps, mechanics, team managers, and in terms of riding nobody could have asked for anything better." Yes.

4	112.70mph	112.62mph	
5	112.86mph	112.87mph	

On this lap Mike took the lead by *four-fifths of one second*. Somewhere out there – no-one will ever know which lap, but it might well have been this one – George caught a glimpse of his prey. He saw him only once. "I came round through Kate's Cottage going down The Mountain and he was actually leaving Creg-ny-Baa (about half a mile away.) I guessed it was him because there was no-one else around." Tantalizing, fleeting, insubstantial, all of it; just a man hunched over a motorbike so far away and then gone, but he was – the prey. And in the background a great misunderstanding was being played out...

"When Mike came by me on the start of lap six he had a lead which was like plus 0.2 of a second", Ogborne says. "I put out a board *Plus zero* – dead level. Our total number of signallers was two, me at the pit and one other at Ramsey, and Honda had nine signalling stations. They'd taken over maybe 28 people and they'd signallers all in radio contact.

"Alex George knew everything that was happening. We used to ask if we could use the radio antennae up The Mountain – the one Manx Radio used – and we were told it was illegal. If we'd have had an aerial there we'd have had coverage of the whole of the Isle of Man, but it was not allowed. Honda then got it – and that was important. You can't do it by walkie-talkies because of The Mountain."

Forgive Ogborne this. He was, as all racing people are, absorbed in his own efforts and that of his team; and in life itself it is somehow a natural assumption that the opposition will have more of everything than you have. You're out-numbered and out-gunned, but that doesn't mean you lose the war; and of course the opposition are thinking the same thing.

George: "I had a signaller at the start-finish just like everybody else and only one other, at Sulby Crossroads. A lot of the Honda guys had actually left The Island and others were due to leave very, very shortly afterwards."

The gap at the precise instant of entering the last lap: 0.2 seconds.

At Ballacraine and the turn north an excited voice on *Manx Radio* bayed "and for sure the Isle of Man is no place for anyone who is faint of heart as we look now and the programmes are waving and here he comes and it's yes, you know who ... super neat, super swift ... he keeps his eys on the road, keeps his mind on the business, working away there and we're looking for second-placed man ... we're past 20 seconds and so Mike has got a clear lead ... it's up now to 1.8 seconds, 1.8 seconds we say unofficially, the advantage now to Mike Hailwood."

At Ballaugh and the turn back towards the coast an excited voice on *Manx Radio* bayed "it could all depend on getting jammed up behind a backmarker at Governor's Bridge at the end ... let's hope it doesn't, let's hope it's a straight fight. There's a signalling board being put out, I'm going to stand up for this one, stand up people, this is Hailwood for the last time ... fantastic, there he is and now we've got to wait for the Scot Alex George ... is it going to be Hailwood or is it going to be Alex George? ... 13, 14, 15, 16, 17, 18, here George is ... he's ahead of a backmarker ... 21. They wave to him as well. It's two seconds, Hailwood leads, Hailwood has it by two seconds with 20 miles to go and we've seen the last ever of Mike Hailwood passing through this village on a racing motorcycle."

At Sulby, a mile and a half from Ballaugh, George got his signal, his last signal: *minus three seconds*.

Ogborne: "When Hailwood got to Ramsey he was plus two seconds and that was the last signal he got. That last signal? You have to give a signal you know to be correct. The instant you start cheating on signals you're into hellish places, you have to give what is on the clock. Hailwood always said he was quicker up The Mountain Mile than anybody else. As he got round the Goose Neck" – the right-hander on the climb a mile and a half out of Ramsey – "there was a gaggle of slower riders he had to lap. He said 'I thought to myself should I do it or should I not?' – because if he'd gone through the way he wanted, at the speed of light, he might have put the slower riders on the grass and they'd certainly have had to move out of the way. That was a risk. He chose not to, he thought 'I can make it up'.

"He buttoned himself down, played follow-my-leader through, and in that time Alex George got it back. Honda had a signaller at Windy Corner, the Black

Hut, the Verandah. George knew when he reached the Black Hut that he'd pulled those two seconds back."

George did not know. All he did know was that "it was very, very close. I was giving it ten-tenths and a wee bit more as well, and I was quite sure Mike himself was giving it that, too. I had to pass all the backmarkers he'd passed and I sensed we were both getting the best out of our machines." Yes.

At The Bungalow, just before the highest point of the course, and six and three quarter miles from the line, an excited voice on *Manx Radio* bayed "here he is arriving at The Bungalow ... into the left-hander he goes with lots of road to spare, bends it right under the footbridge, the crowds wave, no response from Mike Hailwood, up the left-hand side of the road he goes tucked behind that streamlining. He's going well, he bends it over to the right, he goes past the warning board towards Brandywell as Alex George comes into the Bungalow bends and the crowds wave yet again and the time interval is ... it's being written down ... 2.3 seconds, Alex George leads by 2.3 seconds."

Ogborne: "Then George got plus whatever at Creg-ny-Baa and Hailwood was still thinking he was plus-two, and of course he wasn't. If we'd had just an extra few people..."

George: "I rode the last bit 'blind', oh yes."

At the start-finish line a very excited voice on *Manx Radio* bayed "we're waiting for the Signpost Corner indicator lights to come on. Who's it going to be? Could a tailender just get in the way of one of them, and with only 2.3 seconds that can make all the difference in the world. The light's not ... yes, Hailwood is there, number six. Mike Hailwood is there. We start the watch. We'll try and get a time difference at Signpost. It's 10, 11, 12, 13, 14, 15, 16, 17 and ... Alex George is there. That would appear to be that, Alex George has a three-second advantage and they've got what, just a mile and a bit to come. Already the crowd in the grandstand are on their feet. All the way along Glencrutchery Road as far as I can see people are looking. Who's it going to be? Mike Hailwood or Alex George? And here's Mike Hailwood now and he's going a tremendous pace and the crowd are waving and we start the watch now. It's seven ... eight ... nine ... 10 ... 11 ... 12 ... 13 and here he is, Alex George is going to do it, Alex George crosses the line *now* and I stopped my watch and I can tell you I make it about 2.8 seconds only. We wait for confirmation."

George: "I crossed the line flat on the tank and after the chequered flag I hit the brakes and I came screeching to a halt just by the entrance to Noble's Park, just before Bray Hill. I stopped the engine. I was concerned – I knew it must be close. Apparently there had been an announcement that it was 3.4 seconds. I lifted my visor and I was unbuckling my helmet and someone said to me '3.4 seconds, 3.4, 3.4.' I said 'Damn, damn I've lost it', and this chap said 'No, no, you've won it by 3.4.' Such a charge of energy went through my body, excitement – utopia. *Satisfaction* came later after it had all sort of quietened down. It was a bit too much to grasp a hold of at first."

Ogborne: "We went down to meet Hailwood and the first thing he said was *'Did I do it? Did I do it?'* Ted Macauley put his arm round his shoulder and said 'No mate, you didn't' and for 30 seconds Hailwood went really quiet. Then he snapped out of it. He said 'Thanks a lot, it would have been nice to end with a win'. Alex George hadn't beaten Hailwood. We knew what had beaten Hailwood. It's called a radio." And that remains the misty legend of The Mountain: what you thought the opposition had and what perhaps they thought you had. The story of every race that's ever been and ever will be. This one, which is only one among so many in the raw-rich tapestry of motorsport, should be chipped out on a stone tablet and left for ever and ever thus:

A. George	(998 Honda)	2h 0m 07.0s	(113.08mph)
M. Hailwood	(500 Suzuki)	2h 0m 10.4s	(113.03mph)
C. Williams	(350 Yamaha)	2h 3m 29.4s	(109.99mph)

Sawyer was there. "He'd had a very exhausting race, he'd ground the front off his boots and there he was hobbling back along the little walkway. A guy stopped him for his autograph. You could see Mike's hands physically jumping an inch from the vibrations he still felt, he was shaking from the effort, and this guy kept persisting, asking him for his autograph, and when Mike said 'No, later' the guy got really shirty. The guy said 'You're a jumped-up stuffed-shirt and full of yourself', and I landed into this guy because he wouldn't accept a quiet 'No'. I had to see him off because he wouldn't leave Mike alone. Mike was very distressed." The invaders of his space were even here, even here.

"Alex was going a bit too quick", Mike would say, magnanimous and selfless at the end and to the end. "It's a great pleasure to finish second to a man like Alex." Question: Is that *it*? "Yes, that's absolutely it. I can never get a ride again like that one."

George: "He was very gracious in his praise. I told him 'I can hardly say I'm sorry – but it could have gone either way'. Mike said 'No, no, the best man won on the day'."

Ogborne revealed to Reynolds that their chain had truly done 12 laps. Reynolds said *"Whaaaat?"*. Ogborne also had a conversation with Mike which went like this. "Until I met you I thought you were a wanker. Hailwood said 'Why's that?'. I said because when I used to know about you finishing races it was always Mike Hailwood on this Honda-six, then it would be Ginger Malloy on a Bultaco, then somebody else, then somebody else and it seemed obvious to me that with six cylinders against one you were always going to win, but, I said, it's not like that, is it? 'No', he said, 'it never was'. I added 'I perceived you as being good because you had good equipment, but *you* are good."

Ogborne's postscript. "In the 500cc race he'd done 114, the next best was I think 112, and that showed the difference between him and normal people."

George's postscript. "I get a chill talking about that race now (1992), I get all tingly talking about it. It was that kind of race, a once-in-a-lifetime race."

3

"He told me things were getting out of hand. After he won the 500 he had an offer from Assen to ride at the Dutch Grand Prix, and apparently they were quoting £25,000. I said are you going to go? He said 'Don't be stupid. With people like Kenny Roberts I'll probably finish about eighth or ninth and get lapped. Here at The Island I'm on my own territory, there I'm not quick enough, not on a short-circuit course. I know that, you know that'," Ogborne says.

"At the end of The Island he said 'I never want to go that fast again' – because he really rode his buns off. 'That's it, thanks a lot, but I'm glad it's over, I'm glad it's ended now. My relationship with The Island is finished.' It was like somebody who had climbed Mount Everest. He knew exactly that that was it. A love-hate relationship, whatever it had been, he'd got it finally out of his system. To try and win that Classic he'd put so much mental effort in, and then unfortunately not to do it – I don't think he ever wanted to go through that again."

Ogborne and Radar headed off for Assen, then Spa a week after that, where the top riders didn't compete because, they claimed, the surface was dangerously slippy. Mike, meanwhile, had been approached to make a farewell appearance at Donington, to be followed by a another at Silverstone.

Re-enter Ogborne and Radar. "We'd got the same Suzuki 500 and in two or three days we had it in short-circuit prep. We went to Donington and I said 'I hope you're wise doing this'. It was something I saw in his eyes. I thought: you're not really into this, but he was too nice, this unassuming guy, to say 'No' to Donington and, anyway, I'd have guessed it was a big money-earner." In fact Mike had promised Tom Wheatcroft, the man in charge at Donington and an old friend, that he'd do it although he hated the very notion of riding again.

"We got the bike ready and I said 'this is completely different to the Isle of Man. Remember how you rode it before? Well, this is short-circuit stuff and this thing is a missile round here. Be careful. Where you have to watch it is Craner Curves" – the sweeping downhill right-and-left – "'don't flick the throttle there'. He went out, five laps later, bang, he fell down at Craner Curves.

"After they'd shovelled him up he knew he'd broken his collarbone in a bad way. He was white. When guys break a bone they're white – he was white going on yellow. He said 'Well, you told me not to touch the throttle at Craner'. They whistled him off to hospital because he was in so much pain he almost passed out.

"This happened, like, 10.20 on a Sunday morning. They brought him back from Derby Infirmary in the afternoon. His arm was in a sling, the bone was poking, but it didn't break the skin. They asked him to do a parade lap, not on a bike of course, because he couldn't do that, but sitting in a car waving. He was in so much pain I thought it was terrible, but he was the sort of bloke who couldn't say no.

"I don't think he wanted people to remember him that way: the last time they saw Mike Hailwood was riding round in an old Bentley with a broken collarbone. He was still white. After the parade lap he limped very gingerly into the pits and he and Ted Macauley disappeared and that was it."

Nor could he ride at Silverstone. "He was terribly depressed", Sawyer says, "because he hadn't been able to fulfil what he wanted to do. I wasn't at Silverstone, but I heard it was a very momentous thing and he was shattered by the way the public responded to him."

That winter Mike and Alex George spent a lot of time together at various dos and presentations and all the rest of it. "We didn't go over the ground of The Classic. We'd smile and talk about other things. I got very little credit for that race, which was a classic in every sense of the word. All the stories afterwards were not about how I'd won it, but how Mike lost it, or how unlucky Mike was. He was a great bloke and all the Press were on his side, and that's understandable. I was philosophical. I had done the job I was paid to do.

"That winter people used to come up to me and say 'You bastard, you beat Hailwood', and I'd say 'Look pal, I was in the race and I finished in front of the man. As far as I'm concerned that doesn't mean I put myself down as winning the race, as beating the great Mike Hailwood.' I used to say 'I didn't beat Hailwood, I only won the race.' That was the quote I used. *I didn't beat Hailwood, I only won the race.*"

4

In May 1980, Valerie Singleton of the BBC interviewed Mike, and with kind permission from both her and the BBC I include all of it because, as with the Brian Johnston interview in the chapter headed Michael, it is extremely eloquent in its content. Singleton, moreover, was a news reporter who knew the technique of the interview.

Singleton: "A few years ago when I was filming on the Isle of Man I negotiated Mad Sunday – that is the Sunday before the races when everybody is allowed out on the course. I raised quite a few laughs because I was the only one doing it on a moped. Of course, the name most associated with TT racing and boyhood hero for many is Mike Hailwood. Mike, good morning. Mad Sunday's fun isn't it? Might not be for you."

Mike: "Well actually we used to go around the track on Mad Sunday and watch the antics of some of these chaps on their motorbikes and it really was very hilarious. As far as I was concerned it was far more amusing than the races themselves."

Singleton: "Are you coming back this year?"

Mike: "Oh, no, no fear, I'm going over to watch, but I'm certainly not riding."

Singleton: "Why did you suddenly decide to come back three years ago? Money?"

Mike: "No, not really, no, hardly. Several reasons really. I had an accident in 1974 in a racing car which left me in the sort of state where I wasn't able to race any more for about a year, but unfortunately I still had the bug and the competitive spirit inside me. We went off to live in New Zealand, and it's a very, very quiet place as you know, and all this stuff was sort of bubbling around inside me. I had the need and the want to come and do something else again in the racing field. Very foolish."

Singleton: "Did it get it out of you?"

Mike: "Well, it did, but not the first time I went back to The Island. I still had it in me even then, and I went back again last year. A couple of my friends were killed just before the TT, a couple of people fell off at another couple of meetings, and I thought, boy, this is not for me, it looks dangerous. And in July last year I had an accident myself. As I was flying through the air I thought *I gotta stop this, I'm really too old for this lark, don't like all this pain and noise.*"

Singleton: "So you think that if you hadn't had the accident when you were racing cars you'd probably still be doing that and you wouldn't have come back to motorbikes?"

Mike: "Yes, I think as you say probably if I hadn't had the accident I'd either be dead or still racing cars."

Singleton: "Had it changed a lot when you went back to it?"

Mike: "Oh yes, a tremendous amount. It's much more glamorous, much more colourful."

Singleton: "Colourful, in what way?"

Mike: "Well, all the lads wear multi-coloured leathers, much more sponsorship, the bikes are a lot faster, they go better and the brakes are better and the suspension and things like that are better technically. They are much advanced. All-round it's improved greatly, except perhaps the fact that the guys who are doing it don't seem to enjoy themselves as much as they used to."

Singleton: "Why not – too competitive now?"

Mike: "Well, not so much that, but I think there is so much money around now involved in the sport. It's the same as anything. When money becomes involved in something it becomes more of a money-grabbing situation rather than something to really enjoy."

Singleton: "How important is that sponsorship? Can one go out and do it on one's own or do you ... well, I mean you had the backing of, well perhaps I can't say ..."

Mike: (chuckle) "Who was it? I can't remember (chuckle). Initially my dad poured a lot of money into my racing efforts, but most people who go bike racing aren't blessed in that way. But, same as everything I suppose, it's becoming very, very expensive to set yourself up properly – something in the region of, oh I don't know, £15,000, £20,000 to get a couple of bikes and a van and go out and do the season."

Singleton: "So you've got to be sponsored?"

Mike: "You really have, yes, because you could never go to your bank manager and say 'Look, lend me 20,000 quid, I'm just going off to race motorbikes'. And in England there is a great shortage of sponsors. This is one of the reasons I think why the Continentals and Americans and so on are much better than we are: because they've been able to raise a sponsorship and go out and do the job properly whereas our lads haven't."

Singleton: "Do we not take motorbike racing as seriously as perhaps other countries do?"

Mike: "I think the lads themselves do, but unfortunately, as I say, the sponsorship is lacking."

Singleton: "How had the Isle of Man course changed, because it's a very dangerous course, isn't it, lot's of complaints about it. Was it improved?"

Mike: "Well, improved in as much as they had resurfaced a lot of it, eased a lot of corners."

Singleton: "What makes it dangerous? Is it the twistiness of it?"

Mike: "It's the sheer speed, the sustained speed and, of course, it is a public road in the Isle of Man, and it's completely surrounded by brick walls, telegraph poles, trees, pavements, drops over mountain sides and things like that, and fences and things like that. Inherently it is very dangerous, yes."

Singleton: "It is described in this book (*Mike The Bike – Again* by Macauley) as a very uncomfortable race, and I wondered what on earth makes you want to go out and be uncomfortable for two hours. What are you getting out of it?"

Mike: "I'm a pure masochist (chuckle)."

Singleton: "Is it the fact you've won, or is there some joy and thrill while you're actually doing it?"

Mike: "Well, I think it always appeared to me as a great challenge, you know, because it is so dangerous and so long and it is so hard on both the man and the machine. To me it was the very ultimate challenge, and if I did well I was very happy and very satisfied. Of course I could have come unstuck along the way, but one doesn't think about things like that."

Singleton: "Are there temptations to push yourself too far, because in 1979 in the Classic you were beaten by three seconds and you said 'I really went over the limits, I went too far'. That presumably is being very dangerous and stupid. What are the temptations to do that when you are actually racing?"

Mike: "The Isle of Man is a peculiar race because you don't race against people

229

on the road. You start off at 10-second intervals and consequently you're really racing against the clock, which is a more controlled situation. But you have the temptation to go perhaps too fast because you don't really know where the opposition is. You get a sign about every 10 minutes so you can fall into the trap of trying too hard, and the Isle of Man is not the sort of place where you should ever over-step the limit because you can get very seriously hurt."

Singleton: "There are a lot of amateur riders in the races, too, aren't there? Do they add to the dangers?"

Mike: "Yes they do, and my excuse was that I lost the race because I was held up by some of the guys that I was lapping at the back of the field. The differential in talent and machine speed in the Isle of Man is extraordinary. My bike was probably doing 60, 70mph faster than the guys at the back, you know. That's no discredit to them, they're enjoying themselves and it's really us who should be responsible, but it does add to the danger, certainly."

Singleton: "What kind of training do you have to do before a race, or is it more a mental attitude than physical training?"

Mike: "When I was racing full-time back in the Sixties we were racing sufficiently that I was able to keep fit without actually doing any physical exercise. When I decided to make the comeback in 1978 I was thoroughly overweight, out of condition, so I went on a very strict training course, not drinking, which I found particularly the hardest, and not eating, which was about the second hardest. The physical exercise was sheer hell, but it had to be done because you can't go into these things in a flabby and overweight condition, really."

Singleton: "Did you enjoy car racing more than motorbike racing?"

Mike: (murmuring) "No. ... no, I didn't enjoy car racing hardly at all when I was racing Formula One. In 1967, when I was racing for Honda, they suddenly pulled the mat out and stopped racing and they left me in a bit of a void. I thought here is an ideal opportunity to get out and try something else, so that's basically why I went car racing."

Singleton: "Of course you've got several medals, including the George Medal for rescuing Clay Regazzoni from a burning car. Is that just something one does without thinking about it?"

Mike: "Oh, absolutely. If you sat back and thought about it coolly and calmly you'd certainly run the other way (little laugh). But you know, when you're in a race you've got the adrenalin going anyway so you're pretty het up and, of course, I was in a situation where the car was burning, certainly, but I had all the fireproof overalls and helmet and breathing apparatus. I really wasn't in any danger, so it was just one of those things you do on the spur of the moment."

Singleton: "So now you sit back to a life with no danger and no excitement and no thrills like that?"

Mike: "Well, I've got a motorcycle dealership in Birmingham, and that gets quite exciting on occasions when you get a few rockers in there."

Singleton: "Different kind of excitement, I imagine."

Mike: "Yes, certainly."

MEMORY

"I am a proud person to say I knew Mike Hailwood, I raced with Mike Hailwood, I was beaten by Mike Hailwood, I adored Mike Hailwood." – Tommy Robb

"It was always very difficult, I found, to decide what actually mattered to him." – Murray Walker

"What did I make of him? Hmmm. I mean, quite a strange guy really, definitely a strange guy." – Mick Grant

"If you met him even briefly he would leave a ray of sunshine dancing about your head." – Alex George

1

"Mike was going to be a courier for one of the Trimby trips. Trimby was the secretary general of IRTA, the International motor racing teams of bikes, a former racer and organizer of trips to the Macau Grand Prix and Daytona. Trimby thought it would be a great idea to go on one of these trips to Daytona with Mike as a sort of courier, which was a joke", Ted Macauley says. "There was no way.

"Mike would take the trip, but he didn't even go on the same plane as the Trimby Trippers. He rang me up – I was covering it for the *Daily Mirror* – and said 'I'll come with you'. We went to Daytona and at one of the hotels they had a motorcycle celebrity night run by some awful American who would introduce these celebrities. All sorts of people were called up on to the stage, Kenny Roberts and so on. Mike, of course, thought he was quite safe in America because nobody would know him.

"There were about 2,000 people in this place, we'd nipped into the bar and the guy on the stage said 'It's a great surprise tonight. Over there in the corner is Mike Hailwood' and the place erupted. I could see the colour draining from Mike's face. He hated that sort of thing and he turned to leave. I had to grab him and pull him back to get him to go on to the stage.

"It put me in mind of when *This is Your Life* was done with Eamonn Andrews. We were all in on the secret and we all knew Mike wouldn't do it. The only way he'd take part, we figured out, was to trap him in a racing car. They did it at a motor show and he couldn't get away. Otherwise he'd just have taken off. He was most upset later on that he'd been done because it was a very emotional *This is Your Life* with Regazzoni on it."[1]

Courier or no, Mike was at the Daytona 200-mile race on March 8, 1981. Nobby Clark was there, too, and Mike said that if he'd got a few days off to please come and stay with him and Pauline.

Mike and Macauley flew back to Britain together. "People attached themselves to him and it was the old reflected glory thing. He wasn't worried about people taking money off him, and a lot of people did. The nicest thing he ever said to me – we were both very drunk on the aeroplane from Daytona – was 'I love you for one reason as much as anything else. You've never wanted to take anything off me'."

Mike had gone into business with Rod Gould selling motorcycles, although Mike was no businessman and claimed a unique talent for losing money, even on houses, even when he put it in Swiss banks.

"He started to ring me up", Sawyer says, "for advice. He wasn't asking for guidance, he was being very astute. He was looking for somebody who could maybe think laterally or see what might create a problem which he hadn't spotted. I helped him along those lines whenever I could.

"It was typical of his character – because of the comeback and everything – that he'd say 'I'm no different to anybody else. Don't think God made me different to anybody else. I've a bit of a talent which allows me to do other things.' He got into a particular period of saying *'Mike who?'*. It became a bit of a joke. He was being Captain Modest, but that was just what he was all about, he was always and forever modest. For some strange reason I asked Mike to sign one of his books for me. He signed it *To Rodders, thanks for everything. Mike (who?) Hailwood*".

Mike signed the book around January 1981, Sawyer isn't exactly an autograph-hunter and looking back on his asking for it he finds a word which is perhaps an inevitable word, the only one.

"Weird."

Rous, who was now living in Northampton, gave a talk to the local vintage motorcycle enthusiasts at the NALGO[2] social club where the Civil Service Motoring Association met. Some while later his phone rang and a voice said "You gave the talk last time. Is it possible for you to get a personality to come next time?"

"I phoned Mike and he said 'Yes', he'd come over. There was no fee, nothing. He arrived prepared to talk about his experiences, but there had been a misunderstanding, it wasn't the motor people at all. I can't remember who they were – it may even have been the fishing society! – but they weren't motorcyclists. He didn't mind, we laughed about it and when he gave the talk they *loved* it. Then we went to the bar and had a little bit of a chat."

Charlie Rous still remembers that drink and that chat. From that moment on, as Mike drove away at the end of the evening, there would be only silence.

---

1. *This is Your Life* was presented by Eamonn Andrews, a sports broadcaster famous for boxing commentaries. Someone, incidentally, did refuse to take part once – Danny Blanchflower, the Spurs and Northern Ireland footballer.
2. National Association of Local Government Officers.

Tommy Robb was "opening my five-star Honda workshop[3] in Warrington and Mike was coming up to perform the ceremony. Pauline was coming, too. 'Yes, I'd love to', Mike had said." Again there was no fee, nothing. Robb eagerly anticipated Mike and Pauline staying with them when the ceremony had been performed. As Robb recounts this 10 years after it should have happened, his eyes look away from mine and he says nothing else.

"We were on road safety together. We organized it with Warwickshire Council, we used to go and give a talk together. The talks would be all over the place. We'd do one in Nuneaton, one in Rugby. People were invited to come along and we'd talk about anything, cars, bikes, road safety", Percy Tait says. "He rang me up and said 'Shall we go out for a meal?'. I said 'Mike, I've got a lot on, but I'll tell you what, on Monday we will after our road safety talk at Stratford."

That was Saturday, March 21, 1981.

Sawyer was due at a dinner party when his phone rang. It was Mike. "We spoke for an hour and a half. He was contemplating calling it a day and getting out of the bike business in Birmingham. He was really down. He was terribly, terribly dejected. Because I knew him so well I detected that. He was very low, very run down, and that's why I stayed on the phone for so long."

That evening Mike took Michelle and David in his Rover to buy some fish and chips. On the way back, on the A435 at a place called Portway, a lorry driver made an illegal U-turn, positioning it to go through a gap in the central reservation to gain the other carriageway. It blocked the road. The Rover bored into it. Michelle was killed almost instantly, Mike died two days later in hospital. David survived. He is, according to Pauline, a Hailwood alright.

The lorry driver was fined £100 with £105 costs.

Rob Walker was asked to read the memorial at Mike's funeral. He declined because he didn't trust himself to be able to get through it. He knew he "would have been overwhelmed".

As I write these words a full decade later there are many people who cannot comprehend or accept what happened, or how or why that evening. As Iain Mackay says "You don't feel as if he's gone".

2

"I started to go out with a man called Max Bissett, brother of the film star Jackie. He wanted me to marry him, and I went to live with him in America, supposedly for six weeks. Max didn't know anything about bike racing. He'd heard of Mike Hailwood, but he didn't know that I'd been out with him all those years ago", Pam Lawton says.

"The first weekend I was there we were driving back to New York and a motorbike suddenly cut Max up in front, Max had to brake and then he said 'Who does he think he is, Mike Hailwood?'. I thought what a funny thing to say.

"We got into his flat, I went into the bathroom and I heard Max turning on his answerphone. I heard a voice which I recognized as a friend of mine, Sandy, but all I heard was the word bulletin, there was going to be another bulletin. My

---

3. An award of excellence from Honda when a workshop reached the highest standard.

immediate thought went to my brother Ian, who used to race motorbikes, but then I thought – this was all flashing through my mind in a split second – it can't be Ian because he's not well-known and there wouldn't be a bulletin.

"I came rushing out of the bathroom and I said *'What's that message, what's that message?'*. Max said 'Wait a minute, there's another one' – because there were more to come. I heard the third message. 'I'm sorry, Pam, to tell you that he died this morning.' Sandy didn't repeat who had died because she'd said it on the previous messages. I said to Max *'Who, who, who?'*. He said 'Look, sit down.' It took him about a minute to tell me. He hadn't known that I'd known Mike, but he did now because of the messages.

"I was stunned to the point where I didn't cry, I didn't do anything, he hadn't died, no, he hadn't. I knew he had because someone told me, but he hadn't. I didn't accept it in my mind, wrong input, wrong information.

"Max had to see a friend, and I said 'You go off on your own and come back later'. I thought: I know I'm going to cry at some stage, I'll do it when Max isn't there. When he'd gone I made myself cry, but they weren't real tears, they were crocodile tears so I could get it out of the way.

"I went to the memorial service and that was pretty bad for me, then a year later I woke up about three in the morning and I kept on thinking of Mike, and I asked myself what I was doing. I couldn't get back to sleep. When I wake up in the middle of the night I close my eyes and try and get back to sleep. But I just couldn't, so I got up and made myself a cup of tea, thinking: I must have been speaking to someone about Mike, that's why he's on my mind, I must have been. Who have I seen, who have I been talking to? Then I thought: hold on a minute, it's March. I went to my diary and it was the day that Mike was killed. I was so shocked I got all my photographs of Mike out and I stood them on my mantelpiece and I sat in my chair and I looked at them, and I cried and cried and cried until about seven in the morning. That's when I cried, and that's when I accepted he'd gone."

3

Faces in a broken mirror, faces in a broken mirror.

If you read fiction the characters are invariably one-dimensional, comfortable to comprehend, neatly parcelled, all the ends tied up. No real human being is recognizably like that.

At the end of many of the interviews for this book I posed a single question. Who was *Mike who*? The answers were often complex, often contradictory, often a rummage and a search which wasn't comfortable, wasn't neat. The answers moved among many dimensions. The man himself lived somewhere within them and perhaps was all of them in different ways at different times to different people.

"One part of him was that he was born and bred into bikes and was pushed by his father, rather like Stirling Moss was with cars. The other part was the natural Mike rebelling against all sorts of establishments. He was a hard man when it came to the police, a very hard man. He hated them, he hated them. He was frightfully drunk in charge outside a London restaurant and they put him in the back of his Citroen-Maserati and told him a police driver would take him home. The Maserati was quick, difficult to drive and unless you knew what you were doing they were all over the road. The policeman started off and Mike said 'If I'm drunk what the hell do you think this driver is?'.

"Another time the police chased him in their Jaguar, he got them really going quickly and then rammed on the brakes. The Jaguar slammed into the back of him and the policeman was sacked. Later Mike was giving a talk to the police somewhere and a policeman came up and said 'Do you remember me?'. 'No, I don't.' 'I'm the policeman you had sacked when I ran into the back of you.' 'Bloody good job, too.' Mike thought, you see, that the police couldn't drive.

"Mike used to tell a story of going into hospital to have cure for the clap, and the nurse said 'What, you again?'. Mike said he didn't dare tell her he'd been to five hospitals in between. Mike never exaggerated.

"When his son was born I asked what Mike was going to call him. 'Fred', he said, and I wondered why. 'Because that's the milkman's name.' He had that sort of sense of humour.

"When Mike retired he used to come down to Poole to test bikes for a friend of mine, and they'd go round a local aerodrome. He rode a Honda which revved at something like 16,000 and he coped with it straight away. I had a gardener who was mad keen on motorbikes and Mike gave him his helmet just like that as a souvenir. When the gardener died I said the one thing I am going to have is that helmet. It is still in my study." – Rob Walker.

My interview took place in the Press Room at Silverstone during the British Grand Prix meeting, mid-summer 1991. It's a vast, modern communications centre plugged into the world electronically, and it hums with the chatter of several hundred journalists. Silverstone has changed, of course Silverstone has changed – everywhere has – although if you glance from the window of this Press Room you still see a straight ribbon of track from the start-finish line laid out exactly as it was on July 20, 1963, when S.M.B. Hailwood (Lotus-Climax) took his position on the fifth row of the grid.

Dickie Attwood: "The Citroen-Maserati was one of those streamlined things, and it went quite well, it made a nice noise, but the great feature for Mike was that it had front-wheel drive, so it was easy to spin the wheels from traffic lights. He loved driving it. He'd be whizzing about London and he'd be stopped by the police and they all knew Mike, they all knew that he drank, where he'd been. They'd say 'Slow it down, Mike, you haven't got far to go'. He had that sort of personality which could get away with anything. He'd see a couple of girls walking along, wind the window down and shout 'Cor, what couldn't I do to you!'. He was outrageous, but it was Mike, it was – (long, reflective pause) – almost natural for him to do that, and I never saw anybody offended by him.

"We had a meal down the King's Road once, the waiter was gay, and a gay record came on. Mike turned to the waiter and said 'This song's about you'. I cringed, but I didn't have to because if any fisticuffs went on Mike was up there and *boof*. But the waiter didn't react.

"He had an appearance to other people of being a very casual, almost flippant character, and one that most people took to be not serious at all in his approach to Formula One or anything else. I think that's what happened with Yamaha on The Island in 1978. In many ways it was unfortunate that his manner didn't portray the seriousness he felt. I knew he was going to do it seriously on The Island, but a lot of people who didn't know him wouldn't. They'd hear him say 'Yeah, yeah, it'll be alright', just passing things off as if there was no problem when others might think there is a big problem – but he was just like that.

"Mike would never ever say how good he was, or how he had done this, that and the other. A lot of the modern guys give you their life history before you've even asked them, and even 30 years ago it didn't do you a lot of good to be seen to be holding back."

Stuart Graham: "Mike could be a hell-raising playboy if you want to call it that, but he was also an extremely serious racer and would never do anything to distract himself from that. Whether he made love to a girl the night before a race or two hours before a race was his choice, and maybe sometimes he'd race with a slight hangover, but it seemed not to affect him in any way. Mike was not as casual about his racing as people thought."

Martin Ogborne: "He was so pleasant, to me almost too pleasant."

Jerry Wood: "He didn't suffer fools gladly, he hated being recognized, he was so incredibly modest. I came from a working-class background and he treated me just like everybody else."

John Watson: "I found him a very easy, unselfish person. He was always genuine. I don't think you can *act* a personality like that, *act* those characteristics."

Chris Barber: "One time I was in Belfast working and he was doing the North West 200 or whatever. We were both staying in the Grand Hotel. I remember people coming along for autographs. I'd sign them and pass them across to him, and he'd pass them back. He wouldn't autograph them because he was so shy. I'd not met anybody quite so shy."

Murray Walker: "It was always very difficult, I found, to decide what actually mattered to him. I used to wonder whether he continued racing because that was all he'd done and he couldn't think of anything else to do, or was that really the burning light in his life? I even wondered if there was a burning light.

"One of the most delightful things about him was that he didn't try and make people think he was something he wasn't. Most people have cabinets made to put their trophies in. He gave his away. They obviously didn't matter to him. It argues that he had not any deep interest in anything. The motorcycling was a way of passing the time.

"Whatever motivated Mike to get into the motorcycle business in Birmingham? Can you imagine Mike Hailwood standing around in a showroom talking to some punter who wants to know what it was like to race a bike, or how his trials machine is going to go compared to the MV Mike rode? Mike would never have had the patience or the interest for that. He was – and I hate to say this – a drifter. He sort of oozed through life. He did not have any targets to meet.

"He never worked at his riding as far as I know. That first day at Oulton Park he must have discovered he had the talent, or certainly Stan did. If it had not been for Stan I don't suppose Mike would have raced a bike anyway. I don't think Mike was racing at Oulton Park because he had a burning desire to do so and had said to Stan 'Can you give me some help, I need a bike'.

"If he hadn't done well that first time I wonder in my heart of hearts if he'd have said 'Never mind, it's only the first time, the light is there, I am going to go on and on'. I don't think Mike would have had the desire and I don't think he would have had the application.

"He became successful as a racing motorcyclist because he had a brilliant natural talent, good reflexes, good eyesight, body co-ordination and all the other human chemistry you need, and he didn't actually apply himself to it very hard.

Mike reacted, I think, to circumstances. He never made things happen. I believe that for ordinary people nothing happens unless you make it, but if you are extraordinary, whether as a violinist or a tap dancer, a bike racer or anything else, the world winds a path to your door. You don't have to do anything.

"That was Mike in his motorcycle and car racing careers. He drifted into them, he was good, he continued to drift, he was pushed into things by other people. He had a natural talent for music, but as far as I know he never actually dedicated himself to developing it. He pranced about with the clarinet or tinkled on the piano.

"When his career stopped so did he, really. I wonder what would have happened to him."

My interview took place in December 1991 at Walker's home, in, specifically, Walker's study. When it was over he foraged and found a book he'd had signed by riders of the Sixties and there was Mike's signature and there was Stan's. Walker handled the book with *reverence*.

Iain Mackay: "We were coming back from a 200-mile race at the Paul Ricard circuit with Yamaha and he happened to be driving back from Monte Carlo. He saw the truck and flagged us down. He sat on the verge of the road chatting. The Japanese mechanics couldn't believe it: here was the great Mike Hailwood who hadn't just sounded his horn and waved as he went by, no, he'd stopped for a chat.

"He was standing in a bar with a friend once and a drunk came up and said to the friend 'I see that chap Hollywood has won another race'. Mike never said a word."

John Cooper: "One year at the Dutch TT we were going to the presentation and Mike said 'I've got no money, can you lend me some? I've forgotten my wallet'. I gave him something like £30. A few weeks later he said 'Oh, I must pay you back that money I owe you'. We were at Mallory Park, his bike lost a cylinder, it was slow. We were lapping him, although Mike would always carry on because he was getting start money and people had paid to watch.

"It was at the hairpin with a couple of laps to go. There were several riders behind me. Mike looked round, saw us coming and when I'd passed him he pulled in front of the others and baulked them. We got back to the pits. He said 'You remember that thirty quid? Shall we call it quits?' I said 'That's not a bad idea' because I'd won the race and I think £50."

My interview with Cooper took place at his office-cum-garage in Derby in autumn 1991. Yes, he had photographs of Mike. We went down some steps into a lumber room and there they were, some in an old filing cabinet, some in boxes: photographs, yellowed Press clippings, programmes, the forgotten residue of a career and a life. *Tempus fugit*, that's all, *tempus fugit*.

Derek Bell: "He was such a contrast in characters. He was such a really nice guy, he was really shy, he could be very, very kind and thoughtful and he could be very, very rude to people if he didn't like them. He didn't suffer fools and if he didn't like somebody he'd make it painfully obvious. I might like them, but people would say Mike doesn't and he's never going to. He made his decisions straight away and that was it.

"We had a mutual friend in Baleira, which is Adriatica – where Enzo Ferrari had a beach house. We met this mutual friend and had a most wonderful 24-hour orgy of food and drink. Mike loved kids. Mine were aged about three and four, he had both of them on his shoulders walking through the garden and I thought: my kids and Mike Hailwood, that's wonderful. He was just an ordinary, soft, father-like figure. And he had his own children, of course, whom he adored. I admired him immensely. He lived life to the full. When you looked at him you didn't think he did, but his eyes gave him away, they always looked a bit debauched.

"In my time I've met three men who went through life doing what they wanted to do and had enough money to do it. They were Steve McQueen,[4] Mike and David Purley.[5] Mike always had enough money to do what he wanted to do. He didn't have to race, but he did. They were a man's man those three, McQueen, Hailwood and Purley.

"Someone would invite us to dinner – say in Italy, *a lovely dinner* (Bell mimicks an Italian accent) and Mike would say 'Sod off, I'm not bloody going'. He had very definite ideas of what he wanted to do. He wasn't being selfish, but if he didn't want to do it he'd say that."

Katsumasa Suzuki: "He always answered our efforts to win races. I wish I could be a mechanic again."

Phil Read: "It was only in his last few years that we got to know each other, 1978, 1979, 1980. We'd be having a party and I'd say 'Stay over, you can have one of my son's beds, I'll just change the sheets', and he'd say 'No, no, the bed's fine'. It was like he wanted to be part of a family."

Guy Edwards: "Funnily enough, the last time I saw him was at the Albert Hall, it was a David Thieme thing.[6] He was living in New Zealand, he seemed much quieter, he'd long been out of racing and he'd settled down into family life. He didn't like all the bullshit around, he really detested that. He didn't take to the politics or the seriousness of motor racing. He would have been better off in Formula One 10 or 20 years earlier in the Mike Hawthorn-Peter Collins era."

Brian Hart: "I never tried to get inside him to see what was there, but he had a motivation to do very well in cars. That's how he and John Surtees achieved so much in the Formula Two year. John had turned constructor, he was up against the established kit-Brabhams and Lotuses and he did a good job. John was the same as Mike, didn't like losing, very determined, just as obstinate."

Mick Grant: "When Tom Herron was killed, a few of us went over to Ireland, Kenny Roberts, Mike, myself for a special night to raise money for his widow Andrea and kids. We did a forum and film show, the normal sort of thing. People were getting Mike to sign his autograph and one of these people came back not a happy man. Mike had upset him. Mike had been writing *Adolf Hitler*. Only he could have got away with it.

---

4. The film actor who was macho and appeared in several car chases as well as the film *Le Mans*. During the filming of that, so the legend goes, McQueen wanted to do some of the driving himself and a couple of the professional drivers (the finger of suspicion points at D. Bell as a culprit) decided to show McQueen what it was really about. Down the Mulsanne Straight one car moved in front of McQueen's and the other behind, holding him in a vice while they took him at *racing speed* all the way down and through the staccato corners thereafter. Alas, I don't know what McQueen said after, or if he could speak at all.
5. Wealthy adventurer, soldier and driver, killed in a flying accident in 1985, who is credited with surviving the greatest impact in a racing car. Driving a Lec-Ford during qualifying for the British Grand Prix at Silverstone in 1977 his throttle jammed open and at the moment of impact against the barrier the deceleration went from 108mph to 0 in 26 inches. The G-force has been put at 179.8.
6. Thieme, of Essex Petroleum, one-time Lotus sponsor.

"We became friends over 1978 and 1979, especially at places like Donington. Perhaps pals is a better word than friends. We went out for meals together. What did I make of him? Hmmm (long pause). I mean, quite a strange guy really, definitely a strange guy. I don't know (long pause). He'd definitely got this thing which is not in abundance these days, he'd definitely got charisma. You liked the guy although he was definitely a little bit odd, no question of it. A little bit odd. I don't know ... a little bit odd. I liked him and I had a lot of time for him. We'd be having dinner, the two of us, and he didn't talk about himself. He was normal, but underneath it all he was ... I don't know.

"We both had a very special common interest and obviously that brought us together, but I wouldn't say I knew him that well. I must admit I'd a feeling – just from odd things he'd say – that there was a side to him I didn't see. He was modest, like a successful businessman. I know people who have made a lot of money and you could go out with them for six meals and never know about it. Mike would never talk about things like that.

"We had a lot of fun. I remember one time a load of us were having dinner and Mike had a little plastic spider which he put in a girl's soup while she was looking away. The next thing she must have scooped it up because her mouth opened and a stream of cream of tomato soup went all over the place. There was that side to him, but you almost think he did that to balance the other side out. I don't know. I'm not really qualified to say."

Tommy Robb: "I think Mike lived his life as a challenge and I think challenge was more important to him than anything else. The challenge was there in whatever he did. He'd had a challenge to overcome, and that was to live like a normal bloke even though he was the son of a millionaire. He met and overcame that challenge. He enjoyed himself with everyday people like the rest of us. I think Mike got his kicks out of the frights that that big Honda gave him, trying to twist itself out from underneath him."

"I am a proud person to say I knew Mike Hailwood, I raced with Mike Hailwood, I was beaten by Mike Hailwood, I adored Mike Hailwood, but then I know that when I say that I am not one in a million, I am one in many millions" – *Tommy Robb* writing in the Ulster Grand Prix programme, 1983.

Ted Macauley: "Mike was the other way round. What people thought of him was a result of his reaction to *them*. It's a stange way to say it but it's the way it was. People would have a view of Mike which was directly according to what he thought of them, and how much of them he allowed into his life, how much he let them see of him. That was instinctive, totally instinctive. He was very dismissive of people he didn't particularly want to spend any time with. He made that very, very obvious inside the bracket of being good-mannered – he didn't want them around or he didn't want to be around them.

"Who was he? He was just a fellow who was gifted with a talent he could never really understand, and which really didn't fit in with the sort of life he'd had. Motorcycle racing was considered rather *infra dig* and there was Mike, Pangbourne, father a millionaire, and Mike with a lot of money to come to him.

"Mike had this honesty of purpose in that he was gifted with such single-mindedness. He could do whatever he wanted to do. Take the clarinet. I'd watch him. He'd put a Sidney Bechet[7] record on and play the clarinet to it sitting by

---

7. An American clarinet and saxophone player who lived in Paris and had his own band.

himself. He wouldn't play it in public. He could play the piano and the guitar and so on, and whatever he did he did with great single-minded determination.

"There was a genius inside him which Mike didn't know, but which co-existed very comfortably with him when he was on a bike or in a racing car. When he couldn't live with it was when he got off the bike or out of the car. He was embarrassed by attention, totally and completely embarrassed by it. He would never take advantage of his fame. He could have been 10 times as wealthy if he'd done a lot of the things I wanted him to do, like sponsorships or advertising. He never wanted to be given anything, he always wanted to work for it himself. He was given a lot by Stan, but he was given a really hard time by Stan, too. Mike succeeded despite Stan rather than because of Stan. There is no question about that.

"Mike pushed himself alright. He was the most self-sufficient man I think I have ever met. He hated to ask anybody to do anything for him, but equally he existed on a platform: If he didn't want to talk to somebody he didn't. He always had that fall-back – *why are you sitting at my table? I don't want you to be there*. He could be like that as well.

"There's a marvellous parallel and it's funny because I drew the parallel the other night. I was out with George Best[8] in Manchester and I'd introduced George to Mike years ago, and Mike was totally fascinated by George, who was then almost passing through the end of his career. In fact there were so many parallels to them in so many ways and it came out that night. George was sitting in the middle of the Midland Hotel in Manchester, and I bet a hundred people asked him for his autograph, just walked over to him with bits of paper. A woman was so drunk she was looking for a pen and she spilled her drink in George's lap. He shrugged his shoulders. I can remember Mike once in the same situation in the Isle of Man, we were in a nightclub and Mike just wanted to have a bit of fun. He was such an idol he couldn't sit without sign, sign, sign, sign. He said 'Come on, let's go to a restaurant', so we went.

"This is a sad and reflective story in many ways. A man and a woman Mike had known for a while were in the restaurant. He'd introduced them to me and they were like a double-act, and Mike thought they were very, very, very funny – but they did the same jokes and you heard them time after time.

"We ate together, five of us including them, and if anybody hesitated anywhere when the bill came Mike would pick it up almost as a reflex. Mike picked up the bill and the woman said something like 'It's about time you paid for something, Hailwood', in what she considered to be a jocular way. Mike looked at her, shrugged, signed the bill and never spoke to her or her husband ever, ever again. They tried to come back in, but it had hurt Mike, who was the most generous guy. And all we'd been trying to do was escape, go for a meal. There was no escape, none.

"He wanted to enjoy himself and that's my abiding memory of him. If ever I could put anything on an epitaph that's what I'd put. He just wanted to have fun. Everyone who got close to him will say that."

---

8. Diminutive Northern Ireland footballer who for a time was as big a name as *The Beatles* and who is still regarded as a football genius. I once saw him score by shooting through the goalkeeper's legs from 25 yards when he was playing for Manchester United at Sunderland, and rather than jeer their own keeper the crowd shook the stadium with applause for this moment of magic. People still remember Best, just as I remember that.

4

There will always be arguments, I suppose, about relative merits. They will always be biased, I suppose, towards what you saw, when you saw it, how you evaluated it and who you were when you saw it. Ignore emotion at your peril. A hero-struck youngster is likely to defend his hero with ferocity all his days because the hero represents a precious era the youngster lived through and quite possibly embodies that youngster's youth, too.

Who dispassionately can surrender that youth by saying things were *worse* then? Who will say, having lived through the tumult of it, that – to take a random example – the Manchester United team of 1968, Law, Charlton and the same George Best, were worse than the Manchester United team of today? But that's where the complications lie. If you were 10 when you saw that team of '68 you're 34 now; if you're younger than 34 you can have but the most distorted of memories. How, then, can you evaluate? Difficult. These days at least you can watch videos, although in many cases they contain no more than fleeting highlights taken by cameras in the distance, the competitors reduced to frantic figurines hunting and harrying and scurrying across a black-and-white landscape.

In all branches of motorsport, however, you have an immediate aide: statistics. You can prove that technology makes things go quicker. The first 100mph lap on the Isle of Man – set by Bob McIntyre in 1957 – was a genuine feat. Now everybody does it, hundreds and hundreds of them. Another random example. In 1985 a rider called Ashley Gardner took a Yamaha round with a fastest lap of 101.15mph in a *newcomers'* 350cc race.

Pole position, as we have seen, was taken by Jim Clark at Mike's first car Grand Prix with 1 minute 34.4 seconds. Surtees set fastest lap in the race, 1 minute 36.0, which was 109.765mph. Silverstone has subsequently been modified twice to slow the cars, and by 1991 included an entirely new 'complex', a very twisty section just before the start–finish straight.

In 1963 Silvertone measured 4.700 kilometres. In 1991 that had become 5.225, and apart from the complex, the previously flat-out section between Stowe and Club Corners had had two bends put in, slowing the cars further.

On lap 43 of the British Grand Prix, on July 14, Nigel Mansell set fastest lap in 1 minute 26.379 seconds, which was 135.325mph. Without belabouring the point, Mansell covered almost half a kilometre more on a deliberately doctored circuit 10 seconds quicker than Surtees had done. Put it another way. If Mansell and Surtees had been able to sustain those lap speeds over the 59 laps of the race – Surtees on the older, faster circuit, Mansell on the new, longer, slower one – Mansell would have won by nearly 10 *minutes*.

All this, of course, only leads to further complications. Technology increases speed, technology allows all manner of permutations to set up a racing bike or a racing car, but where does that take you? Statistics are not a value-judgment, they are only figures and decimal points. Do you need greater skill to drive the Ferrari which Surtees had, or the Williams-Renault that Mansell had? Is it a different skill? Of course, perhaps totally different. And so you come back to the evaluation if you're trying to discover who was the better driver, and it remains difficult, arguably impossible.

You can assemble evidence, though, and there are too many witnesses who all say the same thing to doubt that Mike was alone in being able to take The

Bronco round The Island in 1967; but nobody else tried. What might Roberts or Freddie Spencer or Eddie Lawson or Wayne Gardner have done on it? A hundred and plenty? Fallen off?

The key to Mike's greatness, I believe and insist, is not that he was outstanding in his era – 1961 to 1967 – because somebody is outstanding in most eras in most things. No. It is that, nearing middle-age and in racing terms a cripple, he was able to vault to another era altogether, master a technology so advanced and alien that at first he had no conception of what it was; and of seven races in 1978 and 1979 was only beaten three times when the bikes were functioning properly – and the third of those defeats was by 3.4 seconds after 226 miles riding the crucial final part 'blind' because he had no signals to tell him what he had to make up. As Martin Ogborne has said, beaten by a radio, or the lack of a radio.

It is a legitimate question: which other rider – and you can help yourself to the whole history of it, all the way back to the turn of the century – could have done this?

Broadening the context to embrace the whole of motorsport, Murray Walker points out that the only comparable feat was perhaps Niki Lauda, who retired from Formula One in 1979, returned in 1982, and a season later mastered the entirely new world (to him) of turbo power; Walker does add that, of course, Lauda was only quiescent for three years, Mike essentially for a decade.

There's another legitimate question: what exactly was it that Hailwood had? A word or two of caution from John Cooper. "Mike rode some lovely races. He was always fortunate in that he had faster bikes, but he complemented that by being able to ride them properly. I remember a chap going out in practice with me at a circuit. We were on 500 Matchlesses and he wanted to follow me round. I started to go a bit faster, we were going round a curve and he did everything the same as me at the same time on the same make of bike. I was travelling really hard, but quite safely, and I looked round and I could see he was going over the bank. I said afterwards 'What happened?'. He said 'I don't know, I changed gear the same, I did everything the same and mine let go and yours didn't'. It's just that some people can and some people can't. I don't know why. You could never say why Jackie Stewart went round a corner faster than James Hunt, or today Ayrton Senna goes round faster than some of the others."

Ted Macauley wondered, too. "He had balls when he rode that Honda 500 and it was just impossible. That 500 was a thing only he could have ridden, only he would have dared, only he would have had the balls. How could he do it? There is an X factor about Hailwood that will always exist and I had long conversations with him: what is it you think you've got? Why d'you think you're better? You could never ever get him down to that. He never examined what he had in terms of natural talent any more than he examined his personality or his zest for life. I think the two things are so close together. Nothing ever *fazed* him, things didn't get underneath him."

One clue, perhaps. "When you were dicing with Mike you felt you were doing your best, but anytime now he would come by and disappear. Mike was probably thinking 'Christ, I wish this bloke would slow down a bit, I can't catch him', but you didn't know or feel that. He was a great out-psycher on the line. 'Look, mate', he'd say, 'keep over to the left, I shall be passing you on the right', or 'We'll make a race out of this, we'll mess around for 10 laps and the last lap to count'. He was nervous himself, you see, he was a professional, he'd concentrate his mind on the last lap and ride it to the limit." (Question: What limit? What *was* his limit?)

The quotation above is from Phil Read. When I went to interview him in late 1991 he'd just received a phone call from Pino Allievi, the much respected writer for a famous Italian daily sports newspaper *La Gazetta dello Sport*. Allievi was ringing round old riders for their views so that he could construct a lengthy article on why Agostini was the greatest rider who ever lived. The Allievi-Read conversation was a short one.

"Agostini wasn't", Read said. "Hailwood was."

This is a theme which is almost a theme within a theme. "People always argue who is or was the best", Jim Redman will say. "Is Wayne Rainey better than Hailwood?, and all the rest of it. I sat in a good seat to study quite a few riders. I sat behind or in front of them race after race. I'm thinking about the different classes. Mike would jump on a 125, a 250, a 350, a 500, MV, Gilera, Norton, AJS, NSU, Honda, any bloody thing, all he'd do was jump on and go. He never had to adjust or anything, well, his adjustment was done from when he got on to the first corner and then he was away, you know.

"I saw the tail end of Surtees and Duke and those guys, and to me I hold Mike the best ever, even over Agostini. Ago won the most World Championships by a long way, but it isn't a fair comparison because he had a long easy cruise with MV (when Mike had retired). Agostini used to start casually in the middle of the field, work his way to the front and win by as much as he liked – he'd try and make it a little bit interesting for the crowd. When Mike and I were around there was nothing like that.

"People today ask me 'Did you ever meet Agostini?', and for the first number of years that he raced I didn't even know he was in the race. He came right after three or four or five years or whatever it was. People think Agostini suddenly arrived and hassled Mike and I on the 350s. There's nothing further from the truth. Maybe Agostini improved after I stopped, I don't know, but if it was a straight fight between them I know where I'd put my money. There has never been anyone better than Hailwood."

Alex George, mellowed in the years of it, becalmed after the years of it, is as sharply perceptive as any. "You can't build speed into people. Speed is there and talent is there. He was a hell of a talented guy in everything that he did – an accomplished pianist, and so on, as well. He was just one of those smashing blokes that made everybody feel at home and relaxed, who was a pleasure to talk to. I never ever saw him upset.

"I look round me at all levels of the sport today and I don't see anybody with the same sort of charisma. There are some guys with some of the things. Some guys are fast, some guys have a lot of character, but they're not so fast, some guys have a bit of both, but they're not quite making it to the flag. So I look round me and I see bits of Mike displayed in different riders, but I don't see a complete package, the complete package Mike was, in anybody. That's not being sentimental.

"The guy who impressed me most in all the years I was doing Grand Prix bike racing was the Finn Jarno Saarinen. He had the same kind of qualities as Mike, if you like. He was generous with people, kind to people, very, very aggressive on the track, humorous off it, very funny, relaxed, in control of what he was doing, safe – and so was Mike. A lot of people don't say that about Mike, but he was very, very safe. He took it to the maximum and he could stay there all day long. The only other person who impressed me in the way Mike did was Saarinen. That still holds true. If you met Mike even briefly he would leave a ray of sunshine dancing about your head."

Kiyoshi Kawashima of Honda is no less convinced of the quality of Mike, but expressed it in a slightly different way. "I believe Mike had a talent which few others among Grand Prix riders had. He always said 'Give me a good machine!'. He was not the type of rider who helped develop a machine, but in racing he was a ... genius."

Yes, but how could he still do it at the age of 38? Perhaps quite unconsciously Mick Grant holds that particular clue, and it is culled from his own experiences. "I watched people at the so-called dangerous circuits like Scarborough and the Isle of Man and I'd be quite happy to ride round myself, but I do fear for others. It's much easier when you're doing it yourself.

"The one thing about the Isle of Man is that it is a very precise place. You have to be very precise and you race there in such a way that you're pretty well in control. You're not going to be dicing with other people, there won't be people running underneath you and forcing you wide into walls or whatever. It's not that sort of place.

"I like to think that I think positively, but I've a very negative side to myself which believes in fate. I never ever started a race in my life without thinking: just be careful, don't bloody hurt yourself. A lot of guys go on racing and people say they've lost it, but they haven't lost it at all. They've gone on for years and never seen the danger and one morning they wake up and say: 'I didn't realize it – this is dangerous, be careful'. You never lose the ability, you lose the will to do it, and that's the half a second a lap difference. You can go quick, but it's that last little bit. I won the British Championship when I was 40. I could ride for so long because I'd always known right from day one that it was dangerous. It didn't suddenly come to me one day when I was 34 or 35 or 36."

Mike had been externally nonchalant, deceptively casual all his days, but he had always known too, always known.

Tommy Robb takes the overview. "There is nobody today doing anything which wasn't done in Stanley Woods'[9] day, in John Surtees' day. You still have to be using your ability to the *nth* degree to win a race, perhaps even more so now. That's why I don't usually say anything. If I do I am wrong. Technology has taken over. In those days a man had to make a decision about his race strategy. Someone might say 'If you give the bugger 300 revs more you'll be safely there', but you had to make up your own mind if you could give the bike that 300. Someone might say before the start of a race 'There's oil on that corner', and you hadn't even known. So you cannot compare then and now. I will, however, say that there has never been another man alive able to win on 125, 250, 350 and 500 like Mike did. Never."

Murray Walker expands on that. "I've never seen anyone else with Mike's ability to ride totally different bikes at the *same* meeting and win on all of them, 125 single-cylinders, 350 four-stroke four-cylinder MVs – different characteristics, different engines and different gearchanges."

Surtees, of course, remains the only man to win World Championship titles

---

9. Irishman and the biggest name in riding in the Twenties and Thirties. He won the TT 10 times, and in 1935, when Norton were regarded as invincible, he beat Jimmy Guthrie by four seconds after seven laps – Woods riding a Guzzi. He had already won the 250 on a Guzzi, giving him two out of three. As Murray Walker says, "Not quite equal to Mike in 1961, but not far off!".

in both disciplines, cars and bikes. Will it ever be repeated? Forever is a long time, but it's most unlikely this century and well into the next. The disciplines do not cross-fertilize, each makes more and more demands, each takes many years to master, and if you're doing one you can't be doing the other. The very idea of competing a whole season of both simultaneously, as Surtees and Mike did, would send a team manager today into hysterics or straight to an asylum in a white van. Imagine if Ayrton Senna said to his McLaren boss Ron Dennis that, yes, he'd drive the Formula One car in the 16 Grands Prix, *'but oh, Ron, did I mention that I'll be doing 15 rounds with the other guys on a 500 Honda?'*.

The present day Formula One driver's contract often governs what pastimes he may or may not indulge in. *Don't you dare play table tennis, you might pull a muscle, we're not paying you 10 or 15 million dollars to play table tennis.* OK, I'm being a little flippant, I'm exaggerating a bit. Aren't I?

So Surtees' position is safe. It was achieved by a conjunction of factors: he was good in bikes early, successful early, it was possible to move to cars and he got himself into a good car early, the Ferrari, in only his third full season. Mike might have equalled this, but didn't find the conjunction. He lacked the car, and even if he'd had it that is no guarantee of a World Championship. Only one guy per annum can win it, and the odds are always heavy against. Ask Mansell.

Here is the real perspective: on lap 26 of the United States Grand Prix at Dallas on July 8, 1984, the driver of a Toleman car clipped a wall and retired. He would never drive another Formula One race. A few days later he damaged his legs in a crash at Brands Hatch and his career ended. He was called Johnny Cecotto. In 1975, riding a Yamaha, he had been World 350cc Champion. His Grand Prix car career embraced only 18 races and from them he took but a single point. Cecotto was the first man since Mike to contest cars and bikes at World Championship level. No-one has tried since.

5

Early January 1992 and we're sitting at a corner table in a nice restaurant in a nice little Midlands village, Pauline, David Hobbs and I. Pauline has been spending Christmas with the Hobbs family at their – forgive me, David – country mansion.

At the mansion Hobbs' son Greg has already recounted two relevant though unconnected stories. When Greg was 11 or 12 Mike was visiting and a bunch of people played cricket on the lawn, played it seriously. As a batsman Mike seemed able to just wander along. His eyesight was so keen, his reflexes so quick and controlled that he waited for the ball to reach him and then hit it wherever he fancied, including – to quick deliveries – languid lap shots behind the wicket. Greg had never seen anything like that before.

Greg worked in the Gould-Hailwood business in Birmingham, and when times got hard, he says, Mike arrived in a suit at crack of dawn and was the last to leave. This stands uneasily with what Murray Walker has said, but no matter. Human beings are not, I repeat, cast in one dimension, not neatly parcelled, and the ends are never all tied up.

But now we are sitting in the restaurant, Pauline is dressed casually, but it looks casual-chic. She has a smile which can stun men at 20 paces. The restaurant owner who's Portuguese makes a fuss of her by gushing all round the end of the table, and it takes us some time to shake him off.

Pauline: "Mike was very laid-back, but at the same time he was extremely determined with things that mattered to him. He thought about things, kept things to himself a lot. He wouldn't easily talk about things."

Hobbs: "Mike was the perfect combination of laid-back and the ability to get the job done. The discouraging thing for the rest of us was that he made it look easy, and of course it's not easy at all. I don't think even to him some of it came easy, he had to work at it, he had the ability to work at it whilst at the same time *looking* as if he wasn't working at it."

Pauline: "He didn't lose his temper very often. There was that time with Billy Ivy..."

Hobbs: "He got uptight with me, bloody hell, it was panic. I touched a raw nerve, I said something about the state of his leathers, and that was it, off he went, he accused me of being a snob. (Hobbs fuelled it by laughing, which definitely wasn't the thing to do.) He was in that sensitive transition from bikes to cars and he always felt people who drove cars were inclined to be a bit snobbish."

Pauline: "Occasionally somebody would say something and he'd come back at them and you thought to yourself: *I didn't think he'd be thinking that*. He thought a lot more than people realized. Sometimes he'd come back at me and I'd be absolutely stunned because it showed that he had been thinking deeply about something. He'd totally surprise me, it wasn't what I was expecting."

Hobbs: "He didn't like being taken for granted."

Pauline: "Sometimes, if someone asked him for an autograph he'd say *Mike who?*. I heard that said a few times."

Hobbs: "I remember once we went to a pub at Upper Boddington. I took him. Somebody in there recognized him, and the next thing they're all asking for autographs. That was another time he got a bit miffed with me because he thought I had set him up."

Pauline: "You see. You wouldn't think he'd think that, would you?"

Hobbs: "He thought I'd sent advance warning to the pub that I was going to take Mike Hailwood, whereas actually I hadn't said anything about it at all. He imagined he was going to escape to this quiet village pub where no-one had ever heard of him, but somebody in there obviously recognized him." (No escape again, you see.)

Pauline: "That's exactly what I mean. Knowing you he should have known you wouldn't do that."

Hilton: "Did he get twitchy before a race?"

Pauline: "No, not really. I used to leave him alone, say as little as possible and just let him get on with it. He'd just quietly concentrate. He didn't natter along about things. He wasn't that mad about me going to meetings, I don't think. He had to concentrate on the job in hand and he didn't want to worry if I was bored or whatever. He didn't like taking me to races, especially after the crash at Brands Hatch. That was it, that did it, he wouldn't take me after that."

Hobbs: "It was typical Mike when he rescued Regazzoni and didn't say anything about it afterwards."

Pauline: "It was."

Hobbs: "He was one of the most self-effacing people I ever knew. A lot of people say 'Oh, it was nothing', but I am convinced that when he said it he really meant it."

Pauline: "Yes."

Hilton: "Stan brought women to races. I wonder if Mike, growing up with that, thought that that was the way the world was?"

Pauline: "It's the way they were, the way they were, Mike and Stan. Mike did see the world as it was. I've heard him say to people: 'Oh grow up, this is the real world'. I'm not saying I didn't get angry, I couldn't always keep it under control. Certainly, when we were married, if he fooled around I never knew about it. As long as he kept coming back to me that was all I wanted."

Hilton: "Did he ever speak about his mother?"

Pauline: "No, I think because he couldn't remember much."

Hilton: "Who was he?"

Pauline: "You take the comeback on The Isle of Man. No matter how many years it was down the road he still had his natural ability, he still had his determination to get the best that he could out of something. Such was the ability of the man, I guess. He never thought he was special. He just thought he was an ordinary chap. He didn't know what all the fuss was about. He never really made a fuss about anything. After the Nurburgring there were times, I know, when he must have been in tremendous pain, but if there was anything wrong he wouldn't complain about it. You'd never know. He just didn't make a big deal of things.

"He'd got things fairly sorted out in his mind ... I don't know, maybe (chuckle) he hadn't, maybe he did just sort of bowl along not thinking about it, but I don't think he did really."

[This is the ultimate evidence of the many dimensions, the untied ends which remain untied and we can leave it there.]

6

Faces in the mirror, faces in the mirror.

In January 1992, Yoichi Harada of Honda's Public Relations Division in Tokyo fulfilled his final task in lending so much painstaking and invaluable help to this book. He'd known Mike and "he impressed me a lot". This January day Mr Harada gathered five Honda men who had worked with Mike and invited them to bathe in their memories. They did.

It is touching, almost a kind of pathos, that such people should be reunited so far away in time and distance by the memory of one man. And yet it's not really pathos. It is a celebration of that man.

Those gathered were Mikihiko Aika, currently chief engineer of the Motor Sport Division and a former manager of the bike racing team; Mamoru Haji, currently chief engineer of the power equipment Research and Development centre, former team manager and mechanic; Ikuo Nagashima, currently a technician and former mechanic to Mike's 250cc bike; Katsumasa Suzuki, currently general manager of HRC-E (Europe) and former mechanic to Mike's 350cc bike; Katsutoshi Oshiro, currently staff technician of HRC and former mechanic to Mike's 500cc bike.

These are people who know what they are talking about.

"I was the one who held out a board when Mike's twist grip loosened on the Isle of Man saying *minus 12 seconds*. I thought the race would finish like that, then the MV's chain broke. Mike didn't come back to the pits after the chequered flag and I set off to find the bike. It was leant against a tree. At Monza, in 1967, when he was passed by Agostini and the title was gone, I had to go and find the bike again. This time it was leant against a guardrail.

"Mike wasn't so aggressive with girls, but Agostini was. However girls gathered naturally around him in any country.

"He had a talent on a bike and he practised accelerating and braking, which he would repeat and repeat. He might have been the first man who found such a training method, connecting brain and machine.

"Most of my memories with Mike, other than racing, were at bars. He had a character which didn't allow him to stand still. I wish I could meet him again." – *Katsutoshi Oshiro*.

"Mike thought a trophy would be treated better if he gave it to someone rather than keeping it for himself. Probably he reasoned that giving trophies to his mechanics was the quickest and best way to show his appreciation of them.

"Mike's machine got heavier and heavier, bigger and bigger, when Research and Development responded to his complaints that it wouldn't go straight on the straights. Even so he made many less mistakes compared to average riders. Because of his disposition many riders gathered around him. He was never vulgar, he didn't care about the past. Nobody has a bad memory of him.

"Honda was able to gather fruit when he was there and I was happy to do my job with such a rider. If you're working with someone it's better if that person is superior." – *Mikihiko Aika*.

"Mike fell at a test session at Suzuka in 1966, and I remember that because it was very rare for him to do that. He always talked with the mechanics. After the race in Czechoslovakia in 1966 he stopped his machine, came up and hugged me. And in Spain in 1967, when his machine had trouble in the middle of the race, he came back to our pit, he got very angry and kicked a tyre of the machine. But he didn't show he was upset to the mechanics.

"He often made holes in his shoes. He thought the hole was his sensor for how far over he could bank a machine. His lap times at the Isle of Man were not so different whether it was a fine day or a rainy day. I have worked for many Honda riders, but I felt it was with him I wanted to work the most. I wish I could meet him again if I could." – *Ikuo Nagashima*.

"I have worked with bike riders and car drivers. Mike was a superstar and his behaviour was humane, normal – and superstars can easily lose that. He cared about people. For example, when we were moving around the Continent he often said 'Come over to my caravan'. Once, at Assen, he said that to me, I went, and there were two girls. He said 'You can pick the one you like!'.

"He even gave me a trophy, a silver one from Finland. Nobody was generous like he was. To be honest I had wanted one of his trophies, but I couldn't ask. When he gave it to me I took it back home very carefully. I still have it. I knew some of his girlfriends, but I never heard he gave trophies to them." – *Mamoru Haji*.

"I was given an official crystal trophy after the Czechoslovakian Grand Prix of 1966, when he won the 250, 350 and 500 races." – *Nagashima*.

"I was given four trophies by him and I still keep three of them. The best one is a crystal on a silver base." – *Katsumasa Suzuki*.

"I was given three, after the Dutch and Czech Grands Prix. The latter was bronze with gold plate. He also gave me one after an East German Grand Prix. I display two of them in my living room." – *Oshiro*.

"He rolled tapes up his riding boots at every race. When I asked him why he didn't buy new ones he said 'New ones will not work!'. He had his own measure which told him the limit of his leaning and sliding. His slide-riding looked amazing to everyone, but he was doing it consciously. Somebody worked out that his angle of lean was deeper than the other riders, but he almost never fell. Looking back, only twice did we not win because of his mistakes, the 500cc in Finland in 1967, which was held in heavy rain, and official practice at Assen the same year. Otherwise the machines were *crying* and breaking up because his riding bordered on the performance-limit of the machines.

"Even if he couldn't get pole position he often came back leading after the first lap. I remember Finland and that rain. When I touched his body before the 250cc race he said the pain was because of his tumble in the 500. He said he would go into the 250 just to get the start money. He was leading after the first lap and I thought he would give up on the next. He won the race...

"He was always bright and always playful. I wish I could talk to him to bring back the old memories. I liked the atmosphere around him. If he was alive I'd like to have seen him have a business relationship with Honda, perhaps owning his own team. He could have contributed to the growth of motorcycle racing. He was too good to lose." – *Haji.*

7

Faces in the mirror, faces in the mirror.
Letter (extract)

Morningside
Durban
South Africa

May 15, 1991

Dear Christopher,

I found this request of yours on Mike really hard going. I am not complaining. I would write down in rough certain things which came to mind easily, but in the end I got all my books out and read them to give the brain a bit of a boost.

I have no doubt in my mind he was the greatest rider ever when you look at the bikes he rode and won on. I don't believe Mike ever rode over his limit, and everyone has their own limits, the limits are different rider to rider, bike to bike.

I feel I was very lucky to have known and worked for Mike in an era which was so competitive.

Mike met every challenge square-on, thought it out, planned it and then executed it. He might have asked people for their advice, but he always made the final decision.

I have heard a number of times today's riders state that they have done far more for motorcycle racing than Mike ever did, but most of them forget he did his share on the circuits, racing, and not with his mouth. I have spoken to Agostini often, and he has spoken to me. He has told me he thinks Mike was the greatest rider and acknowledges the fact that Mike taught him a lot.

Yours sincerely,
Nobby Clark.

Letter (extract)

Morningside
Durban
South Africa

May 28, 1991

Dear Christopher,

While watching the Italian Grand Prix on television I heard the commentators mention that Eddie Lawson was the greatest rider ever. Where and how they arrive at such a statement I don't know. I would like to hear why they made it.

I don't think they could have seen Mike ride – or for that matter Carlo Ubbiali, Angelo Nieto, Agostini or Kenny Roberts. In the old times riders rode three times a day, the races were longer, they had one type of tyre for all conditions and the suspension systems, let us say, left a lot to be desired. The above riders each won more races than Eddie Lawson has ever dreamed of winning.

I like to think there are many people, myself included, who are lucky to have seen Mike Hailwood race and privileged to have seen Mike Hailwood race.

Yours sincerely,
Nobby Clark.

Letter (extract)

Bryanston
Johannesburg
South Africa

January 15, 1992

Dear Christopher,

I first met Mike in the winter of 1957–58 when he came to South Africa with Dave Chadwick – christened Davy Crockett. Mike was *very* introverted at that stage. The gang stayed at my place, Red Berry Farm, just outside Johannesburg. Mike spent most of his time in his room strumming on a guitar. He had a wonderful ear and played the guitar, saxophone, piano without reading a note of music. Later, in the Sixties, he'd put a record on and would follow along with whatever instrument he was playing, over and over again.

Mike had a 250 NSU and a 350 Norton back on that first visit. I remember he was loathe to ride the Norton as he thought it was too big, too powerful for him.

Jim Redman and I went to Europe in March 1958, so we were privileged to watch Mike's remarkable progress from scratch. Stan Hailwood sometimes (most times!) entered Mike in four races in a day, 125, 250, 350 and 500! As a result of his prodigious mileage he soon displayed his talents. Strange that a millionaire's son had so much born talent.

In between races, and sometimes before them, Mike was very fond of night-clubbing or jazz-clubbing. He introduced me to the music of such great musicians as Acker Bilk, Chris Barber and Kenny Ball. And of course there were *The Goons*. We spent many a moment on and off the track quoting from Peter Sellers and Spike Milligan in *The Goons* and in fact most of our conversations were 'spiked' with Goon sayings.

Jim Redman christened Mike 'Mickey Hollywood' for his obvious romantic living style. Mike had much charisma, although not a lot of outgoing confidence.

He certainly enjoyed the limelight to a point, but otherwise he was a very private person. The girls loved him – and he them! He had a hang-up about his loss of hair and his 'Punch' profile, but it didn't detract from his obvious desirability; his sparkling smile and blue eyes took care of most female hearts. I stayed with him at his flat at Heston for two months. We partied, boozed, went to his car races in Formula 5000. I was fascinated by the number of women that appeared on his doorstep – some of them well-known to me as wives of other acquaintances! He always gave me a sly grin when they'd left after a 'session' and said 'what must I do?'. It didn't stop him doing! In fact the front doorbell went so often I reckoned they must be queuing-up downstairs and taking tickets...

Within hours of his arrival at Red Berry Farm the phone would start ringing and they'd be coming around.

Whooping it up was some kind of safety valve to Mike. It released a lot of internal tension that he built up whilst racing. He wasn't slow on the booze, either – we always gave it a good tonk until the early hours of the morning. Racing in South Africa was a holiday to Mike, and we didn't mind partying till four in the morning before a race. We could do it in those days. We were young. Can't do it now!

Mike always drove fast cars fast. I was often a passenger and ended up 'braking hard' on the floor when I thought he had cut it a bit fine.

He had a naughty streak in him and coached Agostini in the early days on the correct English phrases to order food. Ago was most confused when the waitresses gave him a mouthful of abuse and stormed off. We roared. Ago thought he'd been ordering supper, but Mike had taught him to ask them to go to bed with him. Poor Ago, he battled with his English!

Mike suffered fools very lightly and could cut people embarrassingly dead, sometimes at very awkward moments.

One time we were in his Iso Grifo going to Cape Town at 100mph-plus. He said calmly 'I wonder what that flashing blue light is way behind us?', and I said, 'Yes, *I* wonder what that flashing blue light is behind us'. He floored the Grifo and we soon lost sight of the blue light.

We used to have water-skiing holidays in early December in Mozambique. Mike was a talented person and took to it like a duck to water.

Mike had no business sense whatever, and it seems that all the ventures he put money into went wrong because he trusted people too much. He lost money in South Africa, New Zealand and the UK with his investments. Enough said.

People sponged off him a good deal, especially in bars and restaurants. They all expected Mike to pay. Aware of this he'd call for the bill, do some arithmatic and say it was 'so much for each one of you'. Everyone put their money in unaware that Mike had arranged the price so that he ate for nothing. It was his way of evening things.

Mike had a few tumbles every season on motorcycles. If you confronted him afterwards he'd say 'I'm OK, I fell on my head'.

Of all the girls, Pauline stuck with him and eventually won through to marry him. A lovely person.

Mike would occasionally appear from his bedroom after a hectic night with some very scruffy bird. He'd shoo her off quickly and explain that 'a bit of rough did you good from time to time!'.

It was my honour to share a factory Chevron in the Springbok series 20 years ago. We finished third behind the two factory Ferraris in the nine-hour race at

Kyalami and won the three-hour race in Bulawayo, Rhodesia as well. Mike would not easily let me drive him anywhere. Although he drove dangerously fast, he didn't trust others to drive him. Someone was driving us back from a party in Cape Town. We were going around some very twisty bends and I was hanging out of the door playing sidecar passenger, urging the driver to go faster. Mike got very cross and demanded that we stop the car! I laughed at him. I couldn't understand his concern when we were only proceeding at a mere 55mph and he regularly drove me at 120mph in his Grifo. Anyway, that was one of his quirks and hard to comprehend. Incidentally, Mike's sportscar drives during the Springbok series were very accomplished.

All the best,
Paddy Driver.

PS. We were fortunate to live and race in the Fifties, Sixties and Seventies – what I feel was the golden age of everything. No sign of AIDS on the horizon.

Mike was not averse to sharing his women, and I suppose I benefited from his appeal to females. I remember once in London he fixed up two dates. One girl was a Swedish *Playboy* playmate who was told to bring a 'friend' for me. On the way back from some jazz supper club I was battling with this lady in the back seat and she was most unco-operative. Mike was obviously watching developments in the rear-view mirror. All of a sudden he lost his cool and screeched to a halt. He berated *Miss Playboy* for organizing such a non-co-operative companion for me: the girls had to get out, they were left somewhere in London and had to find their own way back to wherever they lived. What a mate!

[In the summer of 1991 a book was published by Chris Nixon about the lives and times of two great English drivers, Mike Hawthorn and Peter Collins, who had a catch-phrase between themselves. It was Mon ami, mate – the title of the book.]

PPS. Forgive me the plagiarism, but for me it was *Mon ami, Mike*. I really must say that when Mike died I felt I had lost a brother.

FAX message (verbatim)

President Hotel
Cape Town.

February 1, 1992

Mike and I went through a lot together over the years, the ups and the downs, the laughter and the tears. There is so much more I could have said about Mike and our private life – many people who thought they knew him just wouldn't believe me.

It is impossible to describe the depth of devastation I felt at the loss of Mike and Michelle. Suffice it to say I had no wish to live. But I still had our six-year-old son David, a part of Mike, and he needed me as much as I needed him. So life (of a different kind) went on.

This book has captured the modesty, determination and spirit of Mike very well (goodness knows what repercussions I will have when David reads what a 'hell-raiser' his father was!).

It is also abundantly clear how much Mike treasured his privacy, so I hope you will forgive me for keeping the more personal side of him between David and myself and thereby stay loyal to his wishes and trust. He deserves that.

Pauline.

8

Once upon a time Mike had some words framed. Men do not do such things carelessly. They were a printed version of an inscription set into a tombstone in an American graveyard just after the turn of the century. They had a name, Desiderata. These are those words:

> Go placidly amid the noise and haste
> and remember what peace there may be in silence.
> As far as possible without surrender
> be on good terms with all persons.
> Speak your truth quietly and clearly
> and listen to others, even the dull and ignorant.
> They too have their story.
> Avoid loud and aggressive persons,
> they are a vexation to the spirit.
> If you compare yourself with others
> you may become vain and bitter
> because always there will be greater
> and lesser persons than yourself.
>
> You are a child of the universe.
> No less than the trees and the stars
> you have a right to be here
> and whether or not it is clear to you
> no doubt the universe is unfolding as it should.
>
> Enjoy your achievements as well as your plans,
> keep interested in your own career.
> However humble it is a real possession
> in the changing fortunes of time.
> Exercise caution in your business affairs
> because the world is full of trickery
> but let this not blind you to what virtue there is.
> Many persons strive for high ideals
> and everywhere life is full of heroism.
> Be yourself. Especially do not feign affection
> but neither be cynical about love.
> In the face of all aridity and disenchantment
> it is as perennial as the grass.
> Take kindly to the council of the years
> gracefully surrendering the things of youth.
> Nurture strength of spirit to shield
> yourself from sudden misfortune
> but do not distress yourself with imaginings.
> Many fears are born of fatigue and loneliness.
> Beyond a wholesome discipline, be gentle with yourself.
>
> You are a child of the universe.
> No less than the trees and the stars
> you have a right to be here

and whether or not it is clear to you
no doubt the universe is unfolding as it should.

Therefore be at peace with God
whatever you conceive him to be
and whatever your labours and aspirations
in the noisy confusion of life
keep peace with your soul.
With all its sham, drudgery and broken dreams
it is still a beautiful world.
Be careful. Strive to be happy.

You are a child of the universe.
No less than the trees and the stars
you have a right to be here
and whether or not it is clear to you
no doubt the universe is unfolding as it should.

9

The church of St Mary Magdalene, in Tamworth-in-Arden, was strong and solid and very English, the kind which is woven into the fabric of the country in a timeless way, accepting the generations which come and go, come and go.

The pall-bearers were the men of a life: John Surtees, whose father had raced Stan; Luigi Taveri, who was in that first race on The Island; James Hunt, a kindred spirit – so similar, so different; Dickie Attwood, the competitor who became an admirer, who became a friend; David Hobbs, thinking perhaps of the big, living panorama of Le Mans; Geoff Duke, remembering perhaps the teenager in the hotel who had been so uncertain, so worried; Giacomo Agostini, thinking perhaps of those great, gracious races which will never die.

They all held him now as his memory held them; held him as they moved in lock-step away from the church door in that awkward, unco-ordinated cadence of movement which is bearing a coffin.

The very last journey, from the door to the grave, was not only the shortest, but the slowest of all.

He'd have had something to say about that.

Milestones

1940   Born April 2 near Oxford.

1947   First rides a bike round the lawn.

1954   Attends Pangbourne Naval College, Berkshire.

1957   Leaves Pangbourne and works at King's of Oxford, then the Triumph factory at Meriden, near Birmingham. First competition, the Scottish Six-Day Trial, first race at Oulton Park (11th), first victory in a 250cc race at Cookstown, Northern Ireland. Competes in South Africa in the winter.

1958   Competes in all four classes at the Isle of Man, highest place being third, and wins three out of four Auto-Cycle Union Road Racing Stars (the equivalent of the British Championships).

1960   Only the second rider to lap the Isle of Man at 100mph on a single-cylinder bike, the 500cc Norton. First tests a racing car, a Lotus-Climax, at Silverstone, but spins and crashes.

1961   Wins three TT races in a week. Wins first World Championship, the 250cc on a Honda, and is second in the 500 on a Norton.

1962   Wins World 500cc Championship, second in the 350 Championship, on MVs.

1963   Wins World 500cc Championship, second in the 350, on MVs. First car race in Formula Junior at Brands Hatch (fifth). First car Grand Prix, in a Lotus-Climax, at Silverstone (eighth).

1964   Breaks world one-hour record at Daytona, averaging 144.8mph. Wins World 500cc Championship on an MV. First car Grand Prix point for sixth place at Monaco, driving a Lotus-BRM.

1965   Wins World 500cc Championship, third in the 350, on MVs. Leaves car racing after one Grand Prix at Monaco.

1966   Joins Honda from MV, wins World 250 and 350 Championships, second to Giacomo Agostini in the 500.

1967   Wins World 250 and 350 Championships, second to Agostini in the 500.

1968   Retires from Grand Prix bike racing on the withdrawal of Honda, who pay him a reported £50,000 not to compete for anybody else. Awarded the British Empire Medal.

1969   Races Formula 5000 in a Lola-Chevy, wins at Brands Hatch and is third in the Championship. Drives the Le Mans 24-hour race with David Hobbs, finishes third.

1970   Races Formula 5000 in a Lola-Chevy, third in the Championship again. Drives Le Mans with Hobbs (crashes).

1971   Joins the Surtees team, races Formula 5000, two wins and fourth in the Championship. Two Grand Prix car races in a Surtees-Ford, finishing fourth at Monza. Daughter Michelle born.

1972   European Formula Two Champion in a Surtees-Ford, with five wins. Full Grand Prix season with Surtees, second at Monza, eighth in the table with 13 points.

1973   Full Grand Prix season with Surtees, no points. Awarded the George Medal for bravery after pulling Clay Regazzoni from a burning car during the South African Grand Prix. Drives at Le Mans with John Watson and Rolf Stommelen (Stommelen crashes).

1974   Joins McLaren to drive a Yardley-sponsored car, takes a third place, fourth twice, and fifth once, but a crash at the Nurburgring ends his driving career. Fourth at Le Mans with Derek Bell. Son David born.

1975   Marries Pauline, emigrates to New Zealand.

1978   Returns to the Isle of Man and competes in four classes: wins the Formula One race on an 864cc Ducati; steering damper fails on the Yamaha during the 500cc race; 12th on a Yamaha in the 250; crankshaft breaks on a Yamaha in the Classic.

1979   Competes in three classes at the Isle of Man: fifth on a Ducati in the Formula One race; first on a Suzuki in the 500; second on the same Suzuki in the Classic.

Career totals: 14 wins on the Isle of Man, 76 Grand Prix wins, nine World Championships. Fifty car Grands Prix, one fastest lap, 29 points, highest placing second, at Monza in 1972. Career ends practising on the Suzuki for a farewell appearance at Donington, where he breaks his collarbone.

1981   March 21, crashes at Portway, the Midlands, on the way back from buying fish and chips. March 23, dies in Birmingham Accident Unit.